Diners' Preference towards Restaurants

(An Empirical Study with Special Reference to Coimbatore City)

Dr.K. Prince Paul Antony

Dr.A. Sulekha

Published by

BONFRING®
Intellectual Integrity

Diners' Preference towards Restaurants (An Empirical Study with Special Reference to Coimbatore City)

ISBN 978-93-86176-40-0

Authors

Dr.K. Prince Paul Antony

Dr.A. Sulekha

Bonfring

309, 2nd Floor, 5th Street Extension, Gandhipuram,

Coimbatore-641 012.

Tamilnadu, India.

E-mail: info@bonfring.org | Website: www.bonfring.org

Phone: 0422 4213231

<table>
<tr><th>Chapter</th><th>Contents</th><th>Page No</th></tr>
</table>

CHAPTER I

INTRODUCTION AND RESEARCH DESIGN

1.1. Introduction

Food is one of the basic necessities for the very survival of human beings. Generally, food habits of people changes according to their geographical climates, nature of vegetation available throughout the year and food habits are more influenced by the individual culture and socio-economic status too. It is true, in case of India, as it is a diverse country with variety of religions and cultures, spread over a vast geographic area with wide range of climates and food habits. Wide range of food availability, variety of cuisines and food habits across the Indian sub-continent have been motivating the common man to taste and experiences different food of various culture and societies living across India. Restaurants act as bridge in meeting out the growing desire of common man of tasting different culinary cuisines within their geographical limits.

Since, the economic liberalisation of Indian in 1991, the country has experiences a rapid growth in its services and manufacturing sector. Keeping phase with economic growth, the restaurant services of India have registered a growth of `.247680 crores by the end of the financial year 2013-14 and restaurant services in India is expected to reach a mark of `.408040 crores by 2018[1]. Moreover, Food Service sector is a major contributor to the GDP (Gross Domestic Products) of the Indian economy. Compared to other service sectors of the Indian economy, food service industry. Contributes approximately 2.30 percent of the total GDP. The total market size of the food service industry is bigger than Telecom, Television, Hotels or Film industry and it growing at the rate of 7 per cent per annum[2].

The restaurant sector in India is highly fragmented, roughly, there are 1.5 million eating outlets in India, of which 3000 outlets form part of the organised sectors and rest of 14,97,000 restaurants forms part of unorganised sectors, which is mostly dominated by domestic restaurant owners[3]. Currently, there are 1700 to1800 causal dine outlets spread across India

---

[1]Indian Restaurant Revolution,https://digitalrestro.wordpress.com/2014/07/16/indian-restaurant-revolution/, 16th July, 2014.

[2]Indian Food Service Report (2013),

http://www.hospitalitybizindia.com/detailNews.aspx?aid=17030&sid=20, 5th. July

[3]Feature: Fine dining: A fine experience,Food & Beverages Specials (2012), 12thMarch

http://www.fnbnews.com/article/detnew.asp?articleid=31440§ionid=9

in the affordable and premium segment[4]. The rest are the restaurant establishments in semi-urban and rural areas, which may also include road-side restaurants and dhabas on inter-city roads and highways, may not possessing any license from the authority of regional areas[5]. The unorganised restaurant sector in India is predominantly operated as casual dine restaurants. The casual dine market is led by domestic players, which are largely region-specific.

Dine-in and Dine-out options form an important sales mix strategies of the casual dine segment in India and these casual dine restaurants give more importance for SKU sales mix (i.e., Stock Keeping Units). In casual dining, most of the sales (60 per cent) are through dine-in customers as consumers prefer to sit at restaurants and enjoy the width of available product offerings. Delivery services contribute a healthy 30per cent to sales, followed by takeaway which brings in 10per cent of total sales. This is primarily for outlets located in residential areas, office complexes, etc. where the consumer prefers getting food hand-delivery due to paucity of time. The main meal times of lunch (1.00 pm to 4.00 pm) and dinner (7.00 pm to 11.00 pm) contribute to -85 per cent of the total sales at casual dine outlets. However, the peak business hours of outlets located in office complexes are more skewed towards breakfast and lunch time[6].

With more Middle class Indian consumers are patronising causal dine restaurants; it is the true to claim that restaurant sector is experiencing a high evolution in the country. The number of people dining at restaurants is rising in India as more women are working outside the home, busier lifestyles, increasing disposable income to spend on food dining and the improved standard of living[7]. In short, it can be said that the dining which was earlier used to be occasional is fast changing and settling as recourse to quick meals, entertainment, place for social gathering, family-outing etc[8]. In general, the Indian food choices are a gastronomical delight with each region offering its signature cuisine, but with the growth of restaurants in the

---

[4]Casual Dine, www.restaurantindia.in/article/research-and-events/.../Casual-Dine.a98, 21st January, 2014.

[5]Navjit Ahluwalia, Dushyant Singh, ShyamSuri, Pooran Chandra Pandey and Raj Rajeshwar Sharma (2004), Restaurant Industry in India-Trends and Opportunities-A Study, Published by Secretary General, Federation of Hotel & Restaurant Associations of India.

[6]Ibid. Casual Dine, 21st January, 2014.

[7]Ibid., Yogesh Upadhyay, Shiv Kumar Singh and Dhiraj Sharma (2009).

[8]Kivela, Jaksa, Robert Inbakaran, and John Reece (2000), Consumer Research in the Restaurant Environment- Part 3: Analysis, Findings and Conclusions," International Journal of Contemporary Hospitality Management, Volume.No.12, Issue.No.1, PP:13-30. And Pedraja, M., and Yagüe, J. (2001), What Information do Customers Use When Choosing a Restaurant?, International Journal of Contemporary Hospitality Management, Volume.No.13, Issue.No.6, PP:316-318.

country has put on the table not only diverse local flavours but huge variety of international cuisines like: Chinese, Italian, Persian, etc[9].

From the above discussion, it has been understood that in a country with more than 1.3 billion people, opportunities for restaurant business in India are very prosper. This has led to a rapid growth of the restaurant sector in India. Moreover, dining out has seen explosive growth in recent years as urban consumers seem to have found more occasions to celebrate and more opportunities to dine outside the home, as most of the urban regions India lack space for other entertainments like: sporting, traveling, picnic spots etc[10]. As stated earlier, at present, restaurants have taken over the task for being place for social gatherings, offering novelty and convenience at the same time. Customer service in either causal or fine dining restaurants is of supreme importance, especially in Indian. Customers judge the service of restaurants based units food quality, timely services at affordable cost and these parameters plays a significant role in determining and influencing customer satisfaction[11]. The elaborate theoretical discussion made in this chapter provides required scope and motivation for the conduct of this study. This study aims to analyse diners' preference towards restaurant services in Coimbatore City, as this city is very popular for its restaurant services like: Annapoorna, Anadhas, RHR, Rayappa's, Anjappar and many more to list. Like other tier II cities in India, Coimbatore also lack space for other entertainments like: sporting, traveling, picnic spots etc., thus, restaurants have taken over place for social gatherings, entertainments and place of convenience in this city.

1.2. Significance of the Study

As a nation, hospitality is deep rooted into Indian culture. Indians take real pride of Indian food variety and texture. Although Indian states have a very long history and heritage of its local cuisines, Indian are also very open to adopt new tastes into Indian food menu. Food is not just a need here. In marketing terms, it spans from need to want and beyond when a cook add taste and variety to it. Naturally, when the discussion is about food, on one can just stay within Indian kitchen and dining. Indian never ending passion for taste and variety drives them to restaurants, the ultimate destination every food lover would rush to, to get their desired mix of

---

[9]Fine dining restaurant industry in India, Food & Beverages Specials (2011), Wednesday, 16th November.http://www.fnbnews.com/article/detnews.asp?articleid=31014§ionid=32

[10]Piyush Kumar Sinha (2012), Indian QSR Industry – Opportunities and Strategies to Harness them, working paper series of the IIMA, W.P. No. 2012-06-07, Published by Indian Institute of Management, June.

[11]Fine dining restaurant industry in India, Food & Beverages Specials (2011), Wednesday, 16th November.http://www.fnbnews.com/article/detnews.asp?articleid=31014§ionid=32

products and services. This makes restaurants a perfect industry to analyze from marketing point of view. Now, the restaurants industry is a pretty enormous one in India which makes it a substantially broad topic for research[12].

Casual dining concepts are preferred by a larger number of people as compared to fine dining concepts, largely because India is a price-sensitive market. Having said that, with the increase in disposable income, as consumers are becoming more adventurous and don't mind paying a little bit extra for the experience of a true dining in a restaurant[13].Restaurant managers must understand and satisfy consumers' needs, wants and demands to be successful in the competitive foodservice industry.

1.3.   Statement of Problems

The dining scenario in India has evolved rapidly in the past decades. With the increasing popularity of standalone casual dining restaurants attracting customers are more difficult nowadays due to the challenges of competition and the need to maintain the volume of business that the restaurant have in their geographical region(s). The competition challenge has three major implications on restaurants: (i) to increase their menu choice, (ii) offer greater value of money and (iii) to offer augmented level of service.

To have a timely realisation of the intense competition prevailing in the restaurant sector in India and understanding demanding consumers need and wants, a reasonable concern revolves around what restaurants can do to maintain customer satisfaction. Knowing what the customers want and what makes them come back is important for the restaurant mangers so they can make improvements to the operation of the restaurant. Customers have their own reasons to return to a restaurant. Some of these reasons are seeking quality, value and desirable environment i.e., ambience[14]. Creating positive customer experience by the restaurant managers will enhance the influential factor for customers to dine-in at their favorite restaurants and also motivate them to revisit the restaurant again and again. This is because the eating behavior is a central part of the consumers' daily lives and not just for

---

[12]WahidaShahanTinne (2012), Factors Affecting Selection of Upscale Restaurants in Dhaka City,ASA University Review, Volume No. 6, Issue No. 1, PP:127-138, January–June.

[13]Manjushree Naik (2013), Casual dining is preferred as India is price-sensitive, 1stApril, Monday,http://www.fnbnews.com/Interview/Casual-dining-is-preferred-as-India-is-price-sensitive.

[14]Rasha Ali Eliwa (2006), A study of customer loyalty and the Image of the fine dining restaurant, Submitted to the Faculty of the Graduate College of the Oklahoma State University in partial fulfillment of the requirements for the Degree of Master of Science, Bachelor of Tourism and Hotel Administration, Helwan University, Cairo, Egypt, December.

gaining food nutrition. Moreover, the customers' behavior at restaurant may be influenced by the experiences created at the restaurant at the time of dinning[15].

To create good image about them, casual dine restaurant must aim to meet continuously the varying demands of prospective target customers. The image of a restaurant, as perceived by its potential customers, plays an important role in affecting the customer loyalty behavior as well as in determining its market position within its competitive environment[16]. Above discussed conceptual issues have provoked for the conduct of this study. This empirical study aims to analyse the dinner's preference towards restaurant, the study focused on dinners in Coimbatore city.

1.4. Scope of the Study

The issue of how customers select restaurants has been given considerable attention by both researchers and practitioners. However, surprisingly little research has been generated on the criteria customers use in order to select a restaurant to dine-out. Furthermore, previous studies have not considered the extent to which important choice criteria would differ depending on the restaurant type. It is also important to note that customers with different characteristics tend to use different criteria in choosing restaurants.

Based on the above discussed issues, it is believed that the information provided in this empirical study will be useful to the restaurants owners and managers to identify the appropriate marketing strategies to attract new customers and retain existing customers and also to know about customers preferences towards food variety, quality and nature of services offered at their restaurants and needed changes to be adopt to earn more satisfied and repeated consumers.

1.5. Objectives of the Study

This empirical study aims to analyse the diners' preferences and satisfaction toward selected Restaurants operating in Coimbatore city.

- To study the demographic and socio-economic habits of restaurant diners in Coimbatore city.

---

[15]AzilabintiJaini, Nor Asmabinti Ahmad and SitiZamanirabinti Mat Zaib (2015), Determinant Factors that Influence Customers' Experience in Fast Food Restaurants in Sungai Petani, Kedah, Journal of Entrepreneurship and Business, Volume No. 3, Issue No,1,E-ISSN: 2289-8298, PP: 60-71, June.

[16]Ibid.,Rasha Ali Eliwa (2006).

- To analyse the food consumption habits of Coimbatorians and the factors that determine the restaurant selection by the diners.
- To measure diners' level of perception towards prominent restaurants located at Coimbatore city.
- To measure level of satisfaction experienced by the diners' in the prominent restaurants.
- To evaluate the prevailing gap between diners' level of perception and satisfaction derived by them.

1.6. Hypotheses of the Study

To justify the above stated objectives of the study, following hypotheses are framed:

- Diners' choice of the vegetarian restaurant is purely influenced by their demographic and socio-economic status.
- Diners' choice of the non-vegetarian restaurant is purely influenced by their demographic and socio-economic status.
- There exists no association between food consumption habits of the diners' and factors that motivated them to visit restaurants.
- There exists no differences in the diners' preference towards foods and restaurant service features between vegetarian and non-vegetarian restaurants.
- There exist differences in the diners' perception towards the service features of one restaurant in comparison to the other.
- There exists no differences in the diners' satisfaction towards foods and restaurant service features between vegetarian and non-vegetarian restaurants.
- There exist differences in the diners' satisfaction towards the service features of one restaurant in comparison to the other.
- There exist no differences in diners' perception and satisfaction towards restaurant services.

1.7. Research Methodology

The current study is both explorative and descriptive in nature.

Stage I: The first stage of the research is exploratory in nature. Explorative research form part of desk work carried for collection of review of literature. Through detailed secondary data search on: food consumption, influences of demographic variables on restaurant service selections, consumers' perceptions and satisfaction towards restaurant services were collected and summarised. The collected review of literature forms the basis for preparing the well-structured questionnaire to the next stage of the explorative research.

Stage II: The second stage of the research is descriptive in nature, which was conducted by applying a survey method i.e., fact finding investigation with adequate interpretations. Well-structured questionnaire was framed consisting of five segments comprising, complete details about the socio-economic profile of the restaurant diners, their dining preference, motivating factors for dining practices, their level of perception and satisfaction towards service of restaurant located at Coimbatore city.

1.7.1. *Study Area*

The current study is mainly concentrated on the leading restaurants located at Coimbatore. It is the third largest city of Tamil Nadu (the popular southern state of Indian sub-continent), one of the most industrialised and fastest growing cities in India. Coimbatore is well-known as the textile capital of South India or the Manchester of the South; it is also the primary manufacturing industrial hub for textile spare parts, auto ancillary, electric pumps& motors and various other engineering goods. The city is situated on the banks of the river Noyyal, at the foot-hills of Nilgiris, and it is also known for its pleasant climate, peaceful atmosphere, cosmopolitan outlook, and private enterprise and even for its restaurants and sweets and saviouries shops like: the Annapoorna and Sree Krishna Sweets. Thus, Coimbatore city has been selected as the study area.

1.7.2. *Significance of Area of the Study*

With the increasing competition in large cities, dining chains and restaurants are now bullish on setting up their stores in smaller cities and tier II and III markets. There are 53 TierII cities in India: Bhopal, Kanpur, Jaipur, Nagpur, Lucknow, Patna, Surat, Visakhapatnam, Vijayawada, Kochi, Madurai, Coimbatore, Warangal, Rajkot, Vadodara, Ludhiana, Agra, Meerut, Nashik, Solapur, Faridabad, Varanasi, Jabalpur, Jamshepur, Allahabad, Indore, Gorakhpur, Hubli-Dharwad, Bhavnagar, Rajpur, Mysore, Managalore, Belgaum, Guntur, Bhubaneshwar, Cuttack, Amravati, Aurangabad, Srinagar, Bhilai, Rajahmundry, Kakinada, Nellore, Ranchi, Guwahati, Gwalior, Chandigarh, Patiala, Jodhur, Tiruchirapalli, Pondichery, Salem and Asanso. Coimbatore is the 12th largest Tier II city in India and dining out culture is high at Coimbatore, as the inhabitants of this city have, no better entertainment opportunities other than cinemas. Thus, food dining culture of the people in Coimbatore is very sensitive. Based on the identified significances of food dining practices, Coimbatore has been selected as the study zone.

1.7.3. *Sampling Framework*

For the effective conduct of this study the researcher applied multi-stage sampling techniques. In the first stage of the researcher adopted stratified random sampling techniques for classification and selection of restaurants operating across Coimbatore city and in the second stage, researcher adopted convenience sampling techniques for collection of first-hand information from the diners. There are 214 restaurants currently operating in Coimbatore city. Its list is presented in the following tables:

Table: 1.1: Category of Dining Centers Functioning in Coimbatore City

S.No	Category of Dining Center	Number	Percentage
1.	Bakery	1	0.47
2.	Café Desserts	13	6.07
3.	Causal Dinning	158	73.83
4.	Dessert Parlor	4	1.87
5.	Quick Eat	22	10.28
6.	Fast Foods	7	3.27
7.	Fine Dine	4	1.87
8.	Others	5	2.34
	Total	214	100

Source: https://www.zomato.com/coimbatore/casual-dining, Refer Annexure: I

Current study is purely focused on the 158 casual dine restaurants currently functioning in the city. At the beginning of data collection a pilot survey was conducted among the sample population with two objectives. One to identify the most popular and frequently visited restaurants by the households in Coimbatore city and second, purpose was to test the feasibility and adoptability of the questionnaire framed. Based the pilot survey results five vegetarian and non-vegetarian restaurants were identified, that where more preferred by the Coimbatorians. An option of "others" was provided to gather information about other most preferred and visited casual dine restaurants. Samples of five vegetarian and non-vegetarian restaurants were selected for the effective conduct of the study. The most popular and prominent vegetarian restaurants were chosen for study: Annapoorna's, Anandha's, Aryaa's, Adyar Anandha Bhavanand RHR. Five most popular and prominent non-vegetarian restaurants were chosen for study: Rayappa's, Sampoorna, Haribhavanam, Anjapparand Anjali.

Generally, there are some misconceptions about the required size of a sample across the social-science researchers. One is that sample should not be less than 10 per cent of the population. This rule, commonly known as the 1/10th rule, but it is not relevant to large populations. Statisticians can easily illustrate that when a probability sample reaches a certain size, such as 1000 its efficiency for estimating population parameters is not much different compared with a probability sample of 10000 or even 100000. Another misconception is: 'larger the sample size, greater may be the accuracy of the sample results'. Although an increase in sample size will increase the precision of the sample results, a large sample size does not guarantee the accuracy of the results.

As per the James H. McMillian (1996) a convenience sample is a group of subjects selected because of availability, often this is the only type of sampling possible especially in geographical area based study, where the target group of population is only available for study, and the primary purpose of the research may not be to generalize but to better understand relationships that may exist. Similarly Roscoe (1975) proposed that a sample size of >30 and <500 are appropriate for most research. According to Orme. B (2010)[17] sample size for conjoint studies generally can ranges from about 150 to 1,200 respondents and it largely depends on the purpose of research.

Conjoint analysis is a statistical technique used in Social Science (marketing, management and others) research to determine how people value different attributes (feature, function, benefits) that make up an individual product or service. The author also claims that for investigational work and developing hypotheses about a market, between thirty and sixty respondents may be sufficient. Based on this concept, the sampling framework of the study is constructed. A sample of sixty (60) diners where chose in each category of restaurant, since researcher found it very difficult in identification of restaurant diners and collection of data were restricted on 60 diners from each sample restaurants, which was summed to 600 samples subjects in total.

1.7.4. Data Source

Both primary and secondary data were used for the effective conduct of this study. The primary data for this research were collected through a well-structured questionnaire to find answers for the research questions and objectives. The secondary data needed for the study were sourced from various magazines, journals, internet and thesis works.

---

[17]Orme, B. (2010) Getting Started with Conjoint Analysis: Strategies for Product Design and Pricing Research. Second Edition, Madison, Wis.: Research Publishers LLC.

1.7.5. *Reliability and Validity*

The reliability of an indicator can be defined as its overall quality, i.e. its consistency and its ability to give the same results in repeated measurement. The most outstanding feature of reliability is the test-retest correlation of the specific measure under scrutiny.

Correspondingly, the test-retest correlation for most single-item measures is presented in the following table.

Table 1.2: Data Validity and Reliability Test

General Variables	*No. of Items*	*Range*	*Cronbach's Alpha*
Factors Influencing the Dinners' to Visit Restaurant (S)	11	1-11	.917
Diners' Level of Perception towards Restaurant	7	1-5	.894
Diners' Level of Perception towards the Service Reliability of Restaurant	5	1-5	.894
Diners' Level of Perception towards the Physical Design & Appearance of Restaurant	4	1-5	.892
Diners' Level of Perception towards the Price of Food Items Offered by Restaurant	3	1-5	.895
Diners' Level of Perception towards the Location of Restaurant	6	1-5	.888
Diners' Level of Perception towards the Appearance / Comfort of Restaurant	5	1-5	.890
Diners' Level of Perception towards the Menu offered in Restaurant	5	1-5	.892
Diners' Level of Perception towards the Food Quality of Restaurant	5	1-5	.888
Diners' Level of Perception towards the Service Quality of Restaurant	6	1-5	.887
Diners' Level of Satisfaction towards the Service Features of Restaurant	9	1-9	.885
Overall Score for Sample Adequacy (Kaiser-Meyer-Olkin Measure of Sampling Adequacy)	.928		
Overall Score for Data Reliability (Cronbach's Alpha)	.902		

Source: Computed from Primary Data

The most widely used measure to assess the internal consistency of research instrument constructed is Cronbach's alpha. The generally agreed upon value of Cronbach's alpha is 0.70, although it may decrease to 0.60 in case of exploratory research (Hair et al. 2006; pp.137). In this research the reliability measure for the whole scale is 0.902 which is acceptable. Again the reliability for all the constructs is shown in Table 1.1; the values for all the constructs range between 0.885-0.917, which is acceptable. Similarly, the value of KMO's sample adequacy was rated at 0.928. Hence, construct of both validity and reliability in this research is satisfactory. The result of Cronbach's alpha draws a significant amount of correlation between the variables tested. The validity of a test is the extent to which differences in scores reflect differences in the measured characteristic. Predictive validity is a measure of the usefulness of a measuring instrument as a predictor. Proof of predictive validity is determined by the correlation between results and actual behavior. Construct validity is the extent to which a measuring instrument measures what it intends to measure.

1.8. Operational Concept

Some of the Operational Concepts of the study is briefly discussed in this section of the study.

1. **Food Culture:** It connection to food in a pure and deep sense. It is knows what it takes to bring forth food, rejoicing in times of plenty and people can to help one another in times of scarcity. It is the conversation had around a table three times a day and it is the health given to our bodies from the essence of those plants and animals. Food culture has always existed in rural homes and communities across the world[18].

2. **Food Service:** It is the industry related to making, transporting or selling prepared foods to restaurants, hospitals, schools and lodging establishments[19].

3. **Hospitality:** it refers to the relationship between a guest and a host, wherein the host receives the guest with goodwill, including the reception and entertainment of guests, visitors, or strangers[20].

4. **Restaurant:** Historically, restaurant referred only to places that provided tables where one sit down to eat the meal, typically served by a waiter. In India restaurants range from a regular road side one to an elite high end signature restaurant with specific cuisine specialisation. Restaurant industry in India consists of companies engaged in the operation of restaurants, diners, taverns, pubs, nightclubs, banquet halls, fixed location snack bars, food cart vendors, food service contractors and companies engaged in commercial food service equipment wholesaling[21].

5. **Vegetarian Restaurants:** A huge part of Indian population lives on vegetarian diet. Majority of vegetarians in India are 'lacto-vegetarians', meaning that these people do not eat fish, eggs or meat, but drink milk. The rise in the vegetarian diet in India has prompted in the establishment of numerous vegetarian restaurants. These restaurants

---

[18]Shannon(2013),Defining Food Culture and Where to Find it, https://www.plantoeat.com/blog/2013/01/defining-food-culture-and-where-to-find-it/.

[19]http://www.yourdictionary.com/food-service#uP1xv3T3RuusDogf.99.

[20] https://en.wikipedia.org/wiki/Hospitality

[21]Ibid.,WahidaShahanTinne (2012).

are not only frequently visited by locals but by foreign tourists also[22]. Vegetarianism in India is by and large handed to people by virtue of what religion and/or cast.

6. **Non-Vegetarian Restaurants:** In Indian means a non-vegetarian restaurant as a place where meat, fish, chicken and other animal based foods are served.

7. **Restaurateurs:** is a person who opens and runs restaurants professionally. Although over time the term has come to describe any person who owns a restaurant, traditionally it refers to a highly skilled professional who is proficient in all aspects of the restaurant business[23].

8. **Diner:** Diner is a person who is eating in a restaurant either in casual dine restaurants or in a fine dine restaurants or even in road side vendor stalls[24].

9. **Dining:** The act of consuming food is called as dining[25]. There are different restaurant types to choose from for dining experience by a common man. From street food to fine dining.

10. **Hospitality Industry:** is a broad category of fields within the service industry that includes lodging, event planning, theme parks, transportation, cruise line, and additional fields within the tourism industry. The hospitality industry is a multibillion-dollar industry that depends on the availability of leisure time and disposable income. A hospitality unit such as a restaurant, hotel, or an amusement park consists of multiple groups such as facility maintenance and direct operations (servers, housekeepers, porters, kitchen workers, bartenders, management, marketing, and human resources etc.)[26].

11. **Cuisine:** Cuisine (word derived from French cuisine, "cooking; culinary art; kitchen"; ultimately from Latin coquere, "to cook") is a characteristic style of cooking practices and traditions, often associated with a specific culture. Cuisines are often named after the geographic areas or regions from which they originate. A cuisine is primarily influenced by the ingredients that are available locally or through trade. Religious food laws, such as Islamic dietary laws and Jewish dietary laws, Religious food laws, such as can also exercise a strong influence on cuisine. Regional food preparation traditions, customs and ingredients often combine to create dishes unique to a particular region[27].

---

[22]http://www.mapsofindia.com/restaurants/vegetarian-restaurants.html.

[23]https://en.wikipedia.org/wiki/Restaurateur

[24] http://www.yourdictionary.com/diner#0p6SdyFD3X5m8Gkl.99.

[25]http://www.thefreedictionary.com/dining

[26]https://en.wikipedia.org/wiki/Hospitality_industry

[27]http://en.wikipedia.org/wiki/Cuisine

12. **Culinary Style of Tamil Nadu:** Tamil food is characterized by the use of rice, legumes and lentils, its distinct aroma and flavour achieved by the blending of spices including curry leaves, tamarind, coriander, ginger, garlic, chili, pepper, cinnamon, cloves, cardamom, cumin, nutmeg, coconut and rosewater. The word "curry" is derived from the Tamil word kari which means "an additive to the main course or a side dish". Rice and legumes play an important role in Tamil cuisine. Lentils are also consumed extensively, either accompanying rice preparations, or in the form of independent dishes. Vegetables and dairy products are essential accompaniments. Tamil Nadu is famous for its spicy non vegetarian dishes. The southern regions in Tamil Nadu, namely; Madurai, Kaaraikudi or Chettinaadu are famous for their spicy non-vegetarian dishes[28].

13. **Food Menu:** In a restaurant, a menu is a presentation of food and beverage offerings. A menu may be which guests use to choose from a list of food options[29].

14. **Hotel:** A commercial establishment providing lodging, meals and other guest services[30].

1.9.   Statistical Tools Applied

According to the nature of the data analysis and interpretations required, appropriate statistical tools have been applied. The following tools have been applied in the study: Frequency distribution, Weighted Average, Likert's Scaling, Chi-Square test, ANOVA Test, Independent 'z' test, Paired 'z' test, Reliability and Rotation Factor Analysis.

- The frequency distribution of the variables has helped the researcher to calculate distribution value of variables tested.

- Weighted arithmetic mean and Likert's Summated scales helped in interpreting the averages of the variable used in this study, like: factors influencing the dinners' to visit particular restaurant, dinners' level of perception towards the responsiveness of particular restaurant, dinners' level of perception towards the service reliability of particular restaurant, dinners' level of perception towards the physical design & appearance of particular restaurant, dinners' level of perception towards the price of food items offered by particular restaurant, dinners' level of perception towards the location of particular restaurant, dinners' level of perception towards the appearance/

---

[28]AdamyaShyam (2012), Food habits of India and U.K. http://www.slideshare.net/adamya 2013/ food-habits-of-india-uk, 27th December.

[29]https://en.wikipedia.org/wiki/Menu.

[30]http://www.businessdictionary.com/definition/hotel.html#ixzz3ufICLInt.

comfort of particular restaurant, dinners' level of perception towards the menu offered in particular restaurant, dinners' level of perception towards the food quality of particular restaurant, dinners' level of perception towards the service quality of particular restaurant and dinners' level of satisfaction towards the service features of particular restaurant.

- Chi-Square test has been applied to measure whether the (i) Diners' choice of the vegetarian restaurant is purely influenced by their demographic and socio-economic status and (ii) Diners' choice of the non-vegetarian restaurant is purely influenced by their demographic and socio-economic status.

- ANOVA test was applied to measure whether (i) There exists association between food consumption habits of the diners' and factors that motivated them to visit restaurants

- Independent 'z' test was performed to measure whether (i)There exists differences in the diners' preference towards foods and restaurant service features between vegetarian and non-vegetarian restaurants and (ii) There exists differences in the diners' satisfaction towards foods and restaurant service features between vegetarian and non-vegetarian restaurants.

- Paired 'Z' test was applied to measure whether there exist differences in (i) There exist differences in the diners' perception towards the service features of one restaurant in comparison to the other (ii) There exist differences in the diners' satisfaction towards the service features of one restaurant in comparison to the other and (iii) There exist no differences in diners perception and satisfaction towards restaurant services.

- Rotation factor analysis with Kaiser-Meyer-Oklin (KMO) test and Reliability analysis were applied to establish and reveal the correlation between
(i) diners' perception towards the service features of vegetarian restaurants and their preferences towards particular restaurant,
(ii) diners' perception towards the service features of non-vegetarian restaurants and their preferences towards particular restaurant,
(iii) diners' satisfaction towards the service features of vegetarian restaurants and their preferences towards particular restaurant and
(iv) diners' satisfaction towards the service features of non-vegetarian restaurants and their preferences towards particular restaurant.

1.10. Limitations of the Study

Some of the limitations of the study are as follows:

- The study is specific to the geographical limitation. This study is confined to Coimbatore City only. The geographical and socio-economic setting may not be identical to that of other cities in India, and thus the findings of this study may not be generalized to casual dine restaurants operating in other parts of Tamil Nadu or India or in other countries.

- The perception of the sample respondents who dined in the selected vegetarian and non-vegetarian restaurants may vary many a time based on their time of visit, occasion, company with whom they had visited, diner visit purpose, based on these parameters their perception towards restaurant services may vary, which is not clearly recorded in this study. Therefore, the findings cannot be generalized based on these factors.

1.11. Chapter Organisation Scheme

The framework of this research work has been structured to gain insights into the above purpose and thus includes five chapters namely the introduction and research design, literature review, theoretical discussion on study concepts and issues, analysis and interpretation, summary, findings, Suggestion, conclusion, and future scope for research. The thesis of the study is organized into five major chapters. A brief outline of each of them is given below:

Chapter I: The introductory chapter I deal with the introduction and research design of the study. It includes the introduction, significance of the study, statement of the problem, scope of the study, objectives, hypotheses, research methodology, operational concepts, statistical tools applied, limitations and organization of chapters.

Chapter II: Second chapter focuses on the reviews of the relevant literature on the study subject and issues focused by various researchers in past.

Chapter III: Third chapter is titled as "Overview on restaurant industry in India and consumers' attitude and preferences towards it". The chapter contains detailed theoretical discussion on subject issues.

Chapter IV: Fourth chapter deals with the analysis and interpretation of data collected.

Chapter V: Fifth chapter summaries the findings of the study, suggestions and conclusions of the study.

CHAPTER II

LITERATURE REVIEW

2.1. Introduction

Review of literature helps a researcher(s) to get acquainted with their selected research problem and also may provide some guidelines in selecting a proper research methodology. It is also helpful in finding out the research gaps in the existing literature. Past literature reviews help the researcher in fine-tuning their research problem and methodology. Another advantage of reviewing in the existing literature is that in cases where the research problems are similar, the conclusions and findings may be easily compared. This will help the researcher in determining whether his/her findings are practically viable. The literature under review may be of two types: (i) concerning the conceptual and theoretical framework. (ii) the empirical literature dealing with the studies made in the past which are similar to the one that the researcher intended to undertake. The basic outcomes of such review will be the knowledge as to what data are available for analytical purposes, which will help the researcher to specify his/her own research problem in a more meaningful way. This chapter contains review on

2.2. Food Diversification in India

Indian food is one of the tastiest and subtlest in the world. There is no homogeneity of flavour between North and South or East and West but rather, a wealth of flavours that is simply staggering. Culinary diversity is one of India's treasures[31]. This section briefly discussion on food diversification prevailing in India. Indian cuisine encompasses a wide variety of regional cuisines native to India. Given the range of diversity in soil type, climate, culture, ethnic group and occupations, these cuisines vary significantly from each other and use locally available spices, herbs, vegetables and fruits. Indian food is also heavily influenced by religious and cultural choices and traditions. The development of these cuisines has been shaped by religious beliefs, and in particular by exclusion of pork and vegetarianism, which continues to grow as a dietary trend in Indian society. There has also been Central Asian influence on North Indian cuisine from the years of Mughal rule. Indian cuisine has been and is still evolving, as a result of the nation's cultural interactions with other societies[32].

---

[31]https://www.humanium.org/en/indian-food-diversity/, 2nd August, 2010.

[32] https://en.wikipedia.org/wiki/Indian_cuisine

According to Anita Goyal and N.P. Singh (2007)[33] food diversity in India is an implicit characteristic of India's diversified culture consisting of different regions and states within. Traditionally, Indians like to have home-cooked meals–a concept supported religiously as well as individually. However, with times due to increasing awareness and influence of western culture, there is a slight shift in food consumption patterns among urban Indian families. It started with eating outside and moved on to accepting a wide variety of delicacies from world-over. Liberalization of the Indian economy in the early 1990s and the subsequent entry of new players set a significant change in lifestyles and the food tastes of Indians.

According to a Humanium organisation (2010)[34] Indian food is one of the tastiest and subtlest in the world. There is no homogeneity of flavour between North and South or East and West but rather, a wealth of flavours that is simply staggering. Culinary diversity is one of India's treasures. Each region of this country offers its own culinary distinctive characteristics and numerous traditional dishes.

A study conducted by NCAER (National Council for Applied Economic Research) (2014)[35] had mentioned that the food consumption pattern in India is increasing over the past two decades due to income induced diet diversification, impact of globalization, increasing urbanization and changing lifestyle of people. India's per capita calorie, protein, and fat consumption remains significantly below that of more developed countries such as China and the United States. The implication is that in coming years with rising per capita income and urbanization, India's demand for various superior food products will continue to increase necessitating a possible change in the food production system and agricultural trade. The present study shows that despite rapid economic growth during the past decades, India's average per capita calorie and protein intake has grown only modestly, although the per capita fat consumption has registered a higher growth. Calorie and protein source in the Indian diet is diversifying with fruit/vegetable and animal-based food share increasing and cereal and pulses declining.

According toVikasKhanna (2014)[36] Indian cuisine reflects a 5000-year history of intermingling of various communities and cultures, leading to diverse flavours and regional

---

[33]Anita Goyal and N.P. Singh (2007), *An Empirical Study on Consumer Perception about Fast Food In India*, British Food Journal, Volume. No. 109, Issue. No. 2, PP:182-195, Emerald Group Publishing Limited.

[34] https://www.humanium.org/en/indian-food-diversity/, 2nd August, 2010.

[35]An Analysis of Changing Food Consumption Pattern in India, A research paper prepared under the project Agricultural Outlook and Situation Analysis Reports, National Council of Applied Economic Research, New Delhi. 2014.

[36]VikasKhanna (2014), Cuisine and Diplomacy, Ministry of External Affairs, 18th August.

cuisines. The arrival of the Mughals, the British, and Portuguese further added variety to Indian cuisine. The consequent fusion in cuisines resulted in what is today known as 'Indian Cuisine'. Indian cuisine also means a wide variety of cooking styles. Sometimes it seems referring to it as Indian cuisine is a misnomer, since regional dishes vary tremendously from region to region. Indian cuisine has also shaped the history of international relations; the spice trade between India and Europe is often cited by historians as the primary catalyst for Europe's Age of Discovery. Spices were bought from India and traded around Europe and Asia. It has also influenced other cuisines across the world, especially those from Southeast Asia, the British Isles and the Caribbean. As food influences travelled to India, so has Indian cuisine travelled abroad. Particular dishes have gained popularity or subtle influences through spices have seeped into cuisines the world over.

2.3.   Definition of the Restaurant and its Classification

The historical definition of "restaurant" referred only to places that provided tables where one sits down to dine the meal served by a waiter. The industrial revolution and fast sociological changes led to the rise of fast food and take-out restaurants. The new term was coined for the older "standard" restaurant to, "sit-down restaurant." Most commonly, "sit-down restaurant" refers to a casual dining restaurant with table service, rather than a fast food restaurant, where one orders food at a counter. Sit- down restaurants are often further categorized as "family-style" or "formal". In British English, the term restaurant almost always means a dining establishment with table service. Fast food and takeaway (take-out) outlets with counter service are not normally referred to as restaurants[37].

Othman and Don (2008)[38] opined that restaurants are categories based on certain parameters such as type of services, price offered, market orientation, type of establishment, menu, food specialization, style of operation and ownership. Don (2012)[39] a casual dining restaurant is a restaurant that serves moderately priced food in a casual atmosphere. Every restaurant has their own signature dish to attract customers to their restaurant. As for a Malay restaurant, signature dishes such as Nasidagang, Nasikerabu, Beef rending, Chicken rending and so forth can be found in their menu. However, a restaurant cannot be too dependent on their unique menu alone to be successful and survive in the food business.

---

[37]Types of restaurant, http://en.wikipedia.org/wiki/Types_of_restaurant.

[38]Othman, A.R. and Don, M.S. (2008), Knowledge management and profitability of the casual dining restaurant in Malaysia, The 4th National Human Resource Management Conference.

[39] Don A.R (2012), Knowledge Management and Business Performance of Casual Dinning Restaurants in Malaysia, Knowledge Management International Conference (KMIce), JoherBharu, PP: 115-121.

Bon Brotherton and Roy C. Wood (2008)[40] in his book titled "Handbook of Hospitality Management" had mentions family restaurants represent a slightly smaller segment of the industry but fill an important niche between quick-service restaurants and dinner houses. As the name implies, they are more family-friendly (although more and more restaurant categories are battling for the family share of the foodservice dollar). Family restaurants are typically characterized by: family-friendly dining environments with accommodation for young children; check averages between dinner houses and quick- service, multiple meal periods (usually continuous service from breakfast through dinner, a wide range of menu selection, widespread use of convenience foods; and no alcoholic beverages. The author comments that family dining restaurants are associated with chains as well as being independently owned and operated. They plan an important role in meeting the demands of families (often with various needs) dining out.

According Wikipedia (2014)[41] a restaurant is a business which prepares and serves food and drinks to customers in exchange for money, either paid before the meal, after the meal, or with an open account. Meals are generally served and eaten on premises, but many restaurants also offer take-out and food delivery services. Restaurants vary greatly in appearance and offerings, including a wide variety of cuisines and service models ranging from inexpensive fast food restaurants to high-priced luxury establishments. In Western countries, most mid- to high-range restaurants serve alcoholic beverages such as beer and wine. Some restaurants serve all the major meals, such as breakfast, lunch and dinner (e.g., major fast food chains, hotel restaurants and airport restaurants). Other restaurants may only serve a single meal (e.g., a pancake house may only serve breakfast) or they may serve two meals (e.g., lunch and dinner).

Restaurants may be classified or distinguished in many different ways. The primary factors are usually the food itself (e.g. vegetarian, seafood, steak); the cuisine (e.g. Italian, Chinese, Japanese, Indian, French, Mexican, Thai) and/or the style of offering (e.g. tapas bar, a sushi train, at a stet restaurant, a buffet restaurant or a yum cha restaurant). Beyond this, restaurants may differentiate themselves on factors including speed, formality, location, cost, service, or novelty themes (such as automated restaurants).

Restaurants range from inexpensive and informal lunching or dining places catering to people working nearby, with simple food served in simple settings at low prices, to expensive

---

[40]Bon Brotherton and Roy C. Wood (2008), The SAGE Handbook of Hospitality Management, Editorial arrangement and Introduction, Sage Publications Ltd 2008, ISBN 978-1-4129-0025-6, PP: 425.
[41]Restaurants, https://en.wikipedia.org/wiki/Restaurant.

establishments serving refined food and fine wines in a formal setting. In the former case, customers usually wear casual clothing. In the latter case, depending on culture and local traditions, customers might wear semi-casual, semi-formal or formal wear. Typically, customers sit at tables, their orders are taken by a waiter, who brings the food when it is ready. After eating, the customers then pay the bill. For some time the travelling public has been catered for with ship's messes and railway restaurant cars which are, in effect, travelling restaurants. (Many railways, the world over, also cater for the needs of travellers by providing Railway Refreshment Rooms (a form of restaurant) at railway stations.) In recent times there has been a trend to create a number of travelling restaurants, specifically designed for tourists. These can be found on such diverse places as trams, boats, buses, etc.

RNM and Associates (2015)[42] report that the restaurant services market has been divided into four areas; quick service restaurants, fine dining, casual dining and cafes, bars and pubs. The food and beverage service market has witnessed a compounded annual growth rate of 20per cent. The overall scenario of the food and beverage sector has transformed from a time where a handful of restaurants existed to a time now where consumers are flooded with choices of cuisines, locations and range of prices.

2.4.   Growth of Restaurant Industry in India

India, as a country, has a very diverse range of cuisines to offer. This can be attributed to the varied geographical terrains, cultures, religions and climates that exist in India. Food is an integral part of the overall Indian culture with many ingredients, spices, herbs and inter-regional influence on cooking styles. Over the years, Indian food has evolved and so has the taste preference of its people. Earlier, we preferred to stick to the cuisine we had been brought up on but now we are ready to experiment with our taste buds and willing to explore something new. This urge to try newer cuisines has fuelled the growth of casual and fine-dine industry in India[43]. This section of the growth of restaurant industry India.

Navjit Ahluwalia et.al (2004)[44] research work conducted for Federation of Hotel & Restaurant Associations of India (FHRAI) had mentioned that there are 10 million households in India with average household income of `.46,000 per month and 2 million households with a

---

[42] RNM and Associates (2015), Outlook of the Restaurant Services Market in India, A Research Paper On The Restaurant Services Market In India, PP: 4.

[43]SaurabhSaxena (2015), Food and Beverage News, March.

[44]NavjitAhluwalia, and et.al (2004), Restaurant Industry in India - Trends and Opportunities, A Research Study, Published in April 2004 by: Secretary General, Federation of Hotel & Restaurant Associations of India, Federation of Hotel & Restaurant Associations of India (FHRAI).

household income of Rs 115,000 per month. Eating out has emerged as a trend, which is prevalent within this elite group. Two of out of every five households in this group eat out at least once a month. There are 100 million populations in the age grouping of 17-21 year in India. Sales by Indian food service companies totaled `.350 billion in 2002. The organized sector is responsible for approximately`.20 billion worth of sales. Indian consumers spend only 2.4 percent of their food expenditure in hotels and restaurants (including on premises and take-out sales). American consumers, by comparison spend 46 percent of their food expenditure on away-from-home meals. These demographic numbers represent a young nation which has an increased propensity to spend in restaurant and other food service sectors.

According to Horner and Vinod (2005)[45] the economic growth in the country, which is predicted to grow further, has already meant that the eating habits of urban Indians are moving away from the traditions associated with their cuisine and eating habits. It is predicted that these changes will continue and this, coupled with the expansion of effective food chain systems, will mean that there will be a further explosion of restaurant and contract catering development in the country. New international players will increasingly enter the market and the choices on offer in restaurants will become more varied and international India can also use their traditional cuisine, however, as the basis of tourism development strategies.

According to Gopal.R and Krishna Shetty (2007)[46] Indian restaurant services sector is estimated to be worth `.57,000 crore, out of which only Rs. 3,940 crore i.e., 6.9 percent is accounted for by the organized sector. Thevast unorganized segment mainly comprises street-side stalls/kiosks constituting the majority of consumer food-service units and is characterized by intense fragmentation and a virtual absence of standardization of operations. This segment was `.35,000 crore in 2004, which grew by about 18 per cent to `.41,400 crore in 2005 and in 2006 the segment recorded a growth of nearly 19per cent over previous year and stood at `.49,200 Crore. Major domestic and international players inthe arena have on an average extended their retail reach by 45 percent in 2006 as compared to 2005. Tier II cities are

---

[45]Horner and Vinod (2005), Food and Drink as a Tourist Product – The Relevance for India, Conference paper delivered at the International Food Tourism Conference, PP: 17-19, November

[46]Gopal.R and Krishna Shetty (2007), Innovative entrepreneurship – the key dna for a successful turnaround in the hospitality business , with specific Reference to the Hospitality Sector - Small and Medium sized Hotels in Mumbai. Institute of Management Studies, Navi Mumbai.

http://www.iitk.ac.in/infocell/announce/convention/papers/Industrial%20Economics%20%20Environ ment,%20CSR-02-Krishna%20shetty%20R%20Gopal.pdf.

currently the biggest growth drivers. Additionally investments in supply chain management are another important issue to be focused for the future success.

According to Ball et.al (2007)[47] the economic growth of India, which is predicated to grow further, has already meant that the eating habits of urban Indian are moving away from the traditions associated with their cuisine and eating habits. It is predicted that these changes will continue and this, coupled with the expansion of restaurant and contract catering development in the country. New international players will increasingly enter the market and the choices on offer in restaurants will become more varied and international. India can also use their traditional cuisine for the promotion tourism across the country.

Live Mint PTI New Reports (2010)[48] that National Restaurant Association of India (NRAI) has mentioned that the organised restaurant sector currently enjoys 16per cent market share in the estimated `.43,000-crore restaurant industry. According to the Live Mint report, the total restaurant industry (inclusive of both the organised and the unorganised segment) is expected to grow at over 5per cent in the next three years and is likely to touch `.62,500 crore by 2015. Rise in the disposable income of individuals and changing lifestyle among young Indians are some of the factors contributing to the growth of the sector. The report also stated that a large proportion of the Indian urban population has already moved into an income bracket with a sufficient amount of disposable income and has just started enjoying a lifestyle where eating out is one of the main forms of leisure.

David Williams and Shubhi Mishra (2011)[49] study reported that India's hotel, restaurant and institutional (HRI) sector continues to expand and modernize as domestic and international tourism and business travel increases and Indian consumers increase the frequency with which they consume food outside the home. The study stated that while traditional hotels and restaurants dominate the market, four and five-star hotels and modern

---

[47]Stephen Ball, Susan Horner and Devin Nield, (2007) *Contemporary hospitality & tourism management issues in china and India,* First edition 2007, ISBN : 978-0-7506-6856-9, PP:138.

[48]Organised restaurant market to touch Rs28,000 cr by 2015, Live Mint PTI New Reports,

http://www.livemint.com/Companies/R1dLv7AnHZpc8IOtLfUo6J/Organised-restaurant-market-to-touch-Rs28000-cr-by-2015.html, 9th May 2010,

[49]David Williams and Shubhi Mishra (2011), India Food Service-Hotel Restaurant Institutional, This Report Contains Assessments of Commodity and Trade Issues Made by USDA staff and not necessarily statements of official US Government Policy, GAIN Report: IN1186.

http://gain.fas.usda.gov/Recent%20GAIN%20Publications/Food%20Service%20-%20Hotel%20 Restaurant%20Institutional_New%20Delhi_India_9-15-2011.pdf.

restaurants are benefiting from India's growing economy, a willingness among consumers to try new foods and cuisines and increasing urbanization.

According to Neha Joshi (2012)[50] India is in the midst of the restaurant revolution. The revenues hotel and restaurant industry in 2006-2007 had increased to 22 per cent. The demand for food away from home is dramatically increasing. According to the 2003-04 Indian Household Economic Survey, the average weekly household expenditure on meals away from home increased from US$13.80 in 2000/01 to IS$19.20 in 2003-04 (Ministry of Health, 2006). The growth of demand for food has prompted an expansion of the Indian foodservice industry. The national foodservice industry annual sales rose from US $3,176 million in 2002 to US $4,800 million in 2007 at a nominal growth of 51 percent. The study also comments that since the eating habits of people are changing; the style of cooking and the ingredients used increased the popularity of Indian food all throughout. Indian food had experienced a tremendous change as peoples have started following cooking style and adopted eating habit according to their religion , at present various Indian foods is recognized all over the country. Thus, the restaurants should realise the diners will judge restaurants based on their service quality. Service quality determines an organization success or failure, the satisfaction is a function of consumer, experience and reaction to provide behavior during the service encounter. The level of satisfaction may be influence by various attitudes from internal, external factor.

Ravi Gupta and Lavkush Mishra (2013)[51] are of the opinion that restaurants to stand out in the competitions in the hospitality industry in India, good service quality have become the most Important. Today, everyone recognizes the pervasion consequences of quality, at the same time; everyone seems to be having difficulty in grasping its many dimensions which has becomes a key issue in the management of hospitality industry. There is some misunderstanding in perceiving the service quality between the hospitality industry and tourist in which research has shown that many service industry develop their own perception of what, tourist want, which often differ from what the tourist really want this situation has created a gap between tourist and operators of the industry.

---

[50]Neha Joshi (2012), *A Study on Customer Preference and Satisfaction towards Restaurant in Dehradun City*, Global Journal of Management and Business Research, Volume No.12, Issue.No.21, PP:39-46,Online ISSN: 2249-4588 & Print ISSN: 0975-5853.

[51]Ravi Gupta and Lavkush Mishra (2013), *Relationship Between Guest Satisfaction*, Employee Satisfaction and Manager or Owner Satisfaction for Eateries or Restaurants: Special Reference To Dehradun District, International Journal of Basic And Advanced Research, 2013, Volume No.2, Issue No.4, PP: 97- 102, ISSN: 2278 7143

According DhruvSood and Shubhi Mishra (2014)[52] India's food service sector continues expanding as the number of travellers increases and more consumers dine at restaurants. Traditional venues dominate the market, but four and five-star hotels and modern restaurants are benefiting from altered dininghabits, urbanization, and raised aspirational levels. Traditionally, Indians have tended to eat at home and eat traditional Indian cuisine. Those who ate outside the home often ate street foods from the enormous number of street stalls and informal eateries that are common across India. Eating in a restaurant was reserved for special occasions. However, India appears to be in the early stages of a significant transformation in the restaurant sector. Indian consumers are eating out more frequently and younger Indians are shedding the biases of their elders against international franchises and foreign foods. With only an estimated 100,000 modern, organized restaurants (20 or more seats, wait staff, menus) in India, there is plenty of room for growth in the industry. It is estimated that Indians spend 8 to 10 percent of their food expenditures outside the home in restaurants, cafeterias and other food establishments.

According to Arbind Prasad (2015)[53] Indian Food and Beverage (F&B) service Industry is one of the most vibrant industries that has seen unprecedented growth in the recent past and continues to expand rapidly. This can be attributed to the changing demographics, increase in disposable incomes, urbanisation and growth of organised retail. The F&B service market is worth `.2,04,438 crore and is expected to reach `.3,80,000 crore by 2017. The sector is dominated primarily by the traditional segment. The brands and restaurant chains of both Indian origin and multinationals have not optimally penetrated the market so far. The F&B sector has evolved over the past decade, giving rise to exciting new concepts in food and beverage offerings and new and innovative service elements. Segments such as fine dining, casual dining, quick service restaurants, cafes, etc. have found favour with the consumers. The F&B industry has been at the forefront of attracting investments into India and has played an integral role in portraying India as a land of opportunity.

According Eromonitor report (2015)[54] due to the increasing infrastructure facilities across India, such as increasing state and national highways, which can result in more people travelling, supported the growth of full-service restaurants. Furthermore, the increasing

---

[52]DhruvSood and Shubhi Mishra (2014), Food Service- Hotel Restaurant Institutional, GAIN Report No: IN4118, USDA Foreign Agricultural Services, 29th December.

[53]Arbind Prasad (2015), Unlocking the potential in the food and beverage services sector, Report Jointly Prepared by Grant Thornton nor FICCI ,http://www.ficci.com/spdocument/20589/F&B-Report.pdf.

[54]Full-Service Restaurants in India, http://www.euromonitor.com/full-service-restaurants-in-india/report, September.

presence of international cuisine to smaller cities also supported the growth of full-service restaurants in 2014.The report also mentions that the full-service restaurants are expected to grow by a value CAGR of 4per cent at constant 2014 prices over the forecast period, reaching `.4.3 trillion in 2019. The report identified that increasing disposable incomes and less time for cooking in urban India would be the primary reason of the growth of full-service restaurants. Furthermore, conduct of more social and corporate events in full-service restaurants will also fuel the growth of restaurant business in India.

2.5. Factors Influences Diners in Selection of Restaurants, their Perception and Satisfaction

Creating positive customer experience will enhance the influential factor for customers to dine-in at their favourite restaurants. This is because the eating behaviour is a central part of the consumers' daily lives and not just for gaining food nutritional values. However, the customers' behaviour may be influenced by the experiences created at the time of their visit to specific restaurants. In short it can be said that rrestaurant selection criteria are the most important attributes that customers use in deciding where to dine out. Drawing theoretical views from the above discussion this section of the study aims to summaries reviews on factors that influence diners while selecting a restaurant services, diners' perception and satisfaction towards restaurant services.

Steadman (1991)[55] in his book titled "Restaurant Biz is Show Biz" has stated that people do not go to restaurants just to be fed, but they can order food, take away or get delivered of food, if they haven't cooked food at home. Customers at fine dining restaurants want treat them special by the restaurant operators. The author comments that service quality is a critical component of customers' value perceptions that, in turn, become a determinant of customer satisfaction. Moreover, customers perceive greater value for their money when they experience a high level of quality.

Auty (1992)[56] empirical study aimed to analyse the consumer choice and segmentation in the restaurant industry in Lancaster, England. The study identified the choice factors in the restaurant decision process based on four occasions: a celebration, social occasion, convenience/quick meal, and business Meal. The study findings revealed that food type, food

---

[55]Steadman, D. (1991), *Restaurant Biz is Show Biz*, Whittier Green Publishing Co. Inc., Greenlawn, New York.

[56]Auty, S (1992), *Consumer choice and segmentation in the restaurant industry*, The Service Industries Journal, Volume No.12, Issue No.3, PP:324-339.

quality and value for money were the most important choice variables for consumers when choosing a restaurant. The study mentioned that the order of these choices criteria varied according to dining occasions. The study suggested that if the consumers perceived that restaurants provide comparable food type, food quality and price, they would consider these criteria while selecting the same restaurant in future.

Knutson and Patton (1993)[57] empirical study focused on assessing the market opportunities available to the restaurants' among the adult consumers who are aged 55 years and more. The study found that older customers are more concerned about their health and the quality of food and they give importance to these criterions while selecting a restaurant service.

Muller and Woods (1994)[58] study aimed to analyse the primary factors that influences diner for selection of restaurant services and their perceptions towards restaurant selections. The study findings revealed that the consumers while selecting restaurants always consider the price of the service as important factor, as the restaurant consumers use price as a measure for the quality of the restaurant. The diners perceive that an expensive restaurant serves better food and offers better quality in comparison to the low priced restaurants.

Lee and Hing (1995)[59] adapted the SERVQUAL instrument in measuring and comparing service quality within the two fine dining restaurants: French and Chinese restaurants. The finding of the study revealed that the highest respondents' expectations were assurance and reliability, and the lowest expectation was tangibles for both French and Chinese restaurants. The respondents' perceptions of the service quality dimension of French restaurant were assurance, reliability, and responsiveness being rated the highest respectively. The respondents' perceptions of the service quality of Chinese restaurant were tangibles, reliability and empathy.

Barsky (1996)[60] study aimed to design services with function analysis with references to hospitality sector. The study stated that the consumers may be excellent sources of information for management on how the organization can provide quality service. Similarly,

---

[57]Knutson, B. J. and Patton, M. E. (1993), *Restaurants can find gold among silver hair: Opportunities in the 55+ market,* Journal of Hospitality and Leisure Marketing,Vloume.No.1, Issue.no.3, PP:79-90.

[58]Muller, C.C. and Woods, R.H. (1994).An Expanded Restaurant Typology, Cornell Hotel and Restaurant Administration Quarterly, Volume. No. 35, Issue.No.3, PP:: 27-37.

[59]Lee. Y. L and Hing N. (1995). Measuring Quality in Restaurant Operations: An Application of the SERVQUAL Instrument. International Journal of Hospitality Management, Volume. No. 14, Issue.No.3/4, PP:293-310.

[60]Barsky, J., 1996. Designing services with function analysis. The Hospitality Research Journal, Volume.No.20, Issue.No.4, PP: 73–100.

according to Gabbie and O'Neil (1996)[61] in the challenging and highly competitive hospitality industry, every organization is forced to run its business in the most effective and efficient manner possible, and only this can ensure the success in the market that the business is entering Offering services that customers prefer is obviously a vital basis for gaining customer satisfaction.

Tucci and Talaga (1997)[62] conjoint analysis study aimed to determine the basic parameter on which a diner evaluates a service of restaurant. The study found that customer evaluates restaurant services based on different parameters like: price, speed of service, quality of food, courtesy of server and service guarantee. The study also observed that customers evaluation norms varies from on category of restaurant to the other and it is not uniform in nature, it changes as per their desirability of the services.

Johns and Howard (1998)[63] study aimed to assess the customer expectations and perceptions towards service performance in the foodservice industry. The study founding revealed that customers definitely regarded price and value considerations as part of the service bundle. Clark and Wood (1998)[64] aimed to explore factors relevant to engendering consumer loyalty in restaurant choice. The study findings mentioned that the quality and range or type of food are key determinants in consumer loyalty, but that the concept of "quality of food" offers a range of that is expressed by the sample diners. Similarly, the study identified that the concept of the "meal experience" as a holistic abstraction in the consumer's mind changes from one's perceptive to other. In, final the study findings reveal that the tangible factors as important customer loyalty determinant in restaurant industry rather than intangible factors.

Dulen (1999)[65] research paper aimed to identify the factors that influence the diners in selection of the full- service restaurant. The study found that there are seven factors that cause

---

[61]Gabbie.O and O'Neil. M. A. (1996), SERVQUAL and the Northern Ireland hotel sector: A comparative analysis—part 1. Managing Service Quality,Volume.No.6, Issue.No.6, PP: 25–32.

[62]Tucci, L.A. and Talaga J. (1997), *Service Guarantees and Consumers Evaluation of Services,* Journal of Services Marketing, Volume No.11, Issue No.1, PP. 10-18.

[63]Johns.N and Howard.A (1998), *Customer expectations versus perceptions of service performance in the foodservice industry.*International Journal of Service Industry Management, Volume.No.9, Issue.No.3, PP: 248-265.

[64]Mona A. Clark and Roy C. Wood, (1998), Consumer loyalty in the restaurant industry - a preliminary exploration of the issues, International Journal of Contemporary Hospitality Management, Volume.No.10 Issue: 4, PP:139 – 144.

[65]Dulen, J. (1999), *Quality control.*Journal of Restaurant and Institution,Volume No. 109, Issue No.5PP. 38-44.

consumer to choose particular full-service restaurant which are: food quality cleanliness, service, value, menu variety, convenience, and atmosphere inside the restaurants.

Kivela, J., et.al (2000)[66] empirical study aimed to analyse difference in consumers' rating towards a resultant selection based on the demographic status. The study divided the restaurants into four categories based on their differentiation in price, location, theme/ambience, service level, cuisine and style. The study found that restaurant selection varies across age groups, income levels, and restaurant types. The study found that ambience factor as an important determining choice of restaurants among the 25-34 year old young diner. The result of the study also observed that the interior is another important satisfier when the customer stays for some time in the environment and when their motive is to seek pleasure.

Mattila(2001)[67] study aimed examines the relationship between restaurant ambience and customer satisfaction in the Arabic restaurants. This study also seeks to determine which restaurant ambience elements highly influence customer satisfaction. The elements of spatial layout, interior design, colour and music were measured in Shah Alam, Selangor. The study found that restaurant colour is an important element that is significantly and mostly influences customers satisfaction and their intention towards restaurant ambience.

Mehta and Maniam (2002)[68] study examined the determinants of customers' attitudes towards selecting a restaurant. Various factors such as service, product, location, physical environment, promotion, price, and image attributes were rated and analysed based on diners importance. The study finding stated that customers pay more preferences for food quality, ambience factors, restaurant image and friendly staff while selecting a fine dining restaurant.

Soriano (2002)[69] research study aimed to analyse the Spanish consumers' expectation from the restaurant services offered in their country. The study found that young diners does not pay more importance to the food quality while selecting a restaurant, whereas the customers over 60 years of age due considered food quality as the primary determinant factor. The study

---

[66]Kivela, J., Inbakaran, R. and Reece, J., (2000), *Consumer Research in the Restaurant Environment- Part 3: Analysis,* Findings and Conclusions, International Journal of Contemporary Hospitality Management, 12/1, PP. 13-30.

[67]Mattila.A.S (2001), Emotional bonding and restaurant loyalty. Journal Cornell Hotel and Restaurant Administration Quarterly, Volume.No.42, Issue.No.6, PP: 73-79.

[68]Mehta, S.S. and Maniam, B. (2002), *Marketing Determinants of Customers Attitude Towards Selecting a Restaurant,* Academy of Marketing Studies Journal, Volume No.6, Issue No.1, PP.27-44.

[69]Soriano, D. R. (2002), *Customers' expectations factors in restaurants: The situation in Spai,.* International Journal of Quality and Reliability Management, Volume.No.19, Issue No. 8/9, PP: 1055-1067.

also established the fact the male and female consumers does not consider the brand of the restaurant in a same manner, moreover,   Customers have their own reason whether to revisit to any restaurant in the future or not. Their future repeat visits to a restaurant are dependent on their work pressure, quality of service expectations and their mood for relaxation.

Yu¨ksel and Yu¨ksel (2002)[70] study aimed to analyse the tourist satisfaction towards restaurant services in Turkey. The study had constructed 42 variables to measure the tourist level of satisfaction. It was found that tourists were found to be satisfied with the restaurant's service quality, product quality, menu diversity, hygiene, convenience and location, noise, service speed, price and value, facilities and atmosphere.

Sullivan's (2002)[71] empirical study aimed to analyse consumers' preferences and satisfaction towards restaurant. The study found that well designed environment is important factor that attracts customer and this in turn influences customer satisfaction. The study also found that restaurant cleanliness with appropriate music and lighting also contributes towards the customers satisfactions.

Vincent C.S. Heung and Terry Lam (2003)[72] study examined Chinese customer complaint behaviour towards Hong Kong hotel restaurant services. The main objectives of the study were to identify complaint patterns and the relationships between customers' demographic backgrounds such as age, gender and education levels and their complaint behaviours. The research findings revealed that most customers are like to post private complaint such as word-of-mouth communication and stop patronizing the restaurant. The study highlights that the complaint intentions of Chinese diners were quite low and they were passive about communicating their dissatisfaction to restaurateurs. The study suggests that the restaurateurs can make use their clients' complaints to improve their existing service dimensions.

Cullen's (2004)[73] empirical study aimed analyse the factors influencing restaurant selection in Dublin. The study found that young marriage age with children that are between thirty and

[70]Yu¨ksel, A. and Yu¨ksel, F. (2002), *Measurement of Tourist Satisfaction with Restaurant Services: A Segment-Based Approach*, Journal of Vacation Marketing, Volume No.9, Issue No.1, PP: 52-68.

[71]Sullivan, Malcolm. (2002). The impact of pitch, volume and tempo on the atmospheric effects of music. International Journal of Retail & Distribution Management, Volume No. 30, Issue No. 6, PP: 323-330.

[72]Vincent C.S. Heung and Terry Lam (2003), *Customer complaint behaviour towards hotel restaurant services*, International Journal of Contemporary Hospitality Management, Volume No.15 Issue No.5, PP: 283 – 289.

[73]Cullen, F. (2004), *Factors influencing restaurant selection in Dublin.* Journal of Foodservice Business Research, Volume No.7, Issue No.2, PP:53-85.

thirty-nine and the working people, has different criteria of restaurant selection where a location is the salient attributes and they preferred the restaurants that are near to them. The study also had observed that restaurant's location is not important criterion for retired people.

Sloan. D's (2004)[74] research study aimed to investigate the consumers' preferences towards international restaurant. The study found that the physical environment of the restaurant such as restaurant's atmosphere, ambience, décor, furniture and other facilities can have a great impact on the dining experience and their preferences towards international restaurant.

Sulek and Hensley (2004)[75] aimed to assess the relative importance of food, atmosphere and fairness of wait in determining the customers' satisfaction towards restaurant services. The study found that factors that influence consumers in choosing full-service restaurant are: food quality, atmosphere, quality of the service, and interpersonal skills of the restaurant employee. Cullen (2005)[76] study aimed to investigate the selection process used by consumers when choosing a restaurant to dine. The findings of the research displayed a preference by Dublin consumers for Italian and Chinese styled restaurants and identified quality of the food, type of food, cleanliness of the restaurant, location and the reputation of the restaurant as the key decision variables/attributes used by consumers to select restaurants. The study also established that the importance of the attributes changed, depending on the consumer's age, prior experience, their mood and the occasion involved while selection of restaurant.

Ramapuram and Batra (2006)[77] the study aimed to determine the effect of restaurant attributes on customers' overall perception and return patronage, and whether dining occasions affect return patronage in Ebony Restaurant, Bangalore (India).The finding of the study revealed that there is a correlation between restaurant attributes and customers' overall perception. Results also indicated that there is a relationship between return patronage and restaurant attributes and dining occasions. Managerial implications are addressed and discussed.

[74]Sloan, D. (2004), *Culinary Taste: Consumer Behavior in the International Restaurant Sector,* Oxford: Elsevier Butterworth-Heinemann.

[75]Sulek, J.M., and Hensley, R.L. (2004), *The Relative Importance of Food,* Atmosphere, and Fairness of Wait: The Case of a Full service Restaurant. Volume No. 45, Issue No.3, PP: 235-248.

[76]Frank Cullen (2005), Factors Influencing Restaurant Selection in Dublin, Journal of Foodservice Business Research, Volume.No.7, Issue.No. 2.

[77]Thresi Emmanuel Ramapuram and AdarshBatra (2006), The Effect of Restaurant Attributes on Customers' Overall Perception and Return Patronage: A Case Study on EBONY Restaurant, Bangalore, India, http://www.journal.au.edu/journal_management/2006/jul06/jul06-article04-effect.pdf

Gupta et al.(2007)[78] research paper aimed to assess the guest satisfaction and restaurant performance. The study reviewed various literature studies to understand and draw a linkage between guest satisfaction and restaurant performance. The study reveals evidence of strong relationships between customer satisfaction with various restaurant attributes and repeat-purchase intention.Ladhariet.al (2008)[79] study aimed to investigate and to identify the determinants of dining satisfaction and post-dining behavioral intentions. The study found that perceived service quality influenced customer satisfaction through both positive and negative emotions and that directly influences their post-dinning behaviour.

Han and Ryu (2009)[80] study aimed to analyse the roles of the physical environment, price perception, and customer satisfaction in determining customer loyalty in the restaurant industry. The study findings revealed that physical environment of restaurant significantly influences its selection by the customers. The study suggests that a restaurant firm should carefully design the physical environment to improve the customer's perceived reasonableness of the price. The authors further indicated that creative use of physical design in a restaurant operation would be essential in enhancing specific marketing objectives such as positive customer perception of quality, positive evaluation of experience and positive attitudes.

Kumar et al(2010)[81] study aimed to analyse the influence of restaurant atmospherics on customer value in an emerging market. The study indicated that style enhances the beauty and theatrical feel of a restaurant. The study also stated that the personality and assists in communicating the brand image of restaurant. A visually pleasing design and style in a restaurant can therefore positively influence a customer's mood.

Jang and Namkung.Y (2011)[82] research article aimed to assess effects of authentic atmospherics in ethnic Chinese restaurant. The study found that sit-down restaurants need to consider the improvement of the overall dining atmosphere to end enhance customers'

[78]Gupta.S., McLaughlin.E.and Gomez, M.(2007), Guest satisfaction and restaurant performance. Cornell Hotel and Restaurant Administration Quaterly, Volume.No.48, Issue.No.3, PP:284-298.

[79]Ladhari, R., Brun, I.and Morales, M.(2008). Determinants of dining satisfaction and post-dining behavioural intentions. International Journal of Hospitality Management, Volume.No.27, Issue.No.4, PP:568-573.

[80]Han, H.andRyu, K.(2009), The roles of the physical environment, price perception, and customer satisfaction in determining customer loyalty in the restaurant industry. Journal of Hospitality & Tourism Research, , Volume.No.33, Issue.No.4, PP:487-510.

[81]Kumar, I., Garg, R. &Rahman, Z. (2010), Influence of retail atmospherics on customer value in an emerging market, Great Lakes Herald,Volume.No.4, Issue.No.1, PP:1-13.

[82]Jang, S., Liu, Y. &Namkung, Y. (2011), Effects of authentic atmospherics in ethnic restaurants: investigating Chinese restaurants, International Journal of Contemporary Hospitality Management, Volume.No.23, Issue.No.5, PP: 662–680.

satisfaction. The study suggested that dining atmospherics can typically be improved by optimising the design and layout of the restaurant, implementing the most fitting colour schemes and furniture (based on the type of establishment), and creating the desired ambience by means of effective light use.

Malik and Kumar (2012)[83] research paper intends to assess factors affecting menu planning in hotels of North India. The study results revealed that financial condition of diner, theme of restaurant, guests' spending power and age group, and costs i.e., labour and food costs are considered as primary factors while restaurants while planning their menu.

Deshwal and Khanna's (2013)[84] study aimed to assess service experience of restaurant customers in Delhi. The study found that most of the customer prefers visiting restaurants to have a good meal with their family members or friends and they want to have good relaxing time as they are stressed with number of tensions in their life and stress of work. Shylaja.S and Eahambaram (2013)[85] study aimed to analyse the customer satisfaction towards four season restaurant in Coimbatore city. The found that customers were satisfied with service provided by the restaurant. But they were found to be dissatisfaction with the price of the items, parking facilities, serving time and washing facilities. The study suggests that the management of the restaurant should take necessary steps to solve these problems. If they do so, that will increase their satisfaction level of customers.

Muthukumaranet.al(2013)[86] study aimed to assess the customer preference and satisfaction towards chat out restaurants in Chennai City. The study findings revealed that menu in the chat out restaurants have attracts the customer and tempt to taste and 62per cent of the respondents highly satisfied towards features and service promptness of services. The study findings also reveals that, customers expect varieties of recepies, Promptness of service, delicious food items, good facilities and appearance and total the value for money they spend while visiting restaurant.

---

[83]Sandeep Malik and Sanjeev Kumar (2012), Factors Affecting Menu Planning In Hotels: A Study of North India, Innovative Journal of Business and Management , Volume.No.1, Issue.No.6, ISSN:2277-4947, PP: 97 – 101, November-December

[84]PankajDeshwal and SahilKhanna (2013), Service Experience and Consumer Satisfaction in Restaurants, International Journal of Business and Management Invention, Volume.No.2, Issue.No.10, ISSN (Online): 2319 –8028, ISSN (Print): 2319 –801X, PP:89-95, October.

[85]Shylaja.S and Eahambaram .C (2013), A study on customer satisfaction towards four season restaurant in Coimbatore city, Volume:.No.3, Issue.No.7, ISSN - 2249-555X, PP:143-145.

[86]Muthukumaran .C. K, Sugumar.D and. Angappapillai A.B (2013), Customer Preference and Satisfaction towards Chat Out Restaurants, International Journal of Research In Commerce, Economics & Management, Volume. No. 3, Issue No.5,ISSN 2231-4245, PP:55-60, May.

Kanta and Srivalli.P (2014)[87] study examined the relationship between service quality, satisfaction, and the frequency of patronage in a restaurant setting. The study found that physical environment quality, relative to outcome quality, are more important predictors of service quality. The study findings also established the fact that a high level of service quality is associated with customer satisfaction as well as frequent patronage. However, the study stated that there exist no significant link between satisfaction and repeat patronage.

Latha's (2014)[88] research paper aimed to analyse the consumer perception and satisfaction towards restaurants in Coimbatore city. The study found that the diners were satisfied towards: food portion size served, variety of food/beverage, quality and taste of food, cleanliness of the dining area, value received for the price paid, comfortable and welcoming feeling, timeliness of service, accuracy of order–taking practices, communication skills of the staff, payment of bill, working hours, working of parcel section. However, the study findings also revealed that the diners were neutrally satisfied towards restaurant service features like: temperature of food, convenience of washroom, attentiveness of the staff.

Sabir et.al (2014)[89] research paper aimed to analyse the customer satisfaction in the restaurant industry in Pakistan. The study found that customers were satisfied with the price, product quality, service quality and physical design of the restaurants. The study findings also revealed that dines mostly prefers visiting restaurants either for meal or for social gatherings and as symbol of their prestige and social status.

GoldiPuri and Mahesh Kumar (2014)[90] study highlighted the importance of service quality and customer satisfaction in restaurants. The study comments that the success of any food and service establishment depends on its ability to satisfy their quests by providing a dining. The restaurants' ability to satisfy their guests is the determining factor in customer retention and loyalty. Furthermore, it is a good financial proposition to increase the number of repeating guests and to attract new ones. The restaurant industry in India is large and providing a range of product and services.

---

[87]Kota Neel Mani Kanta and Srivalli.P (2014), A Study on Service Quality in Indian Restaurants with Decision-and Experiential-Oriented Perspectives in India, International Journal of Research and Development-A Management Review (IJRDMR), Volume.No.3, Issue.No.1, ISSN:2319-5479, PP:16-24.

[88]Latha.K (2014),A Study on Consumer Perception and Satisfaction Towards Restaurants in Coimbatore City, Paripex Indian Journal of Research, Voulme.3, Issue.No.7, ISSN:2250-1991, PP:32-34.

[89]Raja IrfanSabir, Muhammad Irfan, NaeemAkhtar, Muhammad Abbas Pervez and AsadurRehman (2014), Customer Satisfaction in the Restaurant Industry; Examining the Model in Local Industry Perspective, Journal of Asian Business Strategy, Volume.No.4, Issue.No.1, PP:18-31.

[90]GoldiPuri and Mahesh Kumar (2014), Importance of service quality and customer satisfaction in restaurants, Volume.No.2, Issue.No.2, IJRMBSS I eISSN: 2321-9874 | ISSN: 2319-6998, PP:51-58, June.

Srivastava (2015)[91] research work aimed to assess reasons for customer preferences regarding restaurant services. The study findings disclosed the fact that the diners select those restaurants that has well appearing ambience, well equipped dining room, rest room, hygiene of the restaurants and its staff, knowledge of the server, personal attention and convenient parking facilities. The study also found that variety in the menu, attentive staff, friendly and helpful employees as act as important attribute in selection of restaurant for dinning by the diners.

Omar et.al (2015)[92] study aimed to examine the relationship between restaurant ambience and customer satisfaction in the Arabic restaurants. This study also seeks to determine which restaurant ambience elements highly influence customer satisfaction. The study findings revealed that spatial layout, interior design, colour and music have significant relationships with customers' satisfaction. The study found that largest contribution to customers' satisfaction is colour followed by spatial layout, music and interior design.

Jun and Arendt (2015)[93] study aimed examine how individual health values influence interest in healthy foods, positive outcome expectations, hedonic expectations, and behaviour intentions. The study results indicated that health value was the key element that inspired customer interest in healthy eating and aroused hedonic and positive outcome expectations, which in turn enhanced intentions to purchase healthy food items. The study suggests to the restaurant managers to establish creative marketing strategies to motivate customer interest in healthy menu items and emphasize benefits of their healthy food items.

Ramli et.al (2015)[94] study aimed to examine to what extent does service provider attentiveness is importance towards customer satisfaction in restaurants in Kuala Lumpur and Selangor. The study findings revealed that customers of each restaurant are satisfied with the overall quality of service delivery, service provider attitude, personal hygiene and restaurant

[91]KalpanaSrivastava (2015), A study of attributes affecting selection of restaurants by selected customers, International Journal of Home Science, Volume.No.1, Issue.No.2, PP: 46-51.

[92]MuhamadSaufiyudin Omar, HashimFadzilAriffin and Rozila Ahmad (2015), The Relationship between Restaurant Ambience and Customers' Satisfaction in Shah Alam Arabic Restaurants, Selangor, International Journal of Administration and Governance, Volume No.1, Issue No.4, ISSN 2077-44,PP:1-8.

[93]Juhee KangJinhyun Jun and Susan W.Arendt (2015), Understanding customers' healthy food choices at casual dining restaurants: Using the Value–Attitude–Behaviour model, International Journal of hospitality Management, Volume.No.48, PP:12-21, July.

[94]NoorazlinRamli, Wan Fatimah Wan MohdNowalid, MalinaHanumMohd Kamal and Wan Nazriah Wan Nawawi(2015), A Study on Determinants of Customer Satisfaction towards Service Providers Attentiveness in Casual Dining Restaurants, Journal of Applied Environmental and Biological Sciences, Volume.No.5, Issue.No.6s, ISSN: 2090-4274, PP:1-4.

environment. Despite these, it was observed that customers were satisfied with service delivery. The study suggests that if the service providers are attentiveness in enhancing the above said attributes that will increase customers' satisfaction and their attention to repeat patronisation.

2.6.   Conclusion

From the elaborate literature reviews discussed above the researcher is able to gather enough knowledge on the growth of restaurant sector in India, classification of restaurants across the world and in India, the primary factors that motivates the diners to visit restaurants, their perception and satisfaction towards restaurant services. The study is able to realise that number of studies on the above mentioned issues i.e., primary factors that motivates the diners to visit a restaurants, their perception and satisfaction towards restaurant services were conducts in the both America, Europe and in South East Asian context. But, not much studied were conducted in the past on Indian context and that too on diners preferences, choice and satisfaction towards casual dine restaurants across India. The identified research dearth has been considered as the primary motivation for the conduct of this study. This aims to analyse diners' preference towards restaurant services in Coimbatore City.

CHAPTER III

OVERVIEW ON RESTAURANT INDUSTRY IN INDIA AND CONSUMERS ATTITUDE AND PREFERENCES TOWARDS IT

Dining etiquette is widely respected in parts of Indian culture, local customs, traditions, and religions. Proper table manners vary from culture to culture, although there are always a few basic rules that are important to follow. Etiquette should be observed when dining in any Indian household or restaurant, though the acceptable standards depend upon the situation[95]. This chapter provides an overview on the restaurant industry in India and consumers' attitude and preferences towards it.

3.1. Food Culture of India

Indian households follow the traditional dining culture which places great value on freshly prepared meals. They eat traditional foods and cook fresh at home for every meal. Vegetables and meats are bought fresh. Meals are prepared fresh every time. A large number of Indian consumers still prefer vegetarian dishes though the demand for non-vegetarian food is on the rise in India, even among conservative households. Indian cuisine is wide-ranging and diverse. Different regions have clearly differentiated tastes and preferences. In recent years consumption of processed and packaged foods has grown strongly in urban areas and among more affluent households that have working women. The number of such households is large but consumption of packaged and convenience foods are still very low even among those households.

Indian consumers often celebrate major religious festivals and they prefer to cook meals at home during these occasions. This is especially true during religious festivals. The main meals as well as the desserts and special celebratory food items are still typically cooked at home. Ordering from restaurants is also on the rise these days across the low, middle and higher income households[96]. An Indian household exhibits a strong preference for Indian flavours and cooking styles. The interest in international dishes is on the rise but most Indian consumers continue to prefer Indian-style dishes. The more popular international cuisines include Chinese, Mexican, Thai, and Middle Eastern. In a large number of cases international dishes are prepared with Indian spices to suit to the local pallets.

---

[95] https://en.wikipedia.org/wiki/Etiquette_of_Indian_dining

[96] White Paper on Indian Restaurant Industry (2010), National Restaurant Association of India Report, PP:33

3.2.   Food Dining Culture among Indian Households

Dining out has seen explosive growth in recent years as urban Indian consumers seem to have found more occasions to celebrate and more opportunities to dine outside the home. Birthdays, wedding anniversaries, graduation parties, Valentine's Day celebrations, reunion parties and many more occasions are celebrated by dining out, at least by affluent consumers. According to the India Leisure and Entertainment Report by the Knowledge Tree company, dining out is now one of the three most popular recreational activities among Indian consumers. This is also due to lack of space in most urban dwellings.

According to a 2011 study conducted on Indian consumers' attitudes toward dining out conducted by the US Department of Agriculture (USDA), says traditional eating habits in India are changing and consumers who traditionally always ate at home are now increasingly dining out. Busy urban workers often pick up a quick breakfast from street stalls located close to office; lunch (and often dinner, too) is often purchased from stalls close to office. But while the vast majority of dining out consists of purchases at street stalls, restaurants have nevertheless accounted for a rapidly growing share. According to the USDA report, dining out in India used to be reserved only for special occasions but increasingly younger consumers and consumers from middle- and upper-income households are dining out more often[97].

Food dining etiquette in India is quite different to Western countries. India has a majority Hindu population, approximately 80per cent, about 14per cent Muslim, 2.4per cent Christian, 2per cent Sikh, 0.7per cent Buddhist, 0.5per cent Jains and 0.4per cent other. Of course we are aware of the enormous impact religion has in influencing the customs, etiquette and eating habits of its followers. Sharing food is part of Indian culture, especially on long train journeys, Indian families will be carrying heaps of food and will invite you to have some. Even when only 2 people are dining in a restaurant it is customary to order two different dishes and in keeping with Indian etiquette, share the dishes between the friends/relatives or co-diner(s)[98].

With changing times, the trends have changed and so have the tastes and preferences of the people. The customers trends are gradually moving from the fine dine to a more casual dining culture. Menu planning and designing is a very important part of a restaurant. And, more often, it is defined as an important marketing tool to gain customers towards a particular restaurant. No one likes to taste the same food over a long period of time. Today everyone believes in tweaking and playing with different flavours. And thus, restaurant owners and chefs believe in revamping their menu and flavours every four-six months to show their creativity in the

---

[97] www.Euromonitor.com

[98] http://www.a-to-z-of-manners-and-etiquette.com/indian-etiquette.html

cuisine that they serve. The Indian consumers are evolving in terms of their food preferences, eating out habits and are becoming more reciprocative towards food experimentation like: South India, Northern Indian, Thai, Chinese, Southern Coastal Indian, Arabic, European, Japanese, Mexican etc. The food experimentation practices of consumers' suits the fine dining as well as the, Casual and Quick dines restaurants[99].

3.3.   Overview of Food and Beverages Industry in India

The Indian Food and Beverage (F&B) service Industry is one of the most vibrant industries that has seen unprecedented growth in the recent past and continues to expand rapidly. The growth of Food and Beverage (F&B) service Industry can be attributed to the changing demographics, increase in disposable incomes, urbanisation and growth of organised retail segment. The F&B service market is worth `.2,04,438 crore in 2015 and is expected to reach `.3,80,000 crore by 2017[100] i.e., `.3.8 trillion in sales. Fast-food joints, which have the largest market share at 45per cent, will grow by 16.6per cent a year, said the report by consulting firm Grant Thornton India and lobby group Federation of Indian Chambers of Commerce and Industry (FICCI), followed by casual dining (32per cent share) expanding 10.1per cent annually. Standalone Restaurants, which comprise 22per cent of the market, is the fastest-growing, the report said, while the cafe segment with 12per cent market share is growing at 10.7per cent a year. Although fine dining constitutes only 3per cent of the market, the segment is seeing a renewed interest, particularly from multinational chains[101].

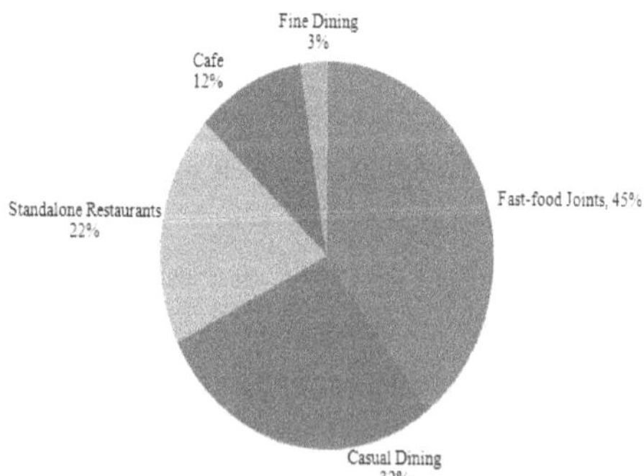

Exhibit 3.1: Classification of Indian Restaurants

Source:http://www.livemint.com/Companies/D6la6rk2jQ77EkOJwemgNO/FB-to-become-a-Rs-38-trillion-industry-by-201617-says-st.html.

---

[99]Archana Sharma (2014), Food for thought, Food & Hospitality World, 18thDecember,
http://www.financialexpress.com/article/fhw/chefs-platter/food-for-thought/20753/
[100]A brief report on tourism in India, January 2015,http://www.cci.in/pdfs/surveys-reports/Tourism-in-India.pdf
[101]http://www.livemint.com/Companies/D6la6rk2jQ77EkOJwemgNO/FB-to-become-a-Rs-38-trillion-industry-by-201617-says-st.html.

This sector is dominated primarily by the traditional segment. The brands and restaurant chains of both Indian origin and multinationals have not optimally penetrated the market so far[102]. The restaurants Industry has contributed between 1.5per cents of the GDP over the last seven to eight years[103]. The Indian food and beverage industry has witnessed healthy growth over the recent years and has illustrated a forward moving approach, resulting in multiple factor that escalates consumption for F&B industry in India. As the purchasing power of the middle class, increase in more nuclear families along with the urbanisation of smaller cities, the demand for quick service restaurants, fine dining and casual dining restaurant have grown manifold in years to come[104]. As stated above the Food and Bevarage service market is dominated by unorganised segment and although it will decline significantly over the next 4-5 years, it is likely to remain more than 60per cent of the market. Brands/chains of both Indian and MNC brands are still less penetrated and there exists a large opportunity in this space to create bigger restaurant chains. The maximum growth being witnessed in the standalone restaurant space where local taste along with uniqueness of concept are the key deciding factors of success[105].

Table 3.1: Indian F & B Food Service Formats

Unorganised Sector (84%)	Organised Sector (16%)		
	Type	Description	Examples
Dhabas: Often referred to as rural India's fast food joints, these are located street side, at truck stops and along highways, Typical fare includes spicy Indian food and snacks, lassi and chai. Characterised by tandoors (pit oven) and chaarpais (cots), dhabas offer the authentic, raw Indian experience.	*Full Service Restaurants*	*Fine Dining:* Offer finest in food, service and ambience; high priced; staff highly trained; usually located in luxury hotels in metropolitan cities	Taj Hotels, The Leela Hotels, Oberoi Hotels, Sheraton Hotels
		Casual: Offer moderately priced food, casual atmosphere, quick table service; some also provide takeaway and home delivery	Saravana Bhavan, T.G.I. Friday's, Punjab Gril, Zambar, FresCo, Asia 7, Street Foods of India, Baker's Street, Chilli's, Great Kabab Factory, California Pizza Kitchen, Hard Rock Cafes, Sbarro, Yellow Chilli, Spaghetti Kitchen, Noodle Bar, Bombay Blue, Copper Chimney

---

[102]Arbind Prasad (2015), Unlocking the potential in the food and beverage services sector, Report Jointly Prepared by Grant Thornton nor FICCI ,http://www.ficci.com/spdocument/20589/F&B-Report.pdf.

[103]A brief report on tourism in India, January 2015,http://www.cci.in/pdfs/surveys-reports/Tourism-in-India.pdf

[104] A Research Paper on the Restaurant Services in India, Marketing Line Industry Profile, 2015, Euromonitor.

[105]Ibid.Arbind Prasad (2015),

Halwais: Confectioners and sweet-makers found mainly in north India. The name is derived from the word halwa, a popular sweet made of flour, ghee, sugar, almonds and raisins. Typical fare includes mithai (sweets) like laddus and burfi and savoury snacks like samosas and pakoras.	*Quick Service Restaurants*	Also called fast food joints; serve processed foods fast at low prices; typical menu items include burgers, pizza, milkshakes, French fries; minimal table service; also provide table service; also provide takeaway and home delivery	McDonald's, Nirula's, Taco Bell, KFC, KaatiZone, Pizza Hut, Domino's, Haldirams, Papa John's, Subway, Quiznos, Café Darshini, South Thindies, Rasna's Devil's, Workshop, Bikanervala, Wimpy, Adiga, Faaso's
	Cafes, Coffee /Tea Bars, Bakery-Cafes	Outlets serving range of coffee and other hot and cold drinks, quick bites such as pastries and sandwiches and breakfast	Café Coffee Day, Barista, Costa Café, Starbucks, Brahmin's Coffee Bar, Gloria Jean's, Coffee Bean and Tea Leaf, Dessert Café, Chai Point, Au Bon Pain, Le Pain Quotidien, Cinnabon, Dunkin'Donuts
Food carts and trolleys: These are stand-alone units run by individuals and typically sell street food and snacks such as grilled corn, boiled or roasted peanuts, chaat, paubhaji, idlis, fruit juices and samosas and tourist spots and tend to move around.	*Bars and Lounges*	Casual or upscale establishment serving alcoholic beverages and food	Mai Tai, Shiro, Aer, Aurus, Some, Wink, Mocha, Esocobar, Vie Deck and Lounge, Enoteca, Flame Le Club, Leather Bar, Zara Tapas, Gallop, Bike and Barrel, Poker, Provogue, Geoffrey's
	Ice Cream and Frozen Yogurt Parlors	Outlets usually exclusively selling ice cream, gelato, sundaes and shakes, sorbet and frozen yogurt	Haagen-Dazs,Hapinezz (Vadilal), Movempick, Swensen's, Baskin Robbins, Amul, Hatsun'sIbacco (formerly Arun), Natural Ice creams, Kwality, Pinkberry
Roadside hawkers/vendors: These are found at street corners and usually set up shop at the same location every day. These vendors sell street foods, juices, lassi, ice cream, snacks and cater to low income populations who want a quick bite on the go.	*Juice Bars*	Stores usually exclusively selling fresh and bottled fruit and vegtable juices, smoothies and juice blends; some also sell soups, salads and wraps	HAS Juice Bar, Tropical Smoothies, Amoretto, Evolution Fresh (from Starbucks), Juice Lounge, Blendz Juice Bar, Fruit Shop on Greams Road, Booster Juice
	Kiosks	Small standalone structures dispensing quick snacks and drinks; typical items include wraps, Indian snacks, sugarcane and fruit juice, Chinese food, corn, ice cream, salads; commonly found in public spaces like shopping malls	Salad Chef, Big Mos's Rolls and Wraps, Yo China, Chai Garam, Chokola, Candy Treat, Sweet World, Mr Orange, Vadaapaa, Burgerman, Nirula's Express, Go Chatzz, GoliVadaaPav, Cane-o-la, Petawrap, Café Coffee Day, Chamosa, Gelato Italiano
Dinners, drive-ins and dives: These are the numerous standalone joints along streets (e.g., at bus stops) serving affordable Indian foods and beverages to the mass market. Many also offer takeaway and home delivery services.	*Food Courts*	A designated area in large public places (shopping malls, airports, hospitals, offices) with several quick service brands serving food at designated stalls	Comesum, Spoon, Yatra, Foodtalk, Polynation, Sagar Ratna, Kailash Parbat

Source: Enterprise Consulting, Athena Infonomics

The overall scenario of the food and beverage sector has transformed from a time where a handful of restaurants existed to a time now where consumers are flooded with choices of cuisines, locations and range of prices. India presents countless opportunities in the restaurant service market being the second most populous country with 65per cent of its population below the age of 35proposing enormous growth prospects for existing and new restaurant businesses. It can also be noted that India is likely to become the world's youngest country, with64per cent of its population in the working age group presenting interesting opportunities for the quick service restaurant and casual dining segment. Growth of the middleclass, supported by the growing Indian youth population is also a driving force in India's rising consumption story. With the increase in spending power, the Indian consumer market is seeking more entertainment options, driving the growth of the restaurant segments.

Moreover, the increasing penetration of the organised sector contributing 8 percent to the total retail in India suggests huge potential for the organised sector to grow. Existing global brands have been popular amongst the Indian consumer market due to their capability of adapting to the local taste of India and continue to penetrate the Indian market[106].

3.4.   Food Trend in India

The development of Indian cuisine has a very long and turbulent history and is ever changing even today as Indians try new cuisines and are exposed to new influences and people from other nations. It can be seen from this historical review that Indian cuisine has developed over centuries and has drawn inspiration from many customs, traditions and religions. This has resulted in a number of features of the cuisine in general, which are very interesting to note:

(i) **Eating Out:** Eating out is a relatively new development in India, which has development despite traditional values because of the growth of the middle and upper classes that have changing work and leisure patterns and the income to eat out in commercial restaurants. This has fuelled the growth of a vast range of restaurants, particularly in the cities of India, offering a full range of international cuisines. Eating out by tourist, particularly in the tourist areas such as Goa, has been an important trend.

(ii) **Links of Food to Culture:** The food eaten by Indians is inextricably linked to the individual's religion, caste, social status and where they live. This includes the

---

[106]Ibid.A Research Paper on the Restaurant Services in India, Marketing Line Industry Profile, 2015.

avoidance of particular foods by religious groups such as Hindus and fasting, which is a part of most religions practiced in India.

(iii) Links of Food to Health: The ancient system of Ayurveda gave the foundation of the idea that food and health are inextricable linked together. The idea that different foods can also be hot or cold depending on their psychological effect is an idea that is thought to have developed in India and then travelled to other countries such as China.

(iv) Links of Caste and Religion with Food Habits: The caste system in India had a major effect on the development of food culture but the major religious groups have also had a major effect on the cuisine as a whole[107].

However, the changing lifestyles with the increasing nuclear families and a rise in the urbanization in India over the past years have also supported the growth of the restaurant market in India. Additionally, the customer preference for the cuisine has seen a transition in India from consuming the traditional Indian food to trying out different cuisines such as the Chinese, Italian and Mexican. Due to the growing exposure to the international cultures and lifestyles, the Indian population has started developing their tastes and is reaching out to restaurants more often which offer different cuisines apart from Indian cuisine. This change in the taste preference of the people in India has motivated many international and Indian players to expand their reach in the Indian restaurant market[108].

Indian Food and Beverage industry has witnessed various new trends in the last two years, where 2013 witnessed trend that made every restaurant try its hands at molecular gastronomy and 2014 was devoted as a year of innovation. According to Restaurant India Research, the year 2015 was filled with food-tech innovations focused on healthy food, prompt delivery and structured supply chain. Some experts believe that traditional Indian cuisines with a blend of modern techniques was on demand as in the last two years, while others were of the opinion that healthy food options with taste and quality was on demand as well[109]. Ancient whole grains are the hottest trend; one would come across Ragi, Jowar, Quinoa, Amaranth, Buckwheat, Rajgira, Nachani and other ancient grains in many restaurant kitchens these days as not only are they healthier options but delicious too and come in various shapes

---

[107]Stephen Ball, Susan Horner, Kevin Nield (2007), Issues in China and India, Today's Dragons and Tigers, Chapter 9, Restaurants fast food and contract food service – India, Contemporary Hospitality and Tourism Management Issues in China and India, Published by Elsevier Ltd, ISBN 978-0-7506-6856-9

[108]India Restaurant Market Outlook to 2018 - Quick Service Restaurants to Drive the Future Growth, http://www.researchandmarkets.com/reports/2585764/.

[109]http://www.restaurantindia.in/article/f-and-b-format/menu-trends/Top-food-trends-that-ruled-India-in-2015.a237/#sthash.ZUuGu1vT.dpuf.

and sizes from tiny Quinoa seeds to large kernels. Restaurant operators believe that it is a decadent way to ensure good health and optimum nutrition[110].

3.5. Classification of Restaurants in India

Historically, restaurant referred only to places that provided tables where one sat down to eat the meal, typically served by awaiter[111]. Following the rise of fast food and take-out restaurants, a retronym for the older "standard" restaurant was created, sitdown restaurant. Most commonly, "sit-down restaurant" refers to a casual dining restaurant with table service, rather than a fast food restaurant, where one orders food at a counter. Sit-down restaurants are often further categorized as "family-style" or "formal". In British English, the term restaurant almost always means an eating establishment with table service, so the "sit-down" qualification is not usually necessary. Fast food and takeaway (take-out) outlets with counter service are not normally referred to as restaurants[112].

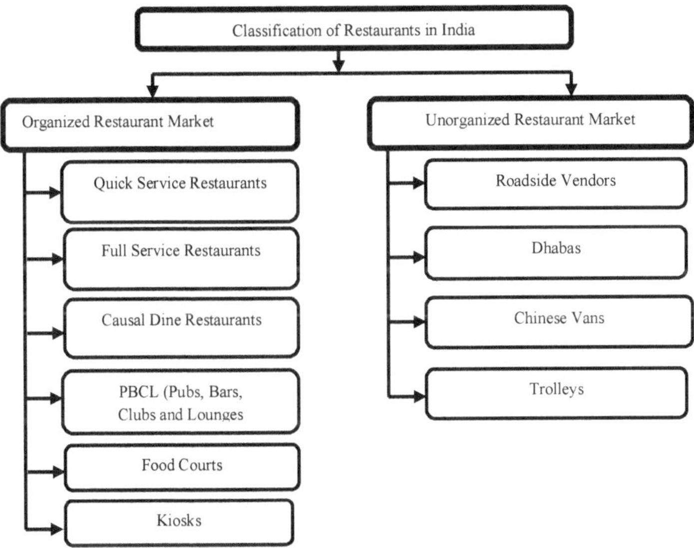

Exhibit 3.2: Classification of Restaurants in India

Source: India Restaurant Market Outlook to 2018-Quick Service Restaurants to Drive the Future Growth, http://www.researchandmarkets.com/reports/2585764/.

---

[110]http://economictimes.indiatimes.com/articleshow/50202445.cms?utm_source=contentofinterest&utm_medium=text&utm_campaign=cppst

[111]http://en.wikipedia.org

[112]White paper on Indian Restaurant Industry, 2010, National Restaurant Association in India.

The unorganized restaurant market includes the roadside vendors, Dhabas, Chinese vans and trolleys. The organized restaurant market includes the Quick Service Restaurants (QSR), the full service restaurants, Causal Dine Restaurants, PBCL(Pubs, Bars, Clubs and Lounges) and the food courts and kiosks[113].

Table 3.2(A): Classification of Restaurants in India

Type	Description
Dhaba	Dhaba is the name given to roadside restaurants in India and Pakistan. They are situated on highways and generally serve local cuisine, and also serve as truck stops. They are most commonly found next to petrol stations, and most are open 24 hours a day. Since many Indian and Pakistani truck drivers are of Punjabi descent, and Punjabi food and music is quite popular throughout India and Pakistan, the word dhaba has come to represent any restaurant that serves Punjabi food, especially the heavily spiced and fried Punjabi fare preferred by many truck drivers. The word has come to represent sub-continental cuisine so much that many Indian restaurant in Europe and America have adopted it as a part of the name. Dhabas were characterized by mud structures and cots to sit upon (called Charpai) while eating. A wooden plank would be placed across the width of the cot on which to place the dishes. With time, the cots were replaced by tables. The food is typically inexpensive and has a 'homemade' feel to it.
Roadside Eateries or Vendor or Trolley	Roadside eateries function on the main roads and the sub-lanes in the Junction, New Bus Stand, Old Bus Stand and other prominent places in various cities. The roadside foods are specialty of Indian cities and reflection of India's culture and tradition, stall vendors of street offers different kinds of delicious and tasty food such as famous cholebhature, Parathas, pitha, chotpoti, puchka, jhalmuri, badam and various fried items. The street vendors of Indian cities also sell sweet items and drinks including Lassi plain or salty,fruit flavored juice, Sherbet, Jaljeera, Neera and other seasonal drinks. Some of major Indian cities are well famous for street food items like Delhi for cholebhature, Indore Pohajalebi, Mumbai for VadaPao and Kolkata for all types of rolls. In Tamil Nadu too, the road side vendors are the crowd pullers and not preferred eating outlets for the poor and low-middle income class people. Roadside eateries that spring up in the late evening hours which bring life to the many city in Tamil Nadu like Madurai, Chennai, Salem, Thirchy and Coimbatore. The main attraction of these eateries is the price and the quick time they take to serve people. An ordinary dosa costs only Rs. 10 and a set of four paniyarams too Rs. 10. They also serve butter dosa, podidosa and tomato dosa . Some serve variety of dishes, including lemon rice and pongal. The side dishes such as coconut chutney, tomato chutney and coriander chutney also provide added taste. A majority of the owners of these eateries are economically and socially downtrodden. These eateries also give part-time employment to many poor youth. Though the business starts only at 7 p.m., the preparation begins right in the evening.
AmmaUnavagam in Tamil Nadu	AmmaUnavagam (meaning "Mother Restaurant" in Tamil) is a food subsidization program run by the Government of Tamil Nadu in India. "Amma" means mother in Tamil but clearly here refers to Chief Minister Ms. J. Jayalalithaa, who introduced this restaurant concept aimed at helping the very poor sections of the society. By convention she is seldom mentioned by her name in the party and government circles but is reverentially referred to as "amma." Under the scheme, municipal corporations of the state run canteens serving subsidized food at low prices. The food chains primarily serve South Indian food namely Idli, Sambar Rice, Curd Rice, Pongal, Lemon Rice, Curry leaf Rice and also Chapathi. The dishes are offered at low prices: `.1 for an Idli, `.5 for a plate of Sambar Rice and `.3 for a plate of Curd Rice, etc.

---

[113]India Restaurant Market Outlook to 2018 - Quick Service Restaurants to Drive the Future Growth, http://www.researchandmarkets.com/reports/2585764/.

Table 3.2(B): Classification of Restaurants in India

Type	Description
Fast food	Fast food restaurants emphasize speed of service. Operations range from small-scale street vendors with carts to mega-corporations like McDonald's. Also known as a QSR or Quick Serve Restaurant.
Fast Casual Restaurants	Usually do not offer full table service, but may offer non-disposable plates and cutlery. The quality of food and prices tend to be higher than those of a conventional fast food restaurant but may be lower than casual dining
Café	Informal restaurants offering a range of hot meals and made-to-order sandwiches. Coffee shops, while similar to cafés, are not restaurants due to the fact that they primarily serve and derive the majority of their revenue from hot drinks. Many cafés are open for breakfast and serve full hot breakfasts. In some areas cafés offer outdoor seating.
Standalone Restaurants	Standalone restaurants range from inexpensive and informal lunching or dining places catering to people working nearby, with simple food served in simple settings at low prices.
Casual Dining	A restaurant that serves moderately-priced food in a casual atmosphere. Except for buffet-style restaurants, casual dining restaurants typically provide table service. Casual dining comprises a market segment between fast food establishments and fine dining restaurants.
Family Style	A type of casual dining restaurants where food is often served on platters and the diners serve themselves
Fine Dining	Full service restaurants with specific dedicated meal courses. Décor of such restaurants feature higher-quality materials, with an eye towards the "atmosphere" desired by the restauranteur, than restaurants featuring lower-quality materials and an eye away from the "atmosphere" desired by the restauranteur. The wait staff is usually highly trained and often wears more formal attire. Fine dining restaurants are almost always small businesses and are generally either single-location operations or have just a few locations. Food portions are visually appealing. Fine dining restaurants have certain rules of dining which visitors are generally expected to follow.
Pub	Mainly in the UK and other countries influenced by British culture, a pub (short for public house) is a bar that sometimes serves simple food fare. Traditionally, pubs were primarily drinking establishments with food in a secondary position, whereas many modern pubs rely on food as well, to the point where gastropubs are often essentially fine-dining establishments, known for their high-quality pub food and concomitantly high prices. A typical pub has a large selection of beers and ales on tap.
Bar	The counter at which drinks are served by a bartender is called "the bar". This term is applied, as a synecdoche to a bar as a business establishment that serves alcoholic drinks — beer, wine, liquor, and cocktails — for consumption on the premises. Bars provide stools or chairs that are placed at tables or counters for their patrons. Some bars have entertainment on a stage, such as a live band, comedians, go-go dancers, or strippers. Bars which offer entertainment or live music are often referred to as music bars or nightclubs.
Chinese Restaurant	Specializes in Chinese cuisine only

3.6.   Dining Preferences towards Casual Dining

Indians are known to be foodies and for not being too open at experimenting with their food. It would be wrong to say that India lacks proper 'fine-dining' culture. Till recent years, fine-dining was a term synonymous with five star hotels in India, however, the independent restaurants sector set up a particular benchmark and clear demarcation between the casual dining and fine dining concepts. Casual dining concepts are preferred by a larger number of people as compared to fine dining concepts, largely because India is a price-sensitive market. Having said that, with the increase in disposable income, consumers are becoming more adventurous and don't mind paying a little bit extra for the experience of a true fine-dine restaurant, hence the growth of this concept in recent years. The Indian restaurant space, in recent years, has seen the advent of many new brands and restaurant chains, however most of them may have created a major uproar in their initial days, they have not managed to live up to the consumer's expectations for varied reasons[114]. Thus, dinner prefer to visit casual dine restaurants than to the fine dine restaurants. Price point is a huge consideration for Indians in every sphere. As a nation, we are obsessed with value for money and would think twice before spending on an expensive meal[115].

3.7.   Contribution of Causal Dine Restaurants to Indian Economy

Casual Dining is an exciting segment that revolves around specific cuisines or themes focusing on elaborate menus, quality of food and increased focus on presentation On the other hand, consumer indulgence is increasingly fuelled by non-occasion outings to these outlets. As stated in Chapter I, in 2013, the size of the chain casual Dine market is estimated at `.3,950 crore(USD760million). It is projected to grow at a CAGR of 18per cent to reach a size of `. 9,035 crore (USD1, 740 million)by 2018.The Casual Dine market is led by domestic players, which are largely region-specific. Currently, there are1700-1800 Casual Dine outlets spread across India .The player spread is the highest in the metros at 45per cent, followed by mini metros with 35per cent of all outlets and across Tier I and Tier II cities, the outlet density is low. In order to achieve sustained growth and attain scale, most of the players across segments are moving to express options that offer a quick and convenient casual dining experience.

3.7.1.   Product Sales and SKU Mix

In the Casual Dine segment, food dominates the SKU and sales mix at 81per centand77per cent followed by beverages and deserts that are mostly side orders. A slight variation is observed in the mix based on formats and the cuisines offered. Overall, the SKU mix is directly proportional to the sales mix.

---

[114]Casual dining is preferred as India is price-sensitive, http://www.fnbnews.com/Interview/Casual-dining-is-preferred-as-India-is-price-sensitive, Monday 1st April, 2013.

[115]SaurabhSaxena (2015), Fine – dine experiences and the Indian Consumer, This article was first published in Food and Beverage News, March.

3.7.2.   Sales Mix- Dine-in & Non- Dine-in

Dine-in and non-Dine-in options form a good mix to sales in the Casual Dine segment. Most of the sales (60per cent) are through dine-in as consumers prefer to sit at restaurants and enjoy the width of available product offerings. Delivery services contribute a healthy 30per cent to sales, followed by takeaway which brings in 10per cent of total sales. This is primarily for outlets located in residential areas, office complexes, etc. where the consumer prefers getting food hand-delivery due to paucity of time.

3.7.3.   Sales Mix – Peak Business Hours

The main meal times of lunch (1pm-4pm) and dinner (7-11P.M) contribute to~85per cent of the total sales at Casual Dine outlets. However, the peak business hours of outlets located in office complexes are more skewed towards lunch time.

3.8.   Diners Expectation and Satisfaction towards Restaurant Services

Eating out is not just food but a lot of experiences. Such consumer behaviours are shaped more out of expectations than the need. While good food is the most desired, the experiences desired by the different segments can be classified as "peak experience" and "consumer or supportive experience". Peak experiences as those activities that are the primary focus of the trip, whereas supportive experiences are those peripheral activities necessary to accomplish the peak experience. In this typology, this has been adapted to a lifestyle setting assuming that eating out behaviours can be similar when compared with touristic behaviours[116]. Consumers also tend to show a variety seeking behaviour both in terms of the outlets, formats and food. The frequency of visit is also lower and it is a planned activity. In addition, in most cases, eating out is the only activity they perform in their outing.

In India, most of the customers visit restaurants with their families and friends and their expenditure in each visit is of primary importance. This makes the eating out a very involved activity across India. Combining the two aspects customers could be classified as in figure below. Each of these segments expects different experiences.

---

[116]Quan, S. and Wang, N. (2004), Towards a structural model of the tourist experience: an illustration from food experiences in tourism, Tourism Management, Volume No. 25, Issue No. 3, PP. 297-305.

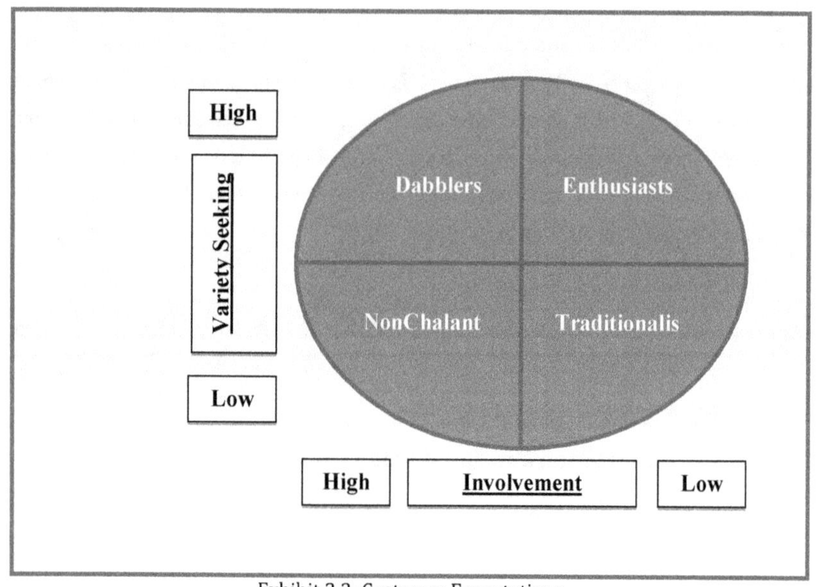

Exhibit 3.3: Customer Expectations

Source: Quan, S. and Wang, N. (2004)

The customers' perception of service quality comes from their evaluation of what they experienced and what they expected. Customer expectation and service-quality perception in the food service industry have revealed certain important attributes, such as low price, food quality (food taste and nutrition properties), value for money, service, location, brand name, and image of the restaurant etc[117].

The restaurant industry is one of the most competitive industries in the world today. The fastest-growing segment of the restaurant industry is casual dining, where sales are increasing at double-digit rates. The restaurant industry has certainly not been exempt from either increased competition or from rising consumer expectations of quality. In the highly competitive food service industry, large chain operators have tended to gain competitive advantages through cost leadership. The industry depends on standardization and economies of arising scale, due to large market shares, where as smaller, independent restaurants attempt to gain advantage through differentiation.

---

[117]Kota Neel Mani Kanta and Srivalli.P (2014), A Study on Service Quality in Indian Restaurants with Decision-and Experiential-Oriented Perspectives in India, International Journal of Research and Development-A Management Review (IJRDMR), Volume.No.3, Issue.No.1, ISSN:2319-5479, PP:16-24.

As the service sector continues to expand, the issue of service quality has received increasingly more attention. The casual dining customer has many choices when dining out in restaurants. The customer is impatient and sophisticated. If the restaurant is not providing satisfaction, service quality, and value for the money, they may leave to another restaurant. Thus, restaurateurs are increasingly concerned with satisfying customers, who are not easily satisfied with the restaurants' service quality but with the food attributes too[118].

To improve customer satisfaction and loyalty, restaurant operators must understand what factors influence customer satisfaction and repeat patronage behaviour Since Indian food market is characterized by regional differences and various types of cuisine. Every region in India has its distinctive cuisines and tastes, which are not easily duplicated. However, such a sample provides the advantage of greater control over sub-cultural effect that might otherwise contaminate the relationships between the factors. The findings on the relationships between service quality, customer satisfaction, and purchasing behaviour offer important practical implications for researchers and practitioners alike[119].

3.9.   Factors Influencing Restaurant Selection Decisions

Restaurant selection criteria are the most important attributes that customers use in deciding where to dine-out. Customers may apply diverse criteria in evaluating the importance of attribute affecting their restaurant choice. There is a wide range of literature concerning the selection of restaurants. For instance, Lewis (1981) considered five factors: food quality, menu variety, price, atmosphere, and convenience factors. Jang and Namkung (2009) suggested three factors: service quality, product quality, and atmospherics as main restaurant attributes affecting perceived quality of restaurant experiences. The total dining experience in a restaurant is comprised of not only food itself, but also the atmosphere (physical aspects) and the service provided[120].

The foodservice industry has become highly competitive as the number of foodservice outlets has increased to meet the demand. In order to succeed in such a competitive industry, restaurant operators need to understand the factors (and their relative importance) that

---

[118]ArisaraSeyanont(2007), A Comparative Study of the Service Quality Of Casual Dining Restaurants in Phuket: Perspective of Thai And International Customers , Thesis submitted in partial fulfilment of the requirements for the Degree of Doctor of Philosophy, Submitted to the Faculty of the Graduate College of the Oklahoma State University, May.

[119]Ibid,. Kota Neel Mani Kanta and Srivalli.P (2014).

[120]Soyeon Kim and Jae-Eun Chung (2009), Restaurant Selection Criteria: Understanding the Roles of Restaurant Type and Customers' Socio-demographic Characteristics.

influence restaurant patrons' decision when selecting a restaurant. Consumers those go to casual dining establishments do not only demand good food but also a complete dining experience. Consumers select their restaurants based on many factors.

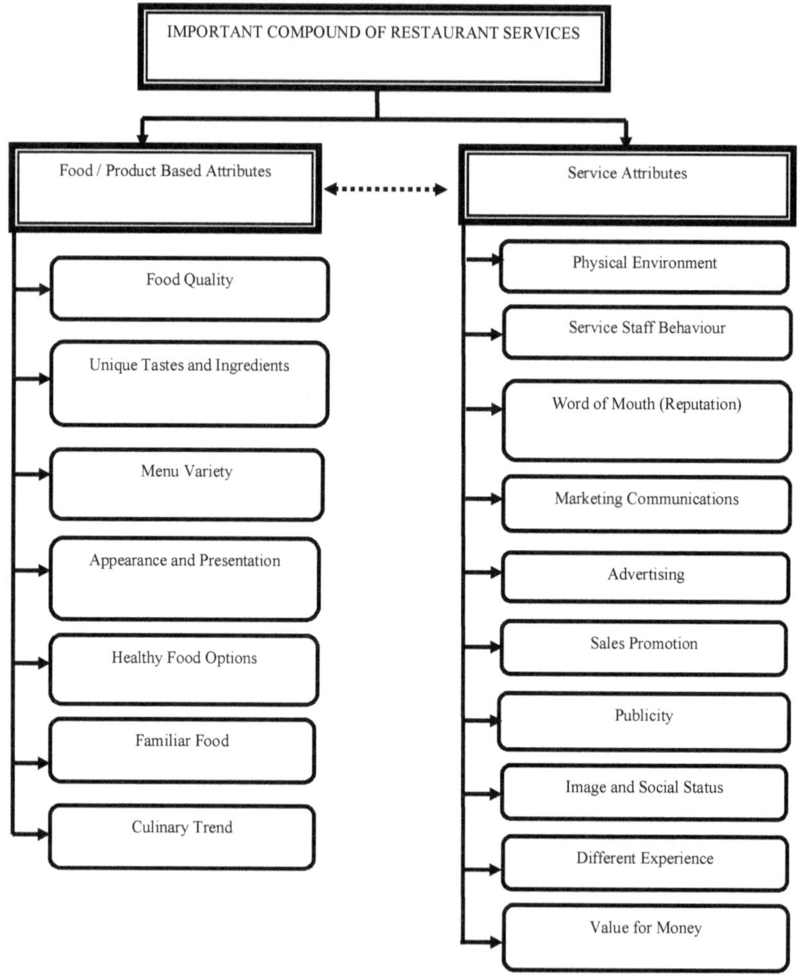

Exhibit 3.4: Factors Influencing Restaurant Selection by Diners

Source: Chirawan Sriwongrat (2008), Consumers' choice factors of an upscale ethnic restaurant, A thesis submitted in partial fulfillment of the requirements for the Degree of Master of Commerce and Management, Lincoln University.

3.9.1. *Food /Product Based Attributes*

Consumers select their restaurants based on food attributes, food quality, unique taste, menu varieties etc.

i.   **Food Quality:** Food quality is rated as the most important attribute influencing restaurant decisions. The elements that constitute food quality are unique tastes and ingredients, menu variety, appearance and presentation, healthy food options, and familiar food.

ii.   **Unique Tastes and Ingredients:** Tastes and ingredients play an important role for consumers when selecting a restaurant. Food taste is regarded as the most important element of food attributes. Unique taste and authentic ingredients are the most important components of their authentic dining experience.

iii. **Menu Variety:** Restaurateurs frequently develop new menus and offer a selection of different menu items to attract customers.

iv.   **Appearance and Presentation:** Appearance and presentation refers to the way food is decorated, it is the most important contributor among food quality attributes in determining customer satisfaction in restaurants.

v.   **Healthy Food Options:** Consumers are more concerned with their health and are therefore driving a growing demand for healthy food choices. In South India, especially in Tamil Nadu a large number of restaurants are adding items and adjusting their menus to accommodate and attract consumers who are concerned about health and nutritional value of a meal.

vi.   **Familiar Food:** Food consumption habits and patterns are components of culture that make an important contribution to the food dining decision consumers make. In some cases, foods of other cultures are accepted if they have familiar ingredients and preparation styles[121].

vii. **Culinary Trend:** The single-biggest factor influencing restaurant services in India is the culinary trends among various populations of different demographics segments. Some important demographic changes have emerged in recent times: increased number of working women with little time to cook at home; a population that travels more and is exposed to international cuisine; a population which is more concerned about its health; an increase in expatriate population; and an increase in disposable

---

[121]ChirawanSriwongrat (2008), Consumers' choice factors of an upscale ethnic restaurant, A thesis submitted in partial fulfillment of the requirements for the Degree of Master of Commerce and Management, Lincoln University.

incomes. And, beyond all these factors, is an indefinable spark that makes one culinary item succeed and another fail. Chefs like Sanveen Kapoor, Malika Bathirinathan, Damu, Venkatesh Bhutt, Vikas Khanna and many more also have influenced that change in culinary trends among Indian households in the recent past[122].

3.9.2. *Service Quality*

Service quality is found to be a salient factor of restaurant selection by the diners.

i.   **Physical Environment:** Physical environment of the restaurant such as restaurant's atmosphere, ambience, décor, furniture, and other facilities can have a great impact on the dining experience   and behavioural intentions. The unique nature of the restaurant service, physical environments could guide consumers in evaluating a restaurant experience.

ii.   **Service Staff Behaviour:** The importance of service staff to the service operators indicated that service staff behaviour was particularly important when the other mechanic clues such as restaurant atmosphere were perceived negatively. In this situation, humanic clues such as impressive employee behaviour could help level up consumers' perception of dining experience. Consumers generally expect restaurant service employees to be attentive, courteous and possess a good knowledge of the menu.

iii.   **Word of Mouth (Reputation):** Word-of-mouth is a critical source of information for a restaurant service if uncertainty and risk are perceived to be high. A recommendation from a friend can greatly contribute to a decision to try a restaurant. Unlike advertising, a suggestion from a friend is not usually based on any gain or profit. Thus, consumers place more trust on their friends' recommendation when making a restaurant choice (Mill, 2007). Besides, consumers can find out about restaurant experience qualities, which are usually difficult to judge through the other non-personal sources, from their friends' personal experience.

iv.   **Marketing Communications:** Services operators use marketing communications as the way to inform, persuade, and remind customers. The marketing communications employed by restaurateurs are advertising, sales promotion, and publicity.

v.   **Advertising:** Advertising includes "any paid form of non-personal presentation and promotion of ideas, goods, or services by an identified sponsor" (Mill, 2007, p. 83).

---

[122]NavjitAhluwalia, and et.al (2004), *Restaurant Industry in India - Trends and Opportunities,* A Research Study, Published in April 2004 by: Secretary General, Federation of Hotel & Restaurant Associations of India, Federation of Hotel & Restaurant Associations of India (FHRAI).

Advertising may come in the form of television, newspaper, radio, magazines, yellow pages, and internet.

vi. **Sales Promotion:** Sales promotions, such as special offers and discounts, can act as short-term incentives motivating consumers to choose a particular service provider. To earn diners patronage restaurants can follow different sale promotion techniques like: coupes, benefits to family diners, couples, early bird concepts etc.

vii. **Publicity:** Publicity refers to non-paid communications such as a press release and press conference. Publicity provides more credibility for consumers as the company (in this context- a restaurant) does not usually have control over critics like it does with paid advertising (Burnett & Moriarty, 1998). Therefore, publicity has the advantage of being able to reach consumers who are particularly cynical about advertising. Positive media relations can create a positive image for a restaurant and thus may be used as another effective marketing communications tool. In India eating in an full service or a casual dine restaurant is a way to experience another culture like South India get a change to taste the foods of North Indian food like: the Punjabi foods (Nanna, Parathas, Tandoori Chickens, Panner Varieties) etc, or Rajasthani Foods,, Gujarati Foods etc. flavour of the cuisine brings diners closer to that particular culture and helps them recall the memories that they had gained during their tours, or while watching a cook programme or while dinning in their neighbours home etc.

viii. **Image and Social Status:** Restaurant dining helped to satisfy diners' deeper emotional desires for social status, image, and belongingness. Some restaurants were regarded as higher in status than others, which was reflected through images the restaurateurs try to communicate with their consumers. The patronage of certain groups of consumers at different classes of restaurant implies that consumers may choose a restaurant based on the restaurant image, as they relate the restaurant experience to their social status.

ix. **Different Experience:** Novelty has specific appeal, and consumers are known to be curious for novelties including experiencing a new food and the new ambience of a restaurant. A new experience emerges as a determinant influencing some consumers to dine at a casual dine restaurant, as they consider such variety of experiences a value in itself. Patrons of traditional food restaurants often seek an authentic experience that is different from their everyday meals at home. Dining at restaurants also offers diners the opportunity to have the similar emotional and symbolic experience of a vacation, without even leaving home town or city.

x. **Value for Money:** Value for money is another factor restaurant patrons take into account when selecting a restaurant. If they perceive that the value received is less than the price paid, they are likely to evaluate the dining experience negatively. If the price value paid by the diners meet their expectation i.e., it offer value for the money paid, it results in positive dining experiences[123].

3.10. Casual Dining Offering and Practices among Diners in India

India, as a country, has a very diverse range of cuisines to offer. This can be attributed to the varied geographical terrains, cultures, religions and climates that exist in India. Food is an integral part of the overall Indian culture with many ingredients, spices, herbs and inter-regional influence on cooking styles. Over the years, Indian food has evolved and so has the taste preference of its people. Earlier, the restaurants preferred to stick to the cuisine they had been brought up on but now the restaurants are ready to experiment with their taste buds and willing to explore something new[124].These days no longer does an Indian restaurant mean either 'North Indian' (butter chicken, naan) or 'South Indian' (idli, dosa, vada) fare as it did a decade or two ago. Now there are eating places serving dishes from almost every state in the country - Kashmir to Kerala, Goa to Nagaland-as well as endless, traditional variations on a single theme, say biryani or kebab. People want to experiment more than before with their food and are also spending more on eating out[125]. Thus, the restaurants managers are planning to launch the first of a chain of restaurants under this brand starting from North India and steadily expand it across the key gourmet regions of the country over the next few years, keeping it largely as a domestic brand[126].

As per National Restaurant Association of India, of those who get food home-delivered, 80per cent of them order-in at least twice a month. Even though rising income, consumerism and increased working population has made the current generation more susceptible to eat outside food, the growth in the sector is over shadowed by growth of ordering-in services[127].Within this organised segment, the traditional 'North Indian' and 'South Indian'

[123]ChirawanSriwongrat (2008), Consumers' choice factors of an upscale ethnic restaurant, A thesis submitted in partial fulfillment of the requirements for the Degree of Master of Commerce and Management, Lincoln University

[124]SaurabhSaxena (2015), Fine – dine experiences and the Indian Consumer, This article was first published in Food and Beverage News, March

[125]SarikaMalhotra (2014),A Bigger Salad Bowl, Restaurant goers' appetite for regional and traditional Indian cuisine is growing rapidly. Business Today, 27th April.

[126]ZorawarKalra (2015), Casual dining is preferred as India is price-sensitive, FnBnews.Com, December

[127]Ibid. SaurabhSaxena (2015).

restaurants, along with Chinese, still comprise 70 per cent of Indian market and the remaining includes both international and regional or traditional players. But there is growth. State-specific restaurants are thriving both in terms of numbers and performance both in South and North India[128].

3.11. Conclusion

Nowadays, with the higher living standard, having dining in restaurants is considered as life-style status among many urban Indians. Dining restaurant is very convenient for working women, officer executives and every one in a family as rest as it place considered for parting, meeting place for socialization, spending evening times during week-ends etc. This chapter provided a detailed theoretical discussion on growth of restaurant industry in India, its classification and also contain an elaborate discussion on the primary factors that motive dine in selection of appropriate restaurant of their choice. Based on the theoretical literature gathered in this Chapter, the following Chapter IV is designed. Chapter IV focuses on analysing and providing empirical evidences on diners' preferences towards restaurant in Coimbatore city.

---

[128]Ibid.,SarikaMalhotra (2014).

CHAPTER IV

ANALYSIS AND INTERPRETATION

4.1. Introduction

The restaurant industry is one of the most competitive industries in the world today. The fastest-growing segment of the restaurant industry is casual dining, where sales are increasing at double-digit rates. The restaurant industry has certainly not been exempt from either increased competition or from rising consumer expectations of towards various food and service dimensions. The casual dining customer has many choices when dining out in restaurants. Casual dine restaurateurs are increasingly concerned with satisfying customers, but it is not an easy task to satisfy a customer. Completely satisfying customers are significantly more likely to influence their revisit intention. To increase customer satisfaction and customer loyalty, casual dining restaurant owners have to strive for better service through offering better food, with more varieties on the menu and with a well-focused service quality. To draw empirical evidences on these issues, this chapter of the study aims to analyse diners' preference towards restaurant services in Coimbatore City.

1. *Life Style Profile of Customers*

Restaurants play a significant role in diner's lifestyle, and dining out is a favorite social activity. Always restaurateur aims to spot emerging culinary trends they go to what they consider the ultimate source-customers. Circumstantial evidence from restaurant customers is only one way to spot trends. The print media and television play a big role in establishing culinary concepts and preferences, with food columnists and TV chefs endorsing one trend over the other. However, the single-biggest factor influencing culinary trends is population demographics. Some important demographic changes have emerged in recent times: increased number of working women with little time to cook at home; a population that travels more and is exposed to international cuisine; a population which is more concerned about its health; an increase in expatriate population; and an increase in disposable incomes. Demographics are statistical information about people such as their age, sex, marital status, average family size, average household income, education levels, ethnic origin, and average annual spending on dining out. This section of the study briefly outlines the life style of the customers' who dine in the popular restaurants of Coimbatore city. Basically eating out is common practices among both male and female consumers in India, the following table provides information on the gender-wise distribution of diners surveyed in Coimbatore city.

Table 4.1: Gender Wise Distribution of Diners

Sl. No	Gender	No. of Respondents	Percentage
1.	Male	291	48.50
2.	Female	309	51.40
	Total	600	100

Source: Primary Data

The above table indicates that, majority i.e., 51.40 per cent of customers' surveyed are female and the rests of 48.50 per cent of respondents' are male.

The study indicated that the food diners in Coimbatore city are evenly poised between the male and female consumers.

The food service industry is witnessing a tremendous growth all over the globe, especially in India with the second largest population in the world. The present day generation is depending largely on the food service operations i.e., restaurant service while on they move up in their career or personal development, especially when they are at work place, when away from home for various reasons and even for relaxing (reduction of job stress), for celebrations, entrainment, socialisation etc. With the wide reasons observed for dining out, the age wise distribution of the diners are presented in the following table.

Table 4.2: Agewise Distribution of Diners

Sl. No	Age	No. of Respondents	Percentage
1.	Below 20 years	144	24.00
2.	21 - 25 years	114	19.00
3.	26 - 30 years	92	15.33
4.	30 - 40 years	71	11.83
5.	40 – 50 years	142	23.67
6.	Above 50 years	37	6.17
	Total	600	100

Source: Primary Data

The above table indicates that out of 600 respondents' surveyed, 24per cent of diners are fall under the age group of below 20 years. Followed by, 23.67 per cent of respondents' belong to the age group of 40-50 years and 19 per cent of them are aged between 21-25 years. Further, it has been observed that 15.33 per cent of respondents' belong to the age group of 26-30 years and 11.83 per cent of sample subjects' are aged between 30-40 years. And the rests of 6.17 per cent of sample subjects' fall under the age category of above 50 years.

The study findings indicates that majority of diners surveyed are young fall within the age grouping of 20 years or less than that to 30-40 years of age i.e., 70.16 per cent. As stated above these category of people prefer restaurant service while on they move up in their career or personal development, especially when they are at work place, when away from home for various reasons and even for relaxing (reduction of job stress), for celebrations, entrainment, socialisation etc. The educational qualification of the sample diners of Coimbatore city is presented in the following table. As it is believed that well-educated modern day youth prefer a cozy ambiences and good restaurant services these days.

Table 4.3: Educational Qualification of the Sample Diners

Sl. No	Qualification	No. of Respondents	Percentage
1.	School Level	118	19.67
2.	Higher Secondary Level	107	17.83
3.	Degree / Diploma	212	35.33
4.	Professionals	163	27.17
	Total	600	100

Source: Primary Data

From the above table it is inferred that, 35.33 per cent of have completed Degree/ Diploma course. Subsequently it has been inferred that 27.17 per cent of respondents' have studied professional courses and19.67 per cent of respondents' have studied upto primary level. Further it has been found that 17.83have completed their higher secondary education.

It has been observed that35.33 per cent of respondents' have gained either Degree or Diploma degrees as their highest level of educational qualification.

Restaurant dining habits among the nuclear and joint family households in briefly discussed in the following table.

Table 4.4: Family Type of the Diners

Sl. No	Family Type	No. of Respondents	Percentage
1.	Nuclear Family	348	58.00
2.	Joint Family	252	42.00
	Total	600	100

Source: Primary Data

The above table clearly indicates that, 58 per cent of respondents' live in nuclear families consisting of a pair of adults with their children. Whereas 42 per cent of respondents' have said that they are part of joint families i.e., a type of extended family composed of parents, their children, and the children's spouses and offspring in one household.

Thus, it has been understood that 58 per cent of respondents' live in nuclear families consisting of a pair of adults with their children. Nuclear families are bigger consumers of products and services.

Occupational status of individual determines their income level and their ability to spend for dining out at restaurants. Following two tables provides information on the occupational status and income class of casual diners surveyed at Coimbatore city.

Table 4.5: Occupational Status of the Diners

Sl. No	Occupation	No. of Respondents	Percentage
1.	Business	112	18.67
2.	Employees	174	29.00
3.	Professional	154	25.67
4.	Home Maker	103	17.17
5.	Student	57	9.50
	Total	600	100

Source: Primary Data

From the above table it has been observed that, 29 percent of the respondents' surveyed are employees working in various public and private organizations. Batch of 25.67per cent of the respondents' are experts in their profession and 18.67per cent of the respondents' are engaged in own business. Further it has been observed that 7.17per cent of the respondents' are home makers and 9.50per cent of the respondents' are found to be students pursuing their studies.

Hence it has been found that 29per cent of the respondents' surveyed are employees working in various public and private organizations. The occupational status of the diners of Coimbatore city clearly depicts the category distribution of the consumers living in this city.

Table 4.6: Monthly Income of the Respondents

Sl. No	Income	No. of Respondents	Percentage
1.	Less than `.10000	170	28.33
2.	`.10001 - `.20000	199	33.17
3.	`.20001 - `.30000	134	22.33
4.	Above `.30000	97	16.17
	Total	600	100

Source: Primary Data

The above table determines the monthly income of the restaurant customers' in Coimbatore city. It has been found that, 33.17 per cent of sample subjects' monthly income ranges between `.10001 to`.20000. Followed by, 28.33 per cent of respondents' earn below`. 10000 per month and 22.33 per cent of respondents' earning ranges between `.20001 to `.30000 per month. Similarly, the remaining 16.17 per cent of customers' earn above `.30000 per month.

It is evident from the above table that 33.17 per cent of sample subjects' monthly income ranges between `.10001 to `.20000.

Dining practices of unmarried individuals and family persons are not unique in nature it varies according to individual status, size of the facilities required, nature of food varieties demanded, frequency of visit, spending capacity of the persons, time spend in a restaurant while dining etc. To draw a detail insight in these dimensions, it is very vital to define and understand the marital status of the diner surveyed in Coimbatore city, the following table depicts the same.

Table 4.7: Marital Status of the Diners

Sl. No	Marital Status	No. of Respondents	Percentage
1.	Married	380	63.33
2.	Unmarried	220	36.67
	Total	600	100

Source: Primary Data

The study observed that majority of the respondents surveyed are married i.e., 63.33 per cent and only 36.67 per cent were found to either bachelors or spinsters or singles.

The family size of the diner, always the provided a vital information to the restaurant owners and manager about the existing and potential customers they have in a market place. Family size constitution of the sample subjects is discussed in the following table.

Table 4.8: Family Size of the Diners

Sl. No	Family Size	No. of Respondents	Percentage
1.	2 member's	49	8.17
2.	3 member's	107	17.83
3.	4 member's	263	43.83
4.	Above 4 member's	181	30.17
	Total	600	100

Source: Primary Data

From the above data discussion it has been observed that, 43.83 per cent of respondents' family size constitutes of four members. Followed by, 30.17 per cent of diners family size consists of 4 members or more than that. Further it has been inferred that 17.83 per cent of sample subjects' have three members in their family and the rests of 8.17 per cent of customers' family constitutes of two members.

Thus it has been concluded that 43.83 per cent of respondents' family size constitutes of four members.

Spending capacity of individual can be accessed through gaining information on their earning status and various income sources they have. Following table provides information on number earning members a sample subject's families have.

Table 4.9: Earning Members of the Respondents

Sl. No	Earning Members	No. of Respondents	Percentage
1.	Husband only	155	25.83
2.	Both Husband and Wife	225	37.50
3.	Others	220	36.67
	Total	600	100

Source: Primary Data

The above table indicates that, 37.50 per cent of respondents' have said that both husband and wife are earning for the family. Similarly 36.67 per cent of respondents' have said that members like their offspring's and other relations are earning for the family needs. And the rests of 25.83 per cent of restaurant customers' have said that only husband i.e., family head is the earning member of the family.

Thus it has been concluded that, 37.50 per cent of respondents' have said that both husband and wife are earning for the family. The duel incomes families are always considered to be frequent diners of casual dine restaurants. Eating out habit of Indians has increased for sure. If a working couple feels they are tired then they go for eating out. Eating out in weekends has now almost become a norm not only in metros but also in Tier-II cities.

The demographic and socio-economic status of the diners surveyed in Coimbatore city provides a brief out-line about the category of consumers hailing in Coimbatore city and their dining at restaurant potentials.

Demographic and socio-economic variations are used in numerous studies to differentiate the market segments of consumers. Moreover, earlier research work had stated that the restaurant selection behaviour was found to vary according to gender, age, educational qualification, family culture, income of the consumers and nature of benefit seekers. Based on the knowledge gained from the previous study following two hypotheses are framed. The two hypotheses aim to measure whether diners' choice of the restaurant is influenced by their demographic and socio-economic status.

H1: Diners' choice of the vegetarian restaurant is purely influenced by their demographic and socio-economic status.

Table 4.10: Demographic Status of the Diners and their Choice of Vegetarian Restaurants

Variables	Annapoorna's			Anandha's			Aryaa's		
	Mean	SD	Rank	Mean	SD	Rank	Mean	SD	Rank
Gender	1.49	.501	8	1.57	.496	8	1.46	.501	8
Age	2.93	1.724	2	3.13	1.558	1	3.14	1.634	1
Educational Qualification	2.62	1.071	4	2.78	1.037	3	2.66	1.097	3
Family Status	1.36	.480	9	1.47	.500	9	1.44	.499	9
Occupations	2.66	1.193	3	2.70	1.214	4	2.56	1.267	4
Income	2.06	1.075	6	2.35	.903	5	2.41	1.105	5
Marital Status	2.05	.807	7	2.12	.714	7	2.04	.701	7
Family Size	2.99	.846	1	2.89	.933	2	2.95	.844	2
Earning Members in the Family	2.08	.821	5	2.16	.763	6	2.09	.734	6

Source: Computed from Primary Data

Table 4.11: Demographic Status of the Diners and their Choice of Restaurants

Variables	Adyar Anandha Bhavan			RHR		
	Mean	SD	Rank	Mean	SD	Rank
Gender	1.52	.503	8	1.59	.495	8
Age	3.46	1.758	1	3.17	1.627	1
Educational Qualification	2.56	1.074	4	2.91	1.147	4
Family Status	1.44	.501	9	1.49	.504	9
Occupations	2.73	1.285	3	3.12	1.219	2
Income	2.19	1.014	5	2.54	1.132	5
Marital Status	2.11	.760	7	2.06	.700	7
Family Size	2.89	.952	2	3.10	.972	3
Earning Members in the Family	2.13	.772	6	2.10	.770	6

Source: Computed from Primary Data

The data presented in the above two tables depicts that there exists vast differences in the diners preferences of vegetarian restaurant selection based on their demographic and socio-economic status.

Table 4.12: Result of Chi-square Demographic Status of the Diners and their Choice of Vegetarian Restaurants

Variables	Chi-square value	DF	Table value	Remark
Gender	13.146	5	11.070	Accepted
Age	37.354	25	37.653	Accepted
Educational Qualification	24.151	15	24.996	Accepted
Family Status	7.683	5	11.070	Accepted
Occupations	27.148	20	31.410	Accepted
Income	50.942	15	24.996	Rejected
Marital Status	8.507	10	18.307	Accepted
Family Size	18.291	15	24.996	Accepted
Earning Members in the Family	10.693	10	18.307	Accepted

Level of Significance: 5 per cent

From the above table it has been inferred that the calculated chi-square values are less than the table values 11.070, 18.307, 24.996 and 31.410 at 5 per cent level of significance. Therefore the hypothesis framed stands accepted and it has been concluded that diners' choice of the vegetarian restaurant is purely influenced by their demographic and socio-economic status. However it is exceptional in the case of income of the diners'.

H2: Diners' choice of the non-vegetarian restaurant is purely influenced by their demographic and socio-economic status.

Table 4.13: Demographic Status of the Diners and their Choice of Non-Vegetarian Restaurants

Variables	Rayappa's			Sampoorna			Hari Bahavanam		
	Mean	SD	Rank	Mean	SD	Rank	Mean	SD	Rank
Gender	1.45	.500	8	1.59	.493	8	1.55	.502	8
Age	3.20	1.703	1	2.89	1.620	3	3.09	1.604	1
Educational Qualification	2.53	1.144	4	2.75	1.071	4	2.79	1.022	3
Family Status	1.34	.476	9	1.45	.499	9	1.48	.504	9
Occupations	2.57	1.158	3	2.93	1.212	2	2.66	1.148	4
Income	2.19	1.040	5	2.27	1.004	5	2.50	1.246	5
Marital Status	2.09	.761	7	2.11	.764	7	2.18	.778	7
Family Size	2.98	.825	2	3.07	.864	1	2.84	1.023	2
Earning Members in the Family	2.11	.765	6	2.17	.786	6	2.21	.789	6

Source: Computed from Primary Data

Table 4.14: Demographic Status of the Diners and their Choice of Non-vegetarian Restaurants

Variables	Anjappar			Anjali		
	Mean	SD	Rank	Mean	SD	Rank
Gender	1.53	.502	8	1.48	.502	8
Age	3.31	1.732	1	3.13	1.664	1
Educational Qualification	2.67	.993	4	2.79	1.098	2
Family Status	1.44	.499	9	1.43	.497	9
Occupations	2.79	1.310	3	2.57	1.239	4
Income	2.24	.984	5	2.44	1.009	5
Marital Status	2.09	.777	6	2.10	.722	7
Family Size	2.94	.930	2	2.73	.973	3
Earning Members in the Family	2.06	.807	7	2.12	.743	6

Source: Computed from Primary Data

The data presented in the above two tables depicts that there exists vast differences in the diners preferences of non-vegetarian restaurant selection based on their demographic and socio-economic status.

Table 4.15: Result of Chi-Square Demographic Status of the Diners and their Choice of Non-vegetarian Restaurants

Variables	Chi-square value	DF	Table value	Remark
Gender	7.787	5	11.070	Accepted
Age	29.237	25	37.653	Accepted
Educational Qualification	16.167	15	24.996	Accepted
Family Status	4.599	5	11.070	Accepted
Occupations	37.367	20	31.410	Accepted
Income	37.361	15	24.996	Rejected
Marital Status	10.876	10	18.307	Accepted
Family Size	34.536	15	24.996	Accepted
Earning Members in the Family	11.855	10	18.307	Accepted

Level of Significance: 5 per cent

From the above table it has been inferred that the calculated chi-square values are less than the table values 11.070, 18.307, 24.996 and 31.410 at 5 per cent level of significance. Therefore the hypothesis framed stands accepted and it has been concluded that diners' choice of the non-vegetarian restaurant is purely influenced by their demographic and socio-economic status. However it is exceptional in the case of income of the diners'.Based on the above two hypotheses findings, the study conclude by stating that people with different demographic characteristics (gender, age, education, income levels, occupational level, family type and size and number of earning) have different traits. These people seek differences in restaurant services according to their traits.

2. *Diners Opinion on Food Consumption Habits (Eating at Outlets)*

Eating out has evolved into a popular trend among Indian households. The sheer variety of gastronomic preferences across the regions, hereditary or acquired of food habits among the Kongu community people and Coimbatorians have gave rise to the casual dine restaurant service in Coimbatore city. Moreover, the casual dine restaurants have been quick to respond to changes in consumer needs by introducing food products that include items avail across the nations cooked both at traditional and innovative manner. Based on this conceptual discussion this section of the study deals with the diners' opinion on food consumption habits (eating at outlets).

The Indian market is typically split into vegetarian (31 percent) and non-vegetarian (69per cent) restaurants. The following table provides information on the diners' preference of restaurant types.

Table 4.16: Food Type Based Restaurants Preferences of Diners

Sl. No	Food	No. of Respondents	Percentage
1.	Pure Vegetarian	116	19.33
2.	Non-Vegetarian	180	30.00
3.	Both	304	50.67
	Total	600	100

Source: Primary Data

It is evident from the above table that, majority i.e., 50.67 per cent of diners prefers to eat both vegetarian and non-vegetarian food items while visiting popular restaurants. On the other hand, 30 per cent of respondents' order onlynon-vegetarian foods while dinning. Whereas the remaining 19.33 per cent of respondents' have said that they are purely vegetarian dinners.

Thus it has been found that majority i.e., 50.67 per cent of diners prefers to eat both vegetarian and non-vegetarian food items while visiting popular restaurants. The data analysis reveals that Indian population in the Southern part of India prefers to eat both vegetarian and non-vegetarian foods.

Frequency of customers visit to restaurant depicts their satisfaction and liking for the food and services offered by the restaurants. The following table depicts on frequency of visit made by the diners to a restaurants.

Table 4.17: Diners Opinion on Frequency of Visiting Restaurants

Sl. No	Frequency	No. of Respondents	Percentage
1.	One in a week	118	19.67
2.	Once in a month	234	39.00
3.	Occasionally	248	41.33
	Total	600	100

Source: Primary Data

Frequent visits to a particular casual dine restaurant is often depend on the factors like taste, ambience, quick service etc. The data presented in the above table infers that, 41.33 per cent of respondents' prefer to visit restaurants during special occasions. Batch of 39 per cent of respondents' have opined that they visit restaurants once in a month and they usually dine out with the entire family. Followed by, 19.67 per cent of diners prefer to eat in restaurants once in every week.

Thus it has been found that 41.33 per cent of respondents' prefer to visit restaurants during special occasionally.

Indian household prefer to living amidst groups of people and this is very much reflected in their dining and hosting practices. Based on this concept a question was raised among the sample diners, with whom do they prefer dining.

Table 4.18: Diners Opinion on Preferred Acquaintance While Visiting Restaurants

Sl. No	Acquaintance	No. of Respondents	Percentage
1.	Alone	27	4.50
2.	With Friends	127	21.17
3.	With Family Members	200	33.33
4.	Both Family Members & Friends	246	41.00
	Total	600	100

Source: Primary Data

The above table clearly indicates that out of 600 respondents' surveyed, 41 per cent of sample populations' like to visit restaurants with both family members & friends to have a pleasant dinning. Subsequently it has been inferred that 33.33 per cent of respondents' prefer to visit restaurants with their family members and 21.17 per cent of sample populations' usually visit restaurants with their peer group i.e., friends. Whereas 4.50 per cent of respondents' have opined that they always visit to visit restaurants singly without any company.

Nowadays, with the higher living standard, having dining in restaurants is considered as life-style status among many urban Indians, thus it has been observed that most of the diners (41 per cent) prefer to visit restaurants with both family members and friends to have a pleasant dining experience.

Branding of casual dine restaurant is very important for attracting more diners, to define the food varieties offered and innovative measures taken and also stay competitive in the market. Following tables provide a brief discussion on diners' preferences towards various restaurants operating in Coimbatore city.

Table 4.19: Diners Preferences towards Branded Vegetarian Restaurants

Sl. No	Vegetarian Hotels	No. of Respondents	Percentage
1.	Annapoorna	210	35.00
2.	Anandha's	165	27.50
3.	Arya's	88	14.67
4.	Adyar Anandha Bhavan (A2B)	67	11.17
5.	RHR	70	11.67
	Total	600	100

Source: Primary Data

It is evident from the above table that, 35 per cent of diners in Coimbatore city often visit Annapoorna hotel for its delicious taste. Batch of 27.50 per cent of respondents' prefer Anandha's and 14.67 per cent of respondents' usually dine in Arya's hotel. Further it has been inferred that 11.67 per cent of respondents' like the taste of RHR food items and 11.17 per cent of sample subjects' frequently visit A2B hotel for its tasty food.

Thus it has been clearly identified that 35 per cent of diners in Coimbatore city often visit the vegetarian restaurant Annapoorna for its delicious taste, unique food varieties and more locational of restaurants across the city.

Table 4.20: Diners Preferences towards Branded Non-vegetarian Restaurants

Sl. No	Non-Vegetarian Hotels	No. of Respondents	Percentage
1.	Rayappa's	138	23.00
2.	Sampoorna	179	29.83
3.	Haribhavanam	71	11.83
4.	Anjappar	92	15.33
5.	Anjali	120	20.00
	Total	600	100

Source: Primary Data

From the above table it has been inferred that, 29.83 per cent of respondents' prefer to visit Sampoorna hotel to dine non-vegetarian dishes. Batch of 23 per cent of diners prefer Rayappa's and 20 per cent of sample populations' like to dine Anjali restaurant for non-veg items. Similarly 15.33 per cent of respondents' usually visit Anjappar hotel and 11.83 per cent of sample subjects' visit Haribhavanam restaurants for having non-vegetarian foods.

From the above data analysis it has been inferred that 29.83 per cent of respondents' prefer to visit Sampoorna hotel to dine non-vegetarian dishes.

Dining occasion at restaurants is influenced by various factors, time period in a day and week. Moreover, dining frequency at restaurants is more determined by the spending power of individual and their intention to spend a specific value of money. Following Table:4.21 to 4.33draw a detailed discussion on these dimensions.

Table 4.21: Diners Opinion on Occasion of Visiting Restaurants

Sl. No	Occasion	No. of Respondents	Percentage
1.	Saturday Evenings	53	8.83
2.	Sundays' (Lunch / Dinner)	148	24.67
3.	Special Occasions	88	14.67
4.	Festive Seasons	95	15.83
5.	Any time	216	36.00
	Total	600	100

Source: Primary Data

The above table describes the diners opinion on preferred occasion of visiting restaurants. Out of 600 respondents' surveyed, 36 per cent of respondents' have said that they visit restaurants at any time as per their wish. Followed by, 24.67 per cent of diners visit restaurants at Sunday's (lunch/dinner) and 15.83 per cent of sample populations' visit hotels on festive seasons with their entire family. Subsequently it has been found that 14.67 per cent of diners make hotel visits on special occasions and the remaining 8.83 per cent of respondents' prefer to dine on Saturday evenings.

Thus it has been clearly identified that 36 per cent of respondents' have said that they visit restaurants at any time as per their wish.

As stated in the Table: 4.17,respondents' prefer to visit restaurants occasionally.

Table 4.22: Diners Opinion Time Preference for Visit Restaurants

Sl. No	Time	No. of Respondents	Percentage
1.	Early Morning	37	6.17
2.	Morning Break – Fast	64	10.67
3.	After – noon Lunch	103	17.17
4.	Early Evening	182	30.33
5.	Late Evening	214	35.67
	Total	60	100

Source: Primary Data

The data presented in the above table clearly indicates that, 35.67 per cent of sample subjects' like to dine in restaurants at late evenings to have a pleasant dinner. Similarly 30.33 per cent of respondents' prefer to go to hotels at early evenings and 17.17 per cent of respondents' have after–noon Lunch at hotels and are usually working individuals. Further it has been inferred that 10.67 per cent of sample populations' visit hotels to have breakfast and 6.17 per cent of them visit restaurants at early morning.

Thus it has been concluded that 35.67 per cent of sample subjects' like to dine in restaurants at late evenings to have a pleasant dinner, especially after completion of their hectic day of work schedules.

Table 4.23: Diners Opinion on Budget Fixation

Sl. No	Budget	No. of Respondents	Percentage
1.	Do Fix Budget	290	48.30
2.	Do Not Fix Budget	310	51.70
	Total	600	100

Source: Primary Data

It is evident from the above table that majority i.e., 51.70 per cent of sample populations' does not fix budgets before visiting restaurants. On the other hand, 48.30 per cent of sample populations' usually plan their expenses while visiting hotels.

Drawing empirical evidences declared in the Table: 4.16 and 4.18, where it was found that 50.67 per cent of diners prefer to eat both vegetarian and non-vegetarian food items while visiting popular restaurants. Similarly, the study confirms that 41 per cent of diners prefer to visit restaurants with both family members and friends to have a pleasant dining experience. Also, Table: 4.17 and 4.21 reveals that respondents' prefer to visit restaurants occasionally, so they may not mind spending money as preference of food varieties from the elaborate menu, ordering of more than one type of food for every individual visiting the restaurants. The study finding declare that majority i.e., Thus it has been observed that majority i.e., 51.70 per cent of sample populations' does not fix budgets before visiting restaurants, rather they spend as per their capacity to spend on that particular occasion.

Table 4.24: Factors Influencing the Diners to Visit a Particular Restaurant

Service Features	Sum	Mean	Rank
Food Quality	5219	8.70	1
Menu Selection (Variety)	4450	7.42	2
Menu Pricing and Value	4217	7.03	3
Waiting Times	3815	6.36	4
Promptness of Service	3730	6.22	5
Professionalism and Friendliness Of Server(S)	3554	5.92	6
Server's Knowledge Of Menu	3022	5.04	9
Decor (Ambience)	2739	4.57	11
Restaurant Location	3275	5.46	7
Special Places For Kids To Play	2778	4.63	10
Overall Restaurant Experience	3179	5.30	8

Source: Primary Data

The data presented in the above table discusses about the factors influencing the diners to visit particular restaurant in Coimbatore city. It has been found that majority of the respondents' have agreed that particular restaurants maintains food quality and so they need not worry about health, so they prefer to visit to the same restaurant again and again. This variable is placed in first rank with an average score of 8.70, respectively. Followed by the respondents' have said that they are influenced by the features like Menu selection (variety), menu pricing, value and waiting times of particular restaurant. These variables are ranked in second, third and fourth rank with the mean score of 7.42, 7.03 and 6.36, accordingly. Similarly the respondents' have stated that they are impressed by the factors like promptness, professionalism, location and overall restaurant experience. These variables are ranked in fifth, sixth, seventh and eighth place with the mean score of 6.22, 5.92, 5.46 and 5.30, respectively. Subsequently it has been observed that the respondents' are influenced by the staff(s) knowledge about the menu, other special arrangements and are also attracted by the ambience of particular restaurant. These factors are placed in ninth, tenth and eleventh rank with an average score of 5.04, 4.63 and 4.57.

The study has observed that diners were influences by restaurant features like: the food quality, menu varieties, price and value for money, least waiting time and prompt services. The study confirms the fact that food aesthetic considerations now heavily weigh on: tastes, preferences, and consumer choices. Food habits undergo continuous change as they adapt to travel, immigration, and the socio-economic environment.

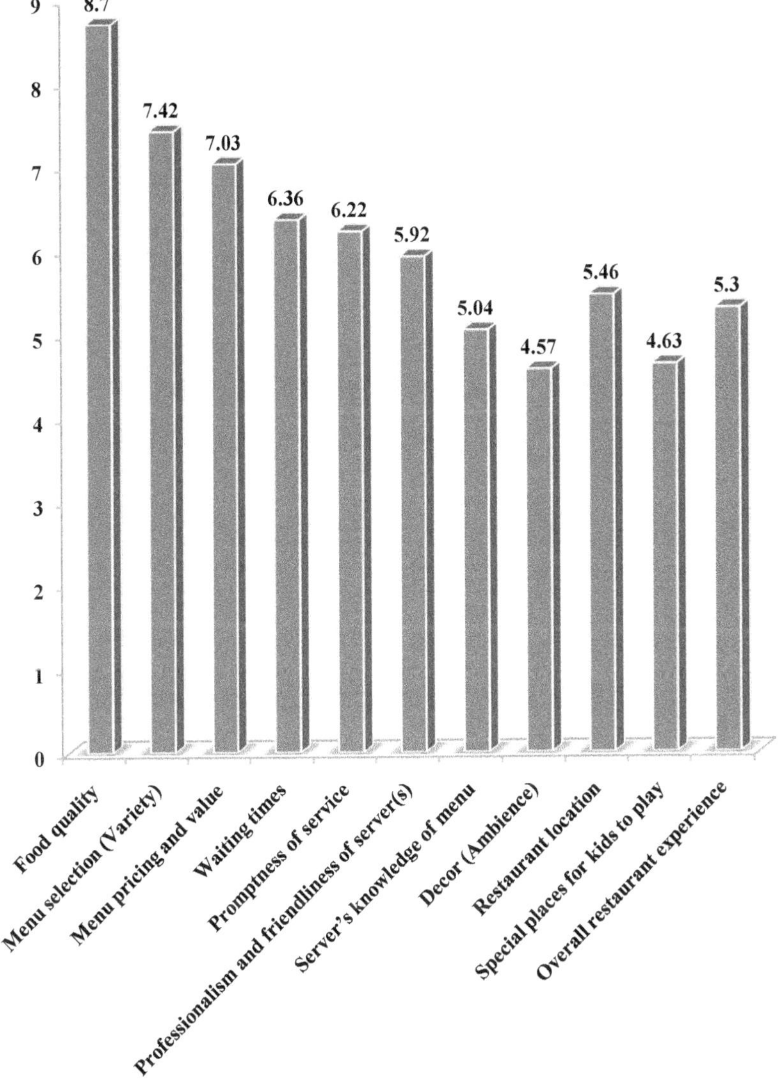

Exhibit 4.1: Factors Influencing the Diners to Visit Particular Restaurant

Table 4.25(A): Factors Influencing the Diners to Visit Particular Vegetarian Restaurant

Variable	Annapoorna			Anandha's			Arya's			Adyar Anandha Bhavan			RHR		
	Sum	Mean	Rank	Sum	Mean	Rank	Sum	Mean	Rank	Sum	Mean	Rank	Sum	Mean	Rank
Food quality	1896	9.12	1	1378	8.56	4	695	8.18	6	558	8.86	2	568	8.23	5
Menu selection (Variety)	1619	7.78	1	1178	7.32	4	614	7.22	5	462	7.33	2	472	6.84	6
Menu pricing and value	1424	6.85	3	1213	7.53	1	610	7.18	2	421	6.68	4	457	6.62	5
Waiting times	1299	6.25	5	1013	6.29	4	594	6.99	2	367	5.83	6	438	6.35	3
Promptness of service	1316	6.33	2	971	6.03	5	531	6.25	3	389	6.17	4	444	6.43	1
Professionalism and friendliness of server(s)	1236	5.94	3	927	5.76	5	491	5.78	4	378	6.00	2	444	6.43	1
Server's knowledge of menu	1044	5.02	4	767	4.76	5	443	5.21	2	321	5.10	3	382	5.54	1
Décor (Ambience)	924	4.44	4	748	4.65	3	343	4.04	6	304	4.83	2	359	5.20	1
Restaurant location	1142	5.49	2	881	5.47	4	459	5.40	5	346	5.49	2	363	5.26	6
Special places for kids to play	936	4.50	5	758	4.71	2	415	4.88	1	296	4.70	3	311	4.51	4
Overall restaurant experience	1057	5.08	5	900	5.59	1	468	5.51	2	327	5.19	4	365	5.29	3

Source: Computed from Primary Data

Table 4.25(B): Factors Influencing the Diners to Visit Particular Non-vegetarian Restaurant

Variable	Rayappa's			Sampoorna			Haribhavanam			Anjappar			Anjali		
	Sum	Mean	Rank	Sum	Mean	Rank	Sum	Mean	Rank	Sum	Mean	Rank	Sum	Mean	Rank
Food quality	1026	8.55	4	1400	8.43	5	468	8.07	6	792	9.32	2	917	8.73	3
Menu selection (Variety)	839	6.99	6	1202	7.24	4	425	7.33	3	701	8.25	1	748	7.12	5
Menu pricing and value	856	7.13	2	1156	6.96	4	406	7.00	3	661	7.78	1	683	6.50	6
Waiting times	733	6.11	6	1028	6.19	5	378	6.52	3	528	6.21	4	687	6.54	2
Promptness of service	774	6.45	1	1043	6.28	3	368	6.34	2	506	5.95	5	649	6.18	4
Professionalism and friendliness of server(s)	698	5.82	4	963	5.80	5	340	5.86	3	483	5.68	6	649	6.18	2
Server's knowledge of menu	603	5.03	4	849	5.11	3	301	5.19	2	407	4.79	5	553	5.27	1
Décor (Ambience)	612	5.10	1	720	4.34	4	257	4.43	3	356	4.19	5	526	5.01	2
Restaurant location	734	6.12	1	954	5.75	2	297	5.12	4	453	5.33	3	503	4.79	6
Special places for kids to play	515	4.29	5	838	5.05	2	297	5.12	1	405	4.76	3	472	4.50	4
Overall restaurant experience	619	5.16	5	940	5.66	2	317	5.47	3	364	4.28	6	596	5.68	1

Source: Computed from Primary Data

The above table discusses about the factors influencing the diners to visit particular vegetarian restaurant in Coimbatore city.

Vegetarian Restaurants

Majority of the respondents' have agreed that Annapoorna hotel offer lots of varieties in menu and maintains the quality standards and it influences them to visit the hotel frequently. Similarly the respondents' prefer Anandha's hotel for its menu and pricing value of food items. Followed by, the diners like to visit Arya's hotel as they have made special arrangements for kids to play. Further it has been inferred that, Adyar Anandha Bhavan customers' have stated that they are influenced by the features like promptness of service, professionalism & friendliness of server, server's knowledge of menu and by the ambience of that restaurant.

Non Vegetarian Restaurants

From the above data analysis it has been observed that, majority of the sample populations' prefer to dine in Rayappas's for its promptness of service, decor (ambience) and for the location of the restaurant. Similarly the diners prefer to visit Haribhavanam hotel for their children as it provides special places for kids to play. Subsequently it has been found that the sample subjects' frequently visit Anjappar as it avails wide variety of items with reasonable price. A batch of sample populations' has opined that they are inspired by the Anjali hotel server's knowledge on menu and are satisfied with the overall services experienced in the restaurant.

Diners as a consumers go to a casual dine restaurant not only for food and service but also for a different dining experience and cultural experience. Various factors like: food quality, menu varieties, hygiene and cleanliness; cleanliness of restrooms; employee friendliness; value for money; efficient service; spicy food; atmosphere; price; vegetarian /non-vegetarian choices; availability of new items; and, cultural familiarity etc. Based on the above discussed theoretical understanding following hypothesis is framed to measure whether There exists association between food consumption habits of the diners' and factors motivated them to visit particular restaurant.

H3: There exists no association between food consumption habits of the diners' and factors that motivated them to visit the restaurants.

In the current study food Consumption habits of diners denotes: type of restaurant selected by diner, frequency of visit to a restaurant, preferred acquaintance accompanying the visit, branded restaurant visited, occasion of visit to the restaurant, time preference of visit and budget fixation attitude of the diners. Thus, the measures of association were assessed between:

- Type of restaurant selected by the dine vs. factors that motivated them to visit the restaurants.
- Frequency of visit to a restaurant vs. factors that motivated them to visit the restaurants
- Preferred acquaintance accompanying the visit vs. factors that motivated them to visit the restaurants

- Branded restaurant visited vs. factors that motivated them to visit the restaurants

- Occasion of visit to the restaurant vs. factors that motivated them to visit the restaurants

- Time preference of visit vs. factors that motivated them to visit the restaurants

- Budget fixation attitude of the diners vs. factors that motivated them to visit the restaurants

Table 4.26: Measure of Dispersion & Result of ANOVA Type of Restaurant Selected Vs Factors Influencing them to Visit the Restaurants

Variables	Pure Vegetarian (N:116)		Non-Vegetarian (N:180)		Both (N:304)		F Value	Sig
	Mean	SD	Mean	SD	Mean	SD		
Food quality	3.16	2.799	3.49	3.037	3.25	3.019	.546	.580
Menu selection (Variety)	4.33	2.781	4.87	2.845	4.51	2.567	1.621	.199
Menu pricing and value	4.95	2.975	5.16	2.946	4.87	2.832	.548	.578
Waiting times	5.82	3.199	5.69	2.839	5.55	2.657	.428	.652
Promptness of service	5.85	2.899	5.68	2.829	5.82	2.588	.181	.834
Professionalism and friendliness of server(s)	6.23	2.691	5.87	3.169	6.14	2.771	.692	.501
Server's knowledge of menu	6.99	2.504	6.89	2.886	6.99	2.842	.078	.925
Decor (Ambience)	7.07	2.861	7.28	2.845	7.66	2.822	2.218	.110
Restaurant location	6.64	2.994	6.78	2.857	6.37	3.124	1.128	.324
Special attraction for kids	7.42	3.110	7.26	3.062	7.42	3.158	.173	.841
Overall restaurant experience	7.07	2.855	6.49	3.223	6.69	3.328	1.158	.315

Level of Significance: 5 per cent

The above table clearly indicates that the vegetarian diners have stated that factors such as waiting time, promptness of service, professionalism and friendliness of server(s), server's knowledge of menu, special attraction for kids and overall restaurant experience are the determinants that influenced them to visit popular restaurants. Similarly the non-vegetarian diners have opined that they are motivated by the features like food quality, menu selection (variety), menu pricing and value and restaurant location of famous restaurants in Coimbatore. Further it has been observed that the respondents' who prefer to dine at both vegetarian and non-vegetarian food have stated that they are attracted by the factors such as server's knowledge of menu, special attraction for kids and decor (ambience) of the popular restaurants in Coimbatore. From the above table it has been inferred that there exists variations in the sample mean values and the probability value of ANOVA at 5 per cent level does not establish good relationship between the variables tested. Therefore, the hypothesis framed stands rejected and it is concluded that there exists close association between type of restaurant selected by the diner and factors that motivated them to visit the restaurants.

Table 4.27: Measure of Dispersion & Result of ANOVA Frequency of Visits to a Restaurant and Factors Influencing them to Visit the Restaurants

Variables	Once in a week (N:118)		Once in a month (N:234)		Occasionally (N:248)		F Value	Sig
	Mean	SD	Mean	SD	Mean	SD		
Food quality	3.54	3.115	3.58	3.174	2.92	2.686	3.437	.033
Menu selection (Variety)	4.91	2.777	4.77	2.871	4.25	2.453	3.350	.036
Menu pricing and value	5.11	2.891	5.00	2.932	4.88	2.864	.259	.772
Waiting times	5.64	3.051	5.65	2.858	5.64	2.679	.002	.998
Promptness of service	5.67	2.844	5.77	2.793	5.85	2.597	.182	.833
Professionalism and friendliness of server(s)	5.90	2.933	5.96	3.020	6.27	2.714	1.011	.365
Server's knowledge of menu	6.83	2.856	6.66	2.738	7.31	2.777	3.529	.030
Decor (Ambience)	7.18	2.928	7.42	2.765	7.57	2.876	.776	.461
Restaurant location	6.68	3.124	6.46	2.934	6.56	3.063	.214	.808
Special places for kids to play	7.04	3.166	7.32	3.163	7.57	3.044	1.207	.300
Overall restaurant experience	6.29	3.171	6.82	3.282	6.79	3.159	1.223	.295

Level of Significance: 5 per cent

It is evident from the above table that the frequent visitors' are influenced by the attributes like menu selection (variety), menu pricing and value and restaurant location of selected restaurants that are considered in the study. Followed by it has been observed that, the monthly visitors' are pleased with the food quality, waiting time and overall services of the popular restaurants. Subsequently, it has been inferred that the occasional visitors' are motivated by the Promptness of service, Professionalism and friendliness of server(s), Server's knowledge of menu, Special attraction for kids and Decor (Ambience) Restaurant location of the popular restaurants that are in Coimbatore.

From the above table it has been inferred that there exists variations in the sample mean values and the probability value of ANOVA at 5 per cent level does not establish good relationship between the variables tested. Therefore, the hypothesis framed stands rejected and it is concluded that there exists close association between frequency of visit to the restaurant by the diners' and factors that motivated them to visit the restaurants. However it is exceptional in the case of food quality, menu selection (variety) and server's knowledge of menu.

Table 4.28: Measure of Dispersion & Result of ANOVA Preferred Acquaintance Accompanying the Visit to the Restaurant Vs Factors Influencing them to Visit the Restaurants

Variables	Alone (N:27)		With Friends (N:127)		With Family Members (N:200)		Both Family Members & Friends(N:246)		F Value	Sig
	Mean	SD	Mean	SD	Mean	SD	Mean	SD		
Food quality	4.70	3.451	3.52	3.157	3.03	2.773	3.26	2.966	2.815	.039
Menu selection (Variety)	5.63	3.140	4.29	2.755	4.36	2.589	4.80	2.672	2.909	.034
Menu pricing and value	5.67	3.013	5.34	3.094	4.61	2.774	5.00	2.842	2.298	.077
Waiting times	5.74	2.863	5.78	2.594	5.31	2.702	5.83	3.009	1.444	.229
Promptness of service	6.56	2.225	5.89	2.694	5.72	2.784	5.70	2.730	.910	.436
Professionalism and friendliness of server(s)	5.37	2.803	6.47	2.828	6.01	2.706	6.01	3.040	1.432	.233
Server's knowledge of menu	7.33	2.922	6.80	2.659	7.32	2.801	6.72	2.815	1.987	.115
Decor (Ambience)	6.33	3.385	7.07	3.143	7.75	2.740	7.49	2.660	2.922	.033
Restaurant location	6.70	2.880	6.99	2.861	6.59	2.983	6.26	3.133	1.719	.162
Special attraction for kids	5.15	3.450	7.51	3.005	7.46	3.159	7.47	3.026	4.893	.002
Overall restaurant experience	5.07	3.339	6.16	3.320	6.89	3.107	7.01	3.153	4.586	.003

Level of Significance: 5 per cent

The data presented in the above table clearly indicates that the respondents' who prefer to dine alone have said that they are attracted by the service features such as food quality, menu selection (variety), menu pricing and value, promptness of service and server's knowledge of menu of famous restaurants. Similarly, the respondents' who dine with their peer group have opined that they are inspired by the professionalism, friendliness of server(s) and also by the decor (ambience) of the popular restaurants' in Coimbatore. Batch of sample populations' who usually dine with their family have opined that they are attracted by the decor (ambience) of popular restaurants. It has been inferred that, the respondents' who prefer to dine with their family and friends have stated that they are influenced by the waiting times, special attraction for kids and by the overall restaurant service.

From the above table it has been inferred that there exists variations in the sample mean values and the probability value of ANOVA at 5 per cent level does not establish good relationship between the variables tested. Therefore, the hypothesis framed stands rejected and it is concluded that there exists close association between preferred acquaintance accompanying the diner visit to a restaurant and factors that motivated them to visit the restaurants. However it is exceptional in the case of food quality, menu selection (variety), decor (ambience), special attraction for kids and overall restaurant experience.

Table 4.29(A): Measure of Dispersion & Result of ANOVA Branded Restaurant Visited Vs Factors Influencing the Diners to Visit Particular Vegetarian the Restaurant

Variables	Annapoorna (N:208)		Anandha's (N:161)		Arya's (N:85)	
	Mean	SD	Mean	SD	Mean	SD
Food quality	2.88	2.587	3.44	3.096	3.82	3.506
Menu selection (Variety)	4.22	2.564	4.68	2.742	4.78	2.701
Menu pricing and value	5.15	2.940	4.47	2.764	4.82	2.709
Waiting times	5.75	2.866	5.71	2.756	5.01	2.500
Promptness of service	5.67	2.775	5.97	2.712	5.75	2.764
Professionalism and friendliness of server(s)	6.06	2.892	6.24	2.876	6.22	2.800
Server's knowledge of menu	6.98	2.757	7.24	2.995	6.79	2.756
Decor (Ambience)	7.56	2.722	7.35	2.851	7.96	2.805
Restaurant location	6.51	3.083	6.53	2.939	6.60	2.691
Special attraction for kids	7.50	3.124	7.29	3.016	7.12	3.462
Overall restaurant experience	6.92	3.017	6.41	3.346	6.49	3.414

Level of Significance: 5 per cent

Table 4.29(B): Measure of Dispersion & Result of ANOVA Branded Restaurant Visited Vs Factors Influencing the Diners to Visit Particular Vegetarian Restaurant

Variables	Adyar Anansha Bhavan (N:63)		RHR (N:69)		Others (N:14)		F Value	Sig
	Mean	SD	Mean	SD	Mean	SD		
Food quality	3.14	2.895	3.77	3.149	3.14	2.770	1.799	.111
Menu selection (Variety)	4.67	2.634	5.16	2.993	4.50	2.565	1.553	.172
Menu pricing and value	5.32	2.961	5.38	2.961	5.43	3.631	1.726	.127
Waiting times	6.17	3.051	5.65	2.945	4.57	2.593	1.797	.111
Promptness of service	5.83	2.820	5.57	2.654	6.36	1.550	.435	.824
Professionalism and friendliness of server(s)	6.00	3.027	5.57	2.794	6.43	3.155	.636	.672
Server's knowledge of menu	6.90	2.360	6.46	2.888	7.36	2.274	.879	.495
Decor (Ambience)	7.17	2.751	6.80	3.184	7.64	3.104	1.516	.183
Restaurant location	6.51	3.262	6.74	3.175	6.00	3.486	.161	.977
Special attraction for kids	7.30	3.046	7.49	3.132	7.57	2.472	.242	.944
Overall restaurant experience	6.81	3.426	6.71	3.097	7.57	2.821	.744	.590

Level of Significance: 5 per cent

From the above tables it has been observed that the sample populations' believe that the food quality of Arya's is better in comparison to the other restaurants surveyed. Followed by, the sample customers' have opined that they are inspired by the quickness of Adyar Anandha Bhavan restaurant in delivering food. Subsequently it has been observed that the sample populations' are influenced by the attributes like menu selection (variety), menu pricing and value and restaurant location of RHR restaurant. It has been found that the visitors' are attracted by the promptness of service, professionalism and friendliness of server(s), server's knowledge of menu, decor (ambience), special attraction for kids and by the overall service features of other restaurants. From the above table it has been inferred that there exists variations in the sample mean values and the probability value of ANOVA at 5 per cent level does not establish good relationship between the variables tested. Therefore, the hypothesis framed stands rejected and it is concluded that there exists close association between branded vegetarian restaurant selected by the diner and factors that motivated them to visit the restaurants.

Table: 4.30(A): Measure of Dispersion & Result of ANOVA Branded Restaurant Visited Vs Factors Influencing the Diners to Visit Particular Non-Vegetarian the Restaurant

Variables	Rayappa's (N:120)		Sampoorna (N:166)		Haribhavanam (N:58)	
	Mean	SD	Mean	SD	Mean	SD
Food quality	3.45	3.059	3.57	3.132	3.93	3.303
Menu selection (Variety)	5.01	2.761	4.76	2.713	4.67	2.671
Menu pricing and value	4.87	3.004	5.04	2.856	5.00	2.847
Waiting times	5.89	2.887	5.81	2.783	5.48	2.624
Promptness of service	5.55	2.822	5.72	2.741	5.66	2.613
Professionalism and friendliness of server(s)	6.18	3.111	6.20	2.871	6.14	2.605
Server's knowledge of menu	6.98	2.693	6.89	2.846	6.81	2.769
Decor (Ambience)	6.90	2.914	7.66	2.832	7.57	2.866
Restaurant location	5.88	3.210	6.25	3.131	6.88	3.304
Special attraction for kids	7.71	2.850	6.95	3.395	6.88	3.540
Overall restaurant experience	6.84	3.183	6.34	3.311	6.53	3.394

Level of Significance: 5 per cent

Table 4.30(B): Measure of Dispersion & Result of ANOVA Branded Restaurant Visited Vs Factors Influencing the Diners to Visit Particular Non-Vegetarian Restaurant

Variables	Anjappar (N:85)		Anjali (N:105)		Others (N:66)		F Value	Sig
	Mean	SD	Mean	SD	Mean	SD		
Food quality	2.68	2.555	3.27	2.900	2.67	2.633	2.195	.053
Menu selection (Variety)	3.75	2.345	4.88	2.827	3.89	2.512	3.544	.004
Menu pricing and value	4.22	2.607	5.50	3.098	5.11	2.718	1.918	.089
Waiting times	5.79	2.786	5.46	2.984	5.02	2.720	1.128	.344
Promptness of service	6.05	2.807	5.82	2.681	6.09	2.558	.552	.737
Professionalism and friendliness of server(s)	6.32	2.748	5.82	2.938	5.62	2.794	.713	.614
Server's knowledge of menu	7.21	2.756	6.73	2.860	7.32	2.813	.550	.738
Decor (Ambience)	7.81	2.486	6.99	3.176	7.94	2.404	2.343	.040
Restaurant location	6.67	2.579	7.21	2.684	6.94	2.945	2.919	.013
Special attraction for kids	7.24	3.089	7.50	2.808	8.20	2.791	2.191	.064
Overall restaurant experience	7.72	3.061	6.32	3.218	6.80	2.802	2.543	.067

Level of Significance: 5 per cent

From the above cross-sectional data analysis it has been observed that the diners' have opined that they are attracted by the menu selection (variety) and waiting times in Rayappa's restaurant. Followed by it has been inferred that, the customers' strongly believe that Haribhavanam restaurant maintain good quality standards. Similarly the customers' have said that they are influenced by the factors like Professionalism and friendliness of server(s), Server's knowledge of menu, Decor (Ambience) and Overall restaurant experience of Anjappar restaurant. Similarly the respondents' have said that they server(s) in Anjali restaurant are prompt and responsiveness. It has been understood that the sample subjects' are influenced by the menu pricing and value, special attraction for kids and restaurant location of the other non-vegetarian restaurants in Coimbatore.

From the above table it has been inferred that there exists variations in the sample mean values and the probability value of ANOVA at 5 per cent level does not establish good relationship between the variables tested. Therefore, the hypothesis framed stands rejected and it is concluded that there exists close association between branded non-vegetarian restaurant selected by the diner and factors that motivated them to visit the restaurants. However it is exceptional in the case of food quality, menu selection (variety), decor (ambience), and restaurant location.

Table 4.31(A): Measure of Dispersion & Result of ANOVA Occassion of Visits of the Restaurant and Factors Influencing them to Visit the Restaurants

Variables	Saturday Evenings (N:53)		Sundays' (N:148)		Special Occasions (N:88)	
	Mean	SD	Mean	SD	Mean	SD
Food quality	4.19	3.258	3.36	3.008	2.84	2.568
Menu selection (Variety)	4.64	2.704	4.60	2.804	4.55	2.528
Menu pricing and value	5.28	3.213	4.84	2.918	5.15	2.911
Waiting times	6.17	2.751	5.46	2.781	5.36	2.763
Promptness of service	5.87	2.962	5.55	2.663	5.33	2.522
Professionalism and friendliness of server(s)	6.25	3.031	6.30	2.962	5.51	2.546
Server's knowledge of menu	6.40	2.670	7.16	2.867	7.49	2.644
Decor (Ambience)	7.09	3.158	7.12	2.878	7.74	2.723
Restaurant location	5.94	3.060	6.68	2.972	7.13	2.892
Special attraction for kids	7.60	3.416	7.15	3.115	7.43	3.151
Overall restaurant experience	5.70	3.220	6.89	3.086	6.98	3.400

Level of Significance: 5 per cent

Table 4.31(B): Measure of Dispersion & Result of ANOVA Occassion of Visits of the
Restaurant and Factors Influencing them to Visit Restaurants

Variables	Festive Seasons (N:95)		Any time (N:216)		F Value	Sig
	Mean	SD	Mean	SD		
Food quality	3.77	3.103	3.02	2.945	2.802	.025
Menu selection (Variety)	4.18	2.836	4.75	2.631	.751	.558
Menu pricing and value	4.67	2.804	5.04	2.834	.589	.671
Waiting times	5.55	2.759	5.79	2.912	1.012	.400
Promptness of service	5.07	2.631	6.42	2.699	5.662	.000
Professionalism and friendliness of server(s)	5.87	2.710	6.20	2.975	1.342	.253
Server's knowledge of menu	6.64	2.717	6.89	2.831	1.875	.113
Decor (Ambience)	7.13	2.757	7.75	2.799	5.761	.122
Restaurant location	7.45	2.708	5.96	3.097	5.761	.000
Special attraction for kids	7.46	3.354	7.40	2.933	.294	.882
Overall restaurant experience	6.80	3.344	6.66	3.134	1.624	.167

Level of Significance: 5 per cent

From the above data discussion it has been observed that, the respondents' who prefer to dine during Saturday evenings have opined that they are pleased with the services like food quality, menu pricing and value, promptness of service, professionalism and friendliness of server(s) in the selected restaurants. Similarly, the sample populations' who prefer to dine on special occasions are influenced by the server's knowledge of menu and overall experience of popular restaurants. Followed by, the respondents' who visit restaurants particularly on festive seasons have said that they are motivated by the Restaurant location and Special arrangements made for kids. From the above table it has been inferred that there exists variations in the sample mean values and the probability value of ANOVA at 5 per cent level does not establish good relationship between the variables tested. Therefore, the hypothesis framed stands rejected and it is concluded that there exists close association between occasion of visit to the restaurant by the diner and factors that motivated them to visit the restaurants. However it is exceptional in the case of food quality, promptness of service and restaurant location.

Table 4.32(A): Measure of Dispersion & Result of ANOVA Factors Influencing the Diners to Visit Particular Restaurant Vs Time Preference of Visit

Variables	Early Morning (N:37)		Morning Break-Fast (N:64)		After-noon Lunch (N:103)	
	Mean	SD	Mean	SD	Mean	SD
Food quality	4.59	3.278	3.39	2.804	2.95	2.935
Menu selection (Variety)	4.68	2.839	4.94	2.754	4.64	2.814
Menu pricing and value	5.76	3.227	5.30	3.120	4.99	2.847
Waiting times	5.38	2.832	6.22	2.634	5.53	2.747
Promptness of service	5.92	2.742	5.67	2.737	5.97	2.659
Professionalism and friendliness of server(s)	6.05	2.494	5.98	3.032	6.50	3.099
Server's knowledge of menu	7.11	2.923	6.97	2.720	7.16	2.608
Decor (Ambience)	6.03	3.420	6.78	3.000	7.31	2.900
Restaurant location	7.22	2.770	7.03	2.851	6.52	2.930
Special attraction for kids	7.22	3.276	7.59	3.245	7.21	2.909
Overall restaurant experience	5.54	3.595	5.77	3.289	6.59	3.368

Level of Significance: 5 per cent

Table 4.32(B): Measure of Dispersion & Result of ANOVA Factors Influencing the Diners to Visit Particular Restaurant Vs Time Preference of Visit

Variables	Early Evening (N:182)		Late Evening (N:214)		F Value	Sig
	Mean	SD	Mean	SD		
Food quality	3.41	3.140	3.13	2.821	2.379	.051
Menu selection (Variety)	4.63	2.713	4.40	2.594	0.563	.690
Menu pricing and value	5.07	2.783	4.64	2.857	1.629	.165
Waiting times	5.53	2.749	5.66	2.968	.865	.485
Promptness of service	5.85	2.754	5.64	2.728	.338	.852
Professionalism and friendliness of server(s)	6.04	2.878	5.94	2.795	.689	.600
Server's knowledge of menu	6.67	2.953	7.09	2.734	.764	.549
Decor (Ambience)	7.54	2.847	7.84	2.551	4.423	.002
Restaurant location	6.60	3.017	6.23	3.143	1.462	.212
Special attraction for kids	7.10	3.148	7.64	3.120	.902	.462
Overall restaurant experience	7.06	3.192	6.93	2.976	3.495	.008

Level of Significance: 5 per cent

The data presented in the above table clearly indicates that, the respondents' who prefer to dine during early mornings have opined that they are inspired by the food quality, menu pricing and value, professionalism and friendliness of server(s) and location of the famous restaurants. It has been clearly identified that the respondents' who prefer to dine morning breakfast in restaurants are influenced by the menu selection (variety) and waiting times, as they rush to their work during mornings. Subsequently it has been observed that the customers' who like to have their lunch in restaurants are motivated by the promptness of service and server's knowledge of menu, since they are food lovers and are passionate towards dining. Followed by, the visitors' who prefer to dine on early evenings are observed to be happy with the overall restaurant experiences, this may be due to their regularity of visits to particular restaurants during evening time. Further it has been observed that the respondents' who visit restaurants on late evenings are influenced by the decor (ambience) and special arrangements that are made for the kids, since these respondents' usually visit for restaurants relaxation they like to have a pleasant dining experience.

From the above table it has been inferred that there exists variations in the sample mean values and the probability value of ANOVA at 5 per cent level does not establish good relationship between the variables tested. Therefore, the hypothesis framed stands rejected and it is concluded that there exists close association between time preferred by diners' for visiting a restaurant and factors that motivated them to visit the restaurants. However it is exceptional in the case of food quality, decor (ambience) and overall restaurant experience.

Table 4.33: Measure of Dispersion & Result of ANOVA Factors Influencing the Diners to Visit Particular Restaurant Vs their Attitude towards Budget Fixation

Variables	Do Fix Budget (N:290)		Does Not Fix Budget (N:310)		F Value	Sig
	Mean	SD	Mean	SD		
Food quality	3.43	3.029	3.18	2.936	1.057	.304
Menu selection (Variety)	4.64	2.731	4.53	2.669	.260	.611
Menu pricing and value	5.07	3.028	4.88	2.761	.681	.410
Waiting times	6.06	2.864	5.25	2.726	12.712	.000
Promptness of service	6.11	2.783	5.48	2.628	8.210	.004
Professionalism and friendliness of server(s)	6.17	2.821	5.99	2.936	.620	.431
Server's knowledge of menu	6.96	2.853	6.97	2.733	.005	.945
Decor (Ambience)	7.27	2.883	7.59	2.799	1.999	.158
Restaurant location	6.39	3.170	6.69	2.873	1.487	.223
Special attraction for kids	7.22	3.147	7.51	3.085	1.230	.268
Overall restaurant experience	6.13	3.105	7.23	3.223	18.011	.000

Level of Significance: 5 per cent

It is evident from the above empirical data analysis that, the diners' who regularly plan their budget are motived by the features like food quality, menu selection (variety), menu pricing and value, waiting times, promptness of service, professionalism and friendliness of server(s) and server's knowledge of menu since, they always have perfect planning before visiting restaurants. Whereas the impulsive visitors' have said that they are attracted by the decor (ambience), restaurant location, special attraction for kids and overall features of eth restaurants.

From the above table it has been inferred that there exists variations in the sample mean values and the probability value of ANOVA at 5 per cent level does not establish good relationship between the variables tested. Therefore, the hypothesis framed stands rejected and it is concluded that there exists close association between budget fixation habits of the diners' while visiting restaurant (s) and factors that motivated them to visit restaurants. However it is exceptional in the case of waiting time, promptness of services and overall restaurant experience.

From the above Tables: 4.25 - 4.32 it has been found that the hypothesis framed stands rejected under the seven parameters tested. Thus, it has been concluded that there exists close association between food consumption habits of the diners' and factors that motivated them to visit restaurants. It is universally known fact that the customers visit a restaurant to enjoy food in pleasant company while experiencing great service. Food and service quality are essential in determining customer satisfaction as well as customers' future behaviour towards the restaurant. This empirical conclusion provided a prelude for the assessing the diners level of perception and satisfaction towards restaurant service in the following section.

3. *Diners Level of Perception and Satisfaction towards Restaurant Service*

There are millions of people away from their homes everyday either by necessity or by choice. The restaurant and catering business has developed to feed this huge number of transients-office employees male and females, schoolchildren, travellers and people out to have a good time. Because there are so many to feed, the restaurant and catering business is one of the largest and fast-growing industries in the world. Those who eat away from home spend vast sums of money for restaurant or to the catered meals. These diners usually have different perception about the restaurant they had visited especially with regards to the food and service, similarly their perception level i.e., taught and believes about a restaurants may influences their satisfaction levels. In this sub section of the study the researcher has made an attempt to analyse the diners level of perception and satisfaction towards restaurant service offered in vegetarian and non-vegetarian restaurants in Coimbatore city.

Food menu extensively represent the personality trait of a restaurant. Following table discussion provided a detailed introspective analysis on diner's perception toward the nature of menu offered by the various vegetarian and non-vegetarian restaurants operating in Coimbatore city.

Table 4.34: Diners Level of Perception towards the Menu Offered in Vegetarian and Non-Vegetarian Restaurants

Factors	Very High	High	Moderately	Low	Very Low	Sum	Mean	Rank
Theme	286(47.67)	181(30.17)	103(17.17)	16(2.67)	14(2.33)	2509	4.18	1
Variety and selection	182(30.33)	287(47.83)	104(17.33)	20(3.33)	7(1.17)	2417	4.03	2
Signature item	181(30.17)	195(32.50)	171(28.50)	45(7.50)	8(1.33)	2296	3.83	3
Price range and value	157(26.17)	217(36.17)	145(24.17)	66(11.00)	15(2.50)	2235	3.73	4
Uniqueness	180(30.00)	166(27.67)	161(26.83)	51(8.50)	42(7.00)	2191	3.65	5

Source: Primary Data

Values in parenthesis are in per cent

From the above empirical data analysis it has been observed that, the diners have said that particular restaurant introduces new dishes with an attractive theme, it is ranked in first position with an average score of 4.18. Similarly the respondents' have stated that particular restaurant is popular for its special features like variety, selection, signature dish, price range and uniqueness in providing services. These variables are placed in second, third, fourth and fifth rank with the mean score of 4.03, 3.83, 3.73 and 3.65, respectively.

The study has concluded that the diners give more preferences and have high perception towards food themes presented in the menu, the type of food varieties listed in the menu and major signature dishes offered by the restaurants. For example, vegetarian restaurants like: Sree Annapoorna is famous for its wide varieties of vegetarian foods and most known for its Sambar and Sambar vadai. Similalray A2B (Adyar Anandha Bhavan) is very famous for its range of foods including wide variety of confectionery, snacks and chaat etc. Ananadha's always offer varieties in their menu, and has a planned menu for all week-day, health food menu for diabetics and sick peoples for the morning and evenings, Arya's is known for its food varieties and menu offering of both North Indian, Tamil Nadu and Kerala dishes and RHR is known for its Idlis varaties, Pongal, Poli, hot jeelabes, string hoppers and hoppers. Similarly, non-vegetarian restaurants like Rayappa's, Anjali and Anjappar offer wide varieties of Chettinadu Cuisines, North India bread varieties and Chinese cuisines. Sampoorna is known for its chicken varieties and Haribhavanam offer menu of spicy Southern Tamil Nadu cuisines.

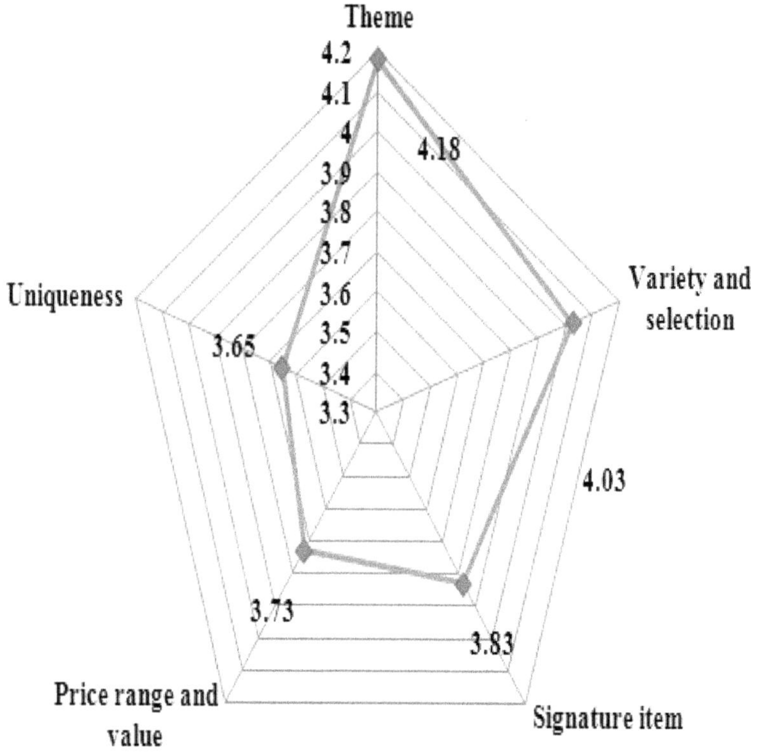

Exhibit 4.2: Diners Level of Perception towards the Menu Offered in Vegetarian and

Non-Vegetarian Restaurants

The above table clearly infers the diners' level of perception towards the menu offered in particular restaurant of Coimbatore. In the vegetarian restaurant category it has been observed that, the respondents' prefer Annapoorna for its uniqueness in customer service.

Arya's offers wide menu variety. Similarly the respondents' are impressed by the theme of innovative menu and signature dishes offered by RHR. As far as non-vegetarian restaurant are concerned, it has been inferred that, majority of the sample subjects' are influenced by the food varieties, price range and unique features of Rayappa's restaurant in comparison to the other non-vegetarian restaurants.

Quality of food is the most important factor in people's evaluation of any of restaurant service and hygiene rating, following table provides a detailed discussion on sample diners' perception towards the food quality in the restaurants they casually dine.

Table 4.35: Diners Level of Perception towards the Food Quality of Vegetarian and Non-vegetarian Restaurants

Factors	Very High	High	Moderately	Low	Very Low	Sum	Mean	Rank
Taste	390(65.00)	160(26.67)	33(5.50)	6(1.00)	11(1.83)	2712	4.52	1
Presentation	164(27.33)	302(50.33)	117(19.50)	9(1.50)	8(1.33)	2405	4.01	2
PortionSize	161(26.83)	196(32.67)	208(34.67)	24(4.00)	11(1.83)	2272	3.79	3
Consistency	153(25.50)	196(32.67)	174(29.00)	66(11.00)	11(1.83)	2214	3.69	4
Health Aspects	199(33.17)	166(27.67)	138(23.00)	40(6.67)	57(9.50)	2210	3.68	5

Source: Primary Data

Values in parenthesis are in per cent

It is evident from the above table that, most of the sample populations' have said that they are influenced by the delicious taste of dishes in particular restaurant, it is ranked in first position with an average score of 4.52. Similarly the diners in Coimbatore have opined that they are attracted by the presentation, size of portions i.e., beverages, consistency and health aspects of food delivered in particular restaurant. These factors are placed in second, third, fourth and fifth rank with an average score of 4.01, 3.79, 3.69 and 3.68, correspondingly.

Hence it has been clearly identified that most of the sample populations' have said that they are influenced by the delicious taste of dishes served in the restaurant, its food presentation manner and portion of food served. The study confines the fact that the food served in the restaurants operating in Coimbatore city are of good quality , the food is served with greater taste, eye-caching presentations and fair enough for individual diner to subside his/her hunger.

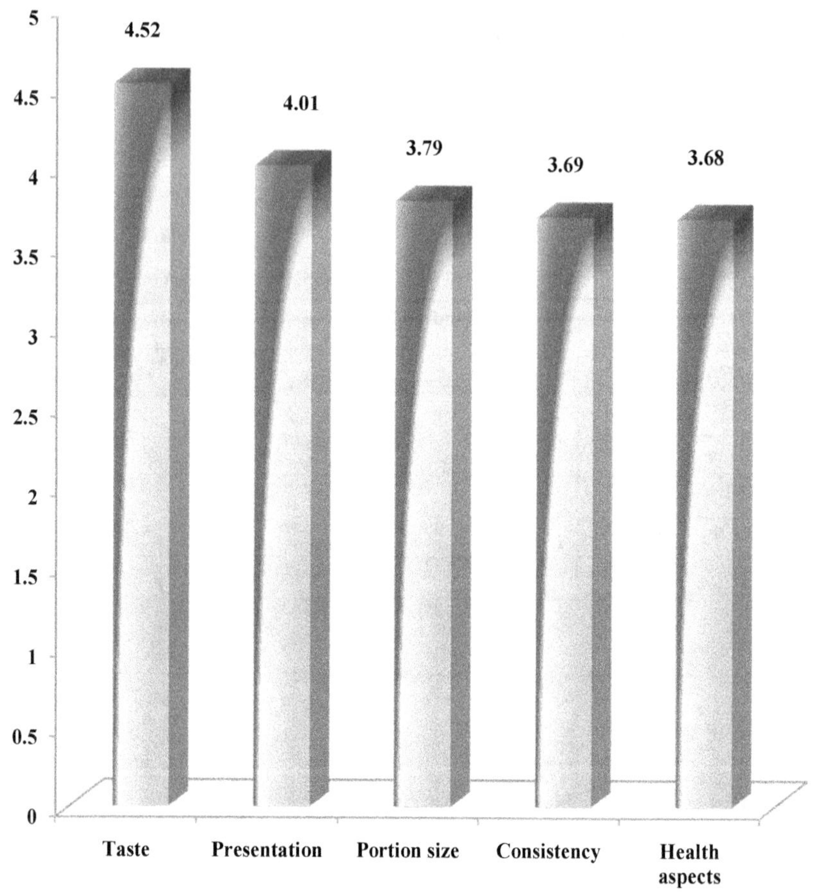

Exhibit 4.3: Diners Level of Perception towards the Food Quality of Vegetarian and Non-Vegetarian Restaurants

Food prices mentioned in the restaurant menu act as important criterion in selection of restaurant services in India, across various demographic and socio-economic class of people. Price is the key element in restaurant sector in India, because customer grades a restaurant and its services based on the price they charge for the service offered. To draw empirical evidences to this statement following table discussion is made.

Table 4.36: Diners Level of Perception towards the Price of Food Items Offered by Vegetarian and Non-Vegetarian Restaurants

Factors	Very High	High	Moderately	Low	Very Low	Sum	Mean	Rank
Economically priced	252(42.00)	178(29.67)	131(21.83)	24(4.00)	15(2.50)	2428	4.05	1
Customers' paid more than they had planned	142(23.67)	253(42.17)	163(27.17)	29(4.83)	13(2.17)	2282	3.80	2
Prices are comparatively competitive	168(28.00)	184(30.67)	185(30.83)	47(7.83)	16(2.67)	2241	3.74	3

Source: Primary Data

Values in parenthesis are in per cent

It is evident from the above table that, most of the respondents' prefer particular hotel to avail food at reasonable and economical price, it is ranked in first place with the mean score of 4.05. Whereas the respondents' complain that specific restaurant price the products competitively and are supposed to pay more than they had planned. These factors are ranked in second and third place with the mean score of 3.80 and 3.74.

Hence it has been clearly identified that most of the respondents' prefer those restaurants that offer economic priced food services, suit to their budget and priced competitively.

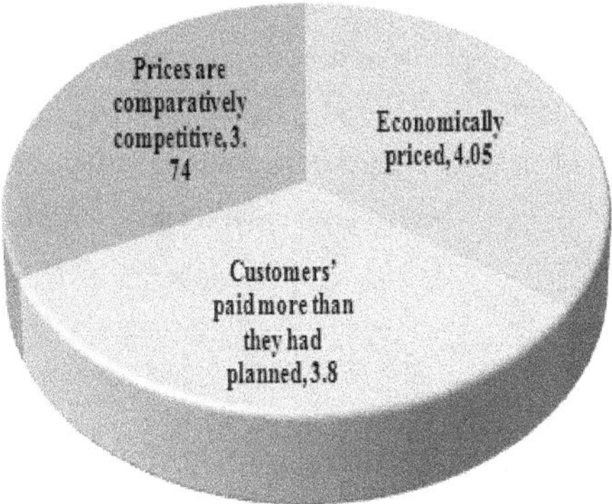

Exhibit 4.4: Diners Level of Perception towards the Price of Food Items Offered by Vegetarian and Non-Vegetarian Restaurants

Restaurant's interior design is an important to remember that before diners smell or taste the food, they judge the restaurant establishment based on the décor and colours surrounding them and how those things make them feel. Following table discussion on the diners' perception towards restaurant appearances and comfort levels they experienced while dining in a restaurants.

Table 4.37: Diners Level of Perception towards the Appearance/Comfort of Vegetarian and Non-Vegetarian Restaurants

Factors	Very High	High	Moderately	Low	Very Low	Sum	Mean	Rank
Exterior appearance and theme	254(42.33)	197(32.83)	115(19.17)	23(3.83)	11(1.83)	2460	4.10	1
Interior appearance and theme	149(24.83)	244(40.67)	160(26.67)	35(5.83)	12(2.00)	2283	3.81	2
Atmosphere	163(27.17)	214(35.67)	171(28.50)	36(6.00)	16(2.67)	2272	3.79	3
Cleanliness	184(30.67)	188(31.33)	150(25.00)	59(9.83)	19(3.17)	2259	3.77	4
Air condition quality	194(32.33)	178(29.67)	140(23.33)	55(9.17)	33(5.50)	2245	3.74	5

Source: Primary Data

Values in parenthesis are in per cent

The above table infers the diners level of perception towards the appearance/comfort of particular restaurant. Majority of the diners in Coimbatore are attracted by the exterior appearance and theme of specific restaurant, it is ranked in first position with an average score of 4.10. Followed by, it has been inferred that the respondents' are influenced by the factors such as interior appearance & theme, atmosphere, cleanliness and air conditioning facilities offered in particular restaurant where they visit regularly. These subjects' are placed in second, third, fourth and fifth rank with an average score of 3.81, 3.79, 3.77 and 3.74, accordingly.

It is evident from the above tables that, majority of the diners in Coimbatore are attracted by the both exterior and interior appearance and theme of specific restaurant.

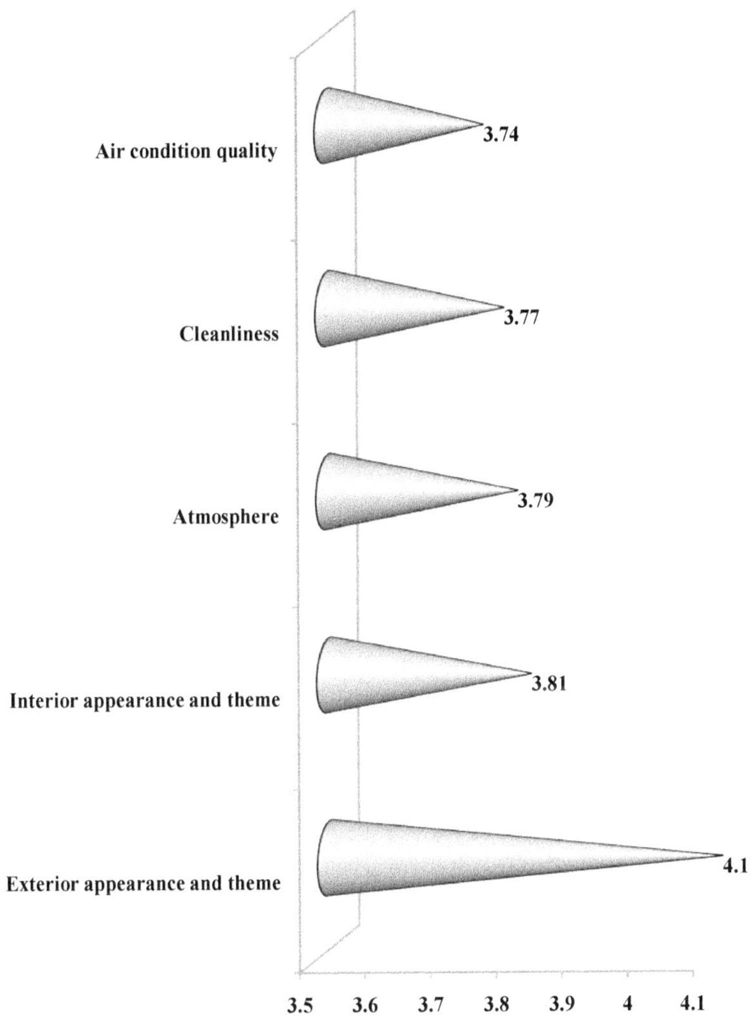

Exhibit 4.5: Diners Level of Perception towards the Appearance/Comfort of Vegetarian and Non-vegetarian Restaurants

Restaurant design significantly influences the diners' perception towards its size, service quality and nature of table service offered in a restaurant. Understanding of customers' psychology plays an important role while designing a restaurant layout. The following table depicts the diners' perception towards physical design on both vegetarian and non-vegetarian restaurants functioning in Coimbatore city.

Table 4.38: Diners Level of Perception towards the Physical Design of Vegetarian and Non-Vegetarian Restaurants

Particulars	*Very High*	*High*	*Moderately*	*Low*	*Very Low*	*Sum*	*Mean*	*Rank*
Lighting in the restaurant	309(51.50)	183(30.50)	86(14.33)	14(2.33)	8(1.33)	2571	4.29	1
Adequate parking facilities	134(22.33)	278(46.33)	150(25.00)	26(4.33)	12(2.00)	2296	3.83	3
Restaurant cleanliness	202(33.67)	187(31.17)	160(26.67)	43(7.17)	8(1.33)	2332	3.89	2
Décor was visibility appealing (Ambiences)	139(23.17)	230(38.33)	160(26.67)	54(9.00)	17(2.83)	2220	3.70	4

Source: Primary Data

Values in parenthesis are in per cent

It is evident from the above table that, most of the diners are attracted by the lightings of particular restaurant; it is ranked in first position with an average score of 4.29. Further it has been understood that the respondents' have said that specific hotels provides clean environment, adequate parking facilities and pleasantly decorated ambience which grabs their attention. These factors are placed in second, third and fourth rank with the mean score of 3.89, 3.83 and 3.70, respectively.

Thus it has been concluded that most of the diners are attracted by the lightings and cleanliness of particular restaurant.

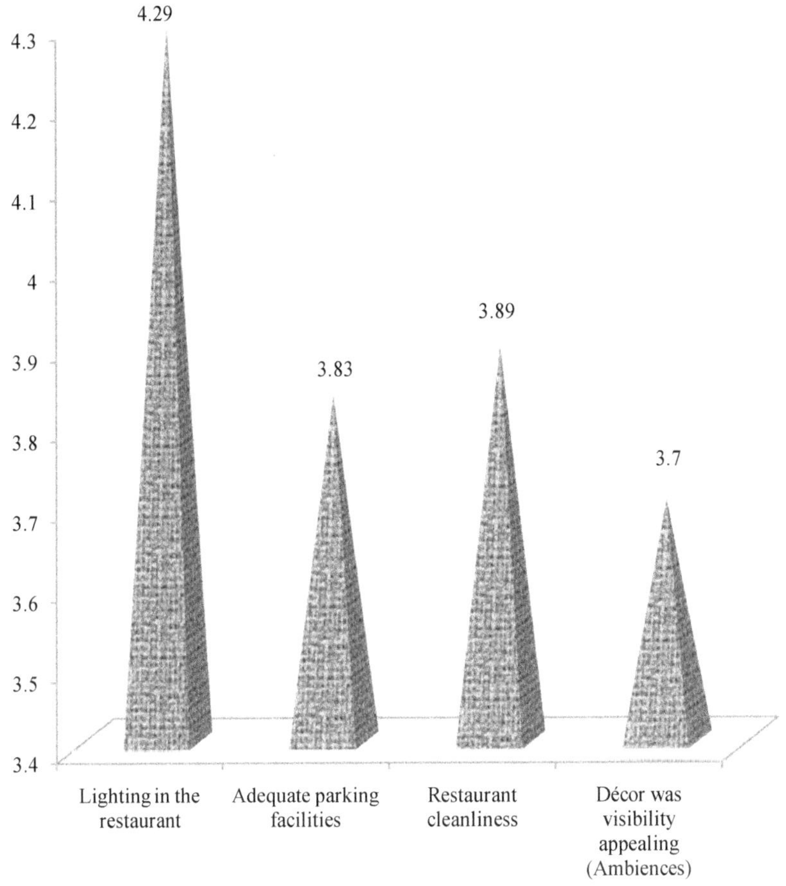

Exhibit 4.6: Diners Level of Perception towards the Physical Design of Particular Restaurant

Various categories of restaurant services need staff for rendering various services like waiters to offer food, attenders for welcoming the guest and taking up the menu and cleaning staff for cleaning the table. The following table discussion is focused on diners level of perception towards the employee responsiveness in various vegetarian and non-vegetarian restaurants in Coimbatore city.

Table 4.39: Diners Level of Perception towards the Responsiveness Vegetarian and

Non-Vegetarian Restaurants

Factors	Very High	High	Moderately	Low	Very Low	Sum	Mean	Rank
Employees attentiveness	285(47.50)	199(33.17)	98(16.33)	14(2.33)	4(0.67)	2547	4.25	1
Employees co-operatives	111(18.50)	295(49.17)	171(28.50)	18(3.00)	5(0.83)	2289	3.82	2
Promptness of service	160(26.67)	190(31.67)	211(35.17)	32(5.33)	7(1.17)	2264	3.77	4
Server's appearance (neat & presentable)	139(23.17)	225(37.50)	160(26.67)	57(9.50)	19 3.17)	2208	3.68	5
Employees understanding towards customers' needs	154(25.67)	200(33.33)	170(28.33)	48(8.00)	28(4.67)	2204	3.67	6
Courtesy of server	110(18.33)	232(38.67)	191(31.83)	48(8.00)	19(3.17)	2166	3.61	7
Server's knowledge about menu	198(33.00)	179(29.83)	151(25.17)	41(6.83)	31(5.17)	2272	3.79	3

Source: Primary Data

Values in parenthesis are in per cent

From the above empirical data analysis it has been observed that, majority of the diners have agreed that the employees are very attentive in particular restaurants and it makes them to visit frequently, it is ranked in first position with mean score of 4.25. The data presented above indicates that the diners are inspired by the co-operation, knowledge and promptness of employees in particular restaurant. These variables are ranked in second, third and fourth place with the mean score of 3.82, 3.79 and 3.77, accordingly.

Similarly the respondents' are influenced by the neat & presentable appearance, understandability and courteous nature of servers in particular restaurant. These factors are ranked in fifth, sixth and seventh place with an average score of 3.68, 3.67 and 3.61, respectively.

Hence it has been found that majority of the diners are inspired by the attentiveness of servers, their co-operation with the diners and servers knowledge about the menu. It can be rightly commented that successful restaurants employ managers and employees who perform at a high level and work to accomplish the restaurant's goals. The secret of many restaurants functioning in Coimbatore city is purely based on these aspects.

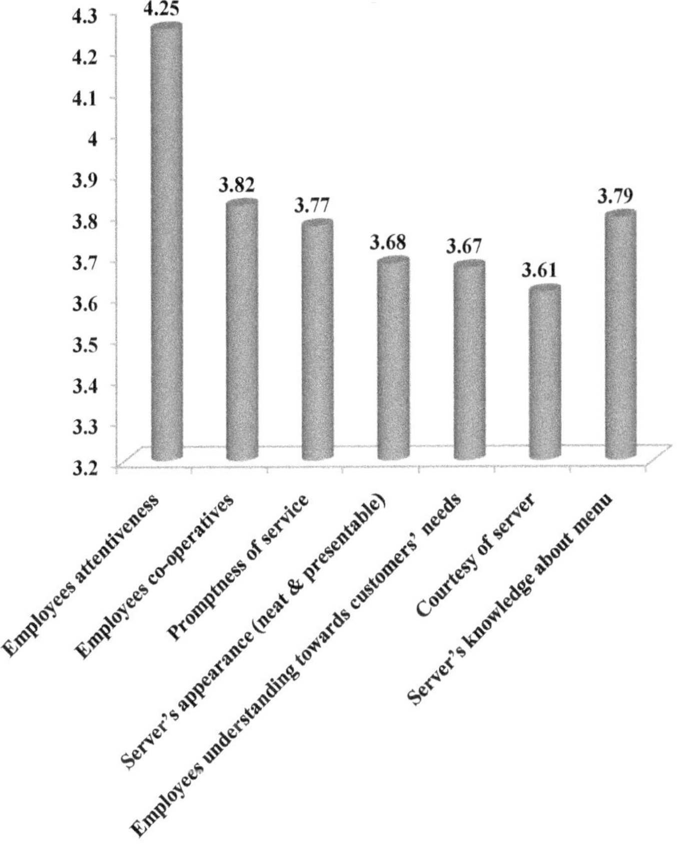

Exhibit 4.7: Diners Level of Perception towards the Responsiveness Vegetarian and Non-Vegetarian Restaurants

Top restaurants operate like well-oiled machines, and busy kitchens can be compared to military operations in terms of efficiency and the chain of command. A diverse range of roles and functions must be filled and performed simultaneously for a restaurant to consistently provide high-quality service to guests. A strict hierarchy of managers, supervisors and individual contributors work together like clockwork to ensure that a restaurant runs smoothly while confronting the challenges of the food-service industry.

Table 4.40: Diners Level of Perception towards the Service Reliability of Vegetarian and Non-vegetarian Restaurants

Factors	Very High	High	Moderately	Low	Very Low	Sum	Mean	Rank
Customers' receives exactly what they ordered the first time	285(47.50)	199(33.17)	94(15.67)	12(2.00)	10(1.67)	2537	4.23	1
Order served are error – free	111(18.50)	298(49.67)	168(28.00)	19(3.17)	4(0.67)	2293	3.82	3
The food was fresh	217(36.17)	177(29.50)	167(27.83)	32(5.33)	7(1.17)	2365	3.94	2
The temperature of the food was just right	137(22.83)	223(37.17)	161(26.83)	57(9.50)	22(3.67)	2196	3.66	5
Foods are Hygienically serviced	208(34.67)	190(31.67)	119(19.83)	47(7.83)	36(6.00)	2287	3.81	4

Source: Primary Data

Values in parenthesis are in per cent

The above table clearly indicates that, the diners in Coimbatore city have said that they prefer specific restaurant delivers exactly what they ordered the first time and are impressed by this quality, it is ranked in first place with the mean score of 4.23. Followed by, it has been observed that the respondents' like to dine in specific restaurant for its service features like freshness, error– free service, hygienically serviced food and for the hotness of food which is prepared and served fresh. These variables are ranked in second, third, fourth and fifth place with the mean score of 3.94, 3.82, 3.81 and 3.66, respectively.

Thus it has been concluded that majority of the diners in Coimbatore city have said that they prefer specific restaurant as it delivers exactly what they ordered the first time and food are served fresh. The consistency of services is the secret of success for many restaurants operating in Coimbatore. Consistency is more related with the timeliness, accuracy in service rendered, courtesy, responsiveness, personalised services, conveniences, variety and many more.

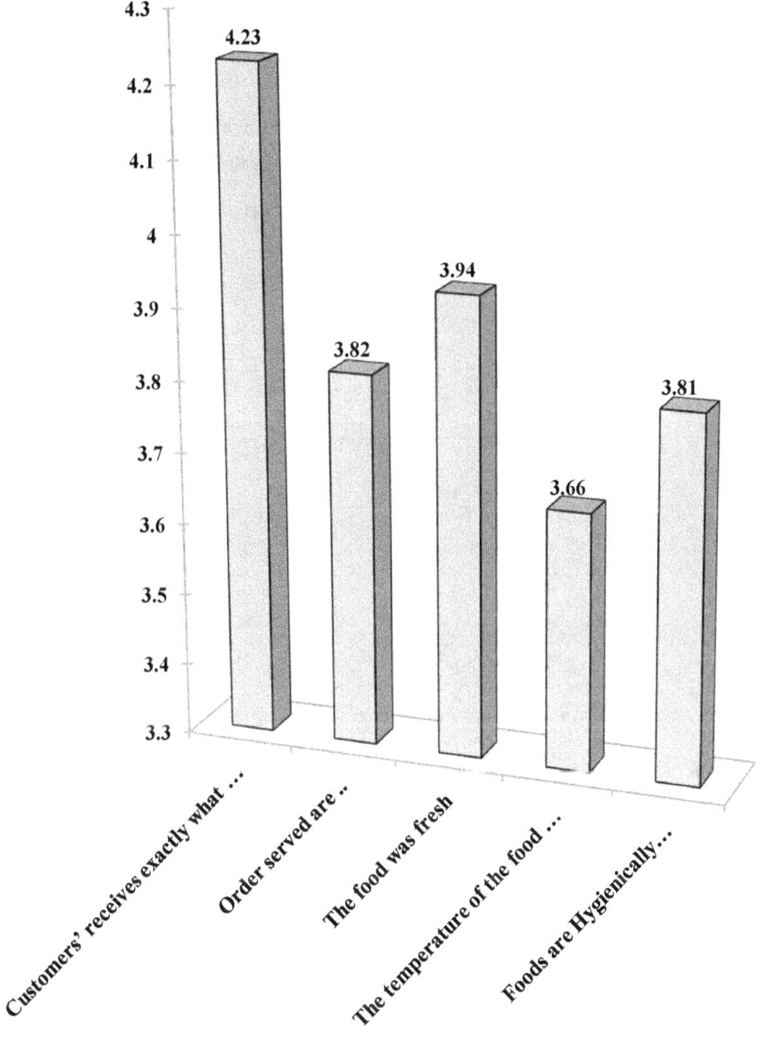

Exhibit 4.8: Diners Level of Perception towards the Service Reliability of Vegetarian and Non-Vegetarian Restaurants

The restaurant industry has not been exempted from either increased competition or customer demand for high service quality. Nowadays, customers have a wide range of restaurant services to choose from and service quality conditions indeed influence a restaurant competitive advantage, thus, service quality is important for restaurant services. The following table reveals the diners level of perception towards the service time quality various vegetarian and non-vegetarian restaurants in Coimbatore.

Table 4.41: Diners Level of Perception towards the Service Time Quality of Vegetarian and Non-Vegetarian Restaurants

Factors	Very High	High	Moderately	Low	Very Low	Sum	Mean	Rank
Days open (7x7 days)	306(51.00)	186(31.00)	77(12.83)	17(2.83)	14(2.33)	2553	4.26	1
Hours of operation	132(22.00)	291(48.50)	150(25.00)	24(4.00)	3(0.50)	2325	3.88	3
Service style	194(32.33)	212(35.33)	152(25.33)	33(5.50)	9(1.50)	2349	3.92	2
Quality of service	184(30.67)	215(35.33)	142(23.67)	46(7.67)	13(2.17)	2311	3.85	4
Speed of service	169(28.17)	191(31.83)	153(25.50)	52(8.67)	35(5.83)	2207	3.68	6
Extra services offered	182(30.33)	166(27.67)	169(28.17)	56(9.33)	27(4.50)	2220	3.70	5

Source: Primary Data

Values in parenthesis are in per cent

From the above table it has been found that, majority of the restaurants have agreed that particular restaurant(s) are open for all 7x7 days, it is ranked in first position with the mean score of 4.26. Subsequently it has been observed that, the respondents' have opined that they are influenced by the factors such as service style, operating time and service quality of particular restaurant in Coimbatore. These subjects' are placed in second, third and fourth rank with the mean score of 3.92, 3.88 and 3.85, respectively. Similarly the sample populations' have opined that they usually dine in specific restaurants for the speediness of services and to avail extra services like combo offers, price discounts, coupons for food festivals etc. These variables are ranked in fifth and sixth position with the mean score of 3.70 and 3.68.

Hence it has been concluded that majority respondents have agreed that they prefer to dine in those restaurants that are opened for all 7x7 days, it has unique service style and long hour of operations i.e., opening. It is public knowledge that service varies by time of delivery, i.e., by the hour, day of the week, day of the month, and month of the year. In restaurant services serving according to customers mood, time of entry into their restaurants and food variation according to the time period of day like: morning coffee/tea, morning break-fast, mid-day brunch, noon-meal, early evening snacking, evening tiffin and dinners and late night serves of supper.

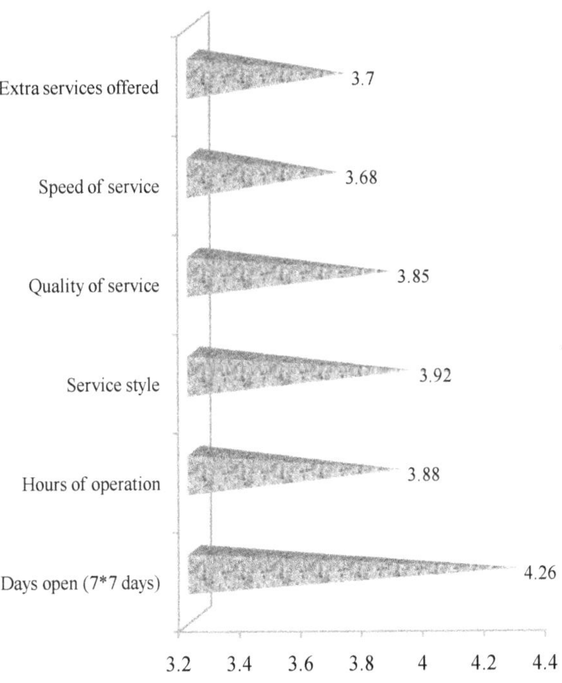

Exhibit 4.9: Diners Level of Perception towards the Service Time Quality of Vegetarian and Non-vegetarian Restaurants

Restaurateurs want the best location to be successful and so site selection is a key factor. Effective and right restaurant location is very important for potential of adequate sales and, therefore, profit; to offset gains made by a competitors choice of location; to minimize the cost of preparing an outlet for operation; and to respond to specific market or community needs. The following table depicts the diners perception towards location of various vegetarian and non-vegetarian restaurants in Coimbatore.

Table 4.42: Diners Level of Perception towards the Location of Vegetarian and Non-Vegetarian Restaurant

Factors	Very High	High	Moderately	Low	Very Low	Sum	Mean	Rank
Proximity to sources of demand	247(41.17)	192(32.00)	128(21.33)	26(4.33)	7(1.17)	2446	4.08	1
Accessibility	161(26.83)	249(41.50)	151(25.17)	35(5.83)	4(0.67)	2328	3.88	2
Visibility	152(25.33)	221(36.83)	179(29.83)	42(7.00)	6(1.00)	2271	3.79	3
Surrounding neighborhood	124(20.67)	188(31.33)	213(35.50)	57(9.50)	18(3.00)	2143	3.57	6
Parking availability	147(24.50)	206(34.33)	155(25.83)	57(9.50)	35(5.83)	2173	3.62	5
Sign visibility (location)	176(29.33)	201(33.50)	143(23.83)	42(7.00)	38(6.33)	2235	3.73	4

Source: Primary Data

Values in parenthesis are in per cent

From the above data analysis it has been inferred that, majority of the diners have opined that particular restaurant located nearby their residence and it is convenient to them, it is ranked in first place with the mean score of 4.08. Similarly the respondents' have said that they are influenced by the features like accessibility, visibility and location of particular hotel in Coimbatore. These variables are ranked in second, third and fourth place with an average score of 3.88, 3.79 and 3.73, respectively. Further it has been observed that the respondents' prefer to visit particular hotel for its parking facility and also for the nearness of the restaurant. These factors are rated in fifth and sixth place with the mean score of 3.62 and 3.57, accordingly. Thus it has been found that majority of the diners have opined that restaurant has proximity in its location i.e., nearby their residence or work place and it is convenient for them to access easily to those restaurant(s) as it is very much visible to traveller and paddlers.

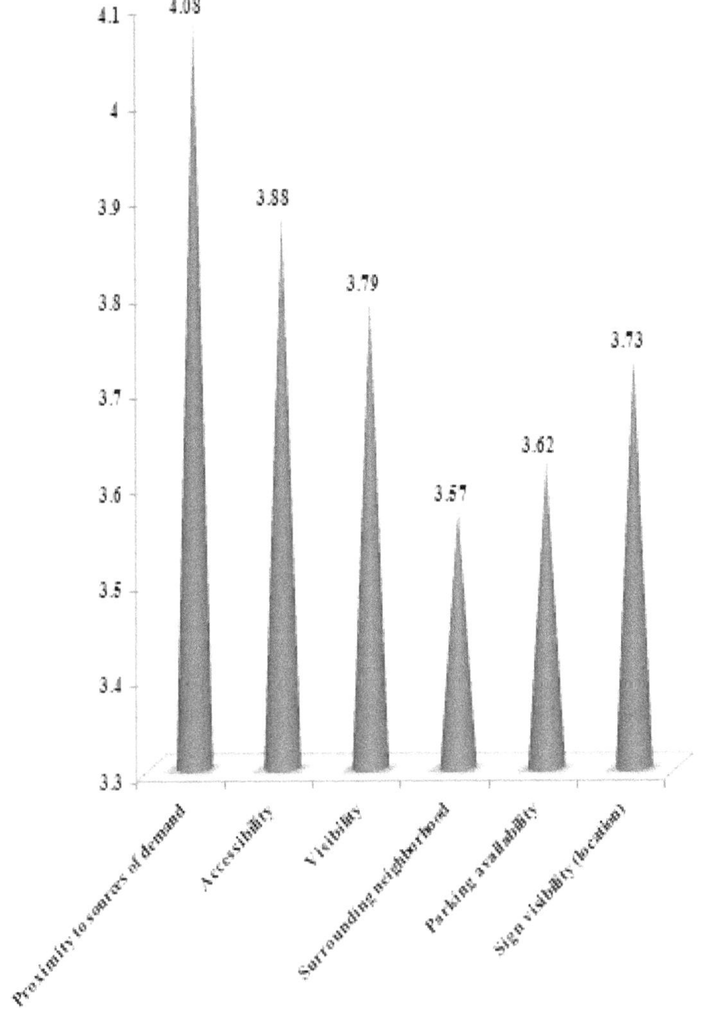

Exhibit 4.10: Diners Level of Perception towards the Location of Vegetarian and Non-vegetarian Restaurant

Table 4.43(A): Diners Level of Perception towards the Menu Offered in Both Vegetarian and Non-Vegetarian Restaurant

Perceptions	Name of the Branded Restaurants				
	Annapoorna	*Anandha's*	*Arya's*	*A2B*	*RHR*
Menu Theme					
Theme (Design)	4.17	4.20	4.00	4.13	4.48
Variety and Selection	4.01	4.03	4.13	3.98	4.01
Signature Item	3.82	3.82	3.89	3.59	3.93
Price Range and Value	3.77	3.65	3.75	3.65	3.71
Uniqueness	3.74	3.60	3.60	3.65	3.61
Food Quality					
Taste	4.59	4.36	4.55	4.57	4.62
Presentation	4.05	4.02	3.94	3.92	4.01
Portion Size	3.80	3.73	3.76	3.87	3.87
Maintaining Taste Consistency	3.78	3.68	3.69	3.63	3.64
Focus on Health Aspects	3.82	3.57	3.78	3.60	3.68
Price of Food					
Economically Priced	4.04	4.14	3.82	4.14	4.14
Customers' Paid More than Planned	3.82	3.81	3.87	3.65	3.91
Prices are Comparatively Competitive	3.80	3.70	3.64	3.73	3.70
Appearance / Comfort					
Exterior appearance and theme	4.08	4.12	4.00	4.25	4.14
Interior appearance and theme	3.74	3.86	3.86	3.79	3.86
Atmosphere	3.80	3.79	4.02	3.54	3.90
Cleanliness	3.90	3.80	3.79	3.44	3.71
Air condition quality	3.84	3.87	3.58	3.90	3.46
Physical Design					
Lighting in the restaurant	4.25	4.32	4.06	4.43	4.45
Adequate parking facilities	3.75	3.96	3.72	3.87	3.87
Restaurant cleanliness	3.91	3.93	3.81	3.98	3.83
Décor was visibility appealing (Ambiences)	3.64	3.82	3.79	3.62	3.68
Employee Responsiveness					
Employees attentiveness	4.18	4.24	4.13	4.54	4.46
Employees co-operatives	3.79	3.89	3.58	3.78	4.01
Promptness of service	3.89	3.70	3.65	3.71	3.88
Server's appearance (neat & presentable)	3.78	3.61	3.67	3.56	3.62
Employees understanding towards customers' needs	3.67	3.58	3.73	3.76	3.84
Courtesy of server	3.58	3.56	3.68	3.60	3.86
Server's knowledge about menu	3.96	3.66	3.73	3.54	3.91

Source: Developed from Primary Data

Table 4.43 (B): Diners Level of Perception towards the Menu Offered in Both Vegetarian and Non-Vegetarian Restaurant

Perceptions	Name of the Branded Restaurants				
	Annapoorna	Anandha's	Arya's	A2B	RHR
Service Reliability					
Customers' receives exactly what they ordered the first time	4.20	4.22	4.13	4.30	4.35
Order served are error–free	3.75	3.92	3.82	3.83	3.81
The food was fresh	4.02	3.81	3.79	4.03	4.09
The temperature of the food was just right	3.68	3.71	3.46	3.70	3.77
Foods are Hygienically serviced	3.84	3.80	3.67	3.87	3.90
Service Time &Quality					
Days open (7 x 7 days)	4.30	4.28	4.18	4.25	4.25
Hours of Operation	3.95	3.91	3.80	3.81	3.74
Service style	3.97	3.89	3.82	3.92	3.94
Quality of Service	3.96	3.78	3.94	3.75	3.68
Speed of service	3.70	3.60	3.65	3.75	3.72
Extra services offered	3.73	3.78	3.62	3.60	3.57
Location					
Proximity to sources of demand	4.05	4.11	4.05	4.10	4.03
Accessibility	3.87	3.93	4.09	3.59	3.84
Visibility	3.87	3.68	3.74	3.81	3.86
Surrounding Neighbourhood	3.63	3.51	3.64	3.44	3.67
Parking Availability	3.69	3.50	3.56	3.90	3.71
Sign Visibility (location)	3.99	3.53	3.82	3.67	3.26

Source: Developed from Primary Data

The competitive status of the various vegetarian restaurants included in the survey is briefly summarised in the above table.

Table 4.44: Strength and Weakness of Vegetarian Restaurant Services

Name of the Restaurant	Strength	Weakness
Annapoorna	Menu Price Range and Value, Uniqueness in Menu, Food Presentation, Maintaining Taste Consistency, Focus on Health Aspects, Cleanliness, Promptness of service, Server's appearance (neat & presentable), Server's knowledge about menu, Days open (7 x 7 days), Hours of Operation, Service style, Quality of Service and Visibility.	Price of Food, Appearance/ Comfort, Physical Design, Service Reliability
Shree Anandha's	Economically Priced, Interior appearance and theme, Adequate parking facilities, Décor was visibility appealing (Ambiences), Order served are error – free and Extra services offered	Menu Theme, Food Quality, Location
Arya's	Variety and Selection, Interior appearance and theme, Atmospheres and Accessibility.	Food Quality, Price of Food, Employee Responsiveness, Service Reliability, Service Time & Quality
A2B	Food Portion Size (Serving), Economically Priced, Exterior appearance and theme, Speed of service and Parking Availability.	Menu Theme, Service Reliability
RHR	Innovative Menu theme, Signature items in menu, Taste, Food Portion Served, Economically Priced, Interior appearance and theme, Lighting in the restaurant, Employees understanding towards customers' needs, Courtesy of server, Employees co-operatives, Foods are Hygienically, serviced, Freshness, Customers' receives exactly what they ordered the first time, Surrounding Neighbourhood	Service Time & Quality

Source: Developed from Descriptive Analysis

The empirical data presented above clearly depicts individual vegetarian restaurant's strength and weakness. Among five restaurants compared it has been observed that Annapoorna has more strength as it is a very popular vegetarian restaurant and an iconic name removed for its food quality, uniqueness and service quality since 1968.

Table 4.45(A): Diners Level of Perception towards the Menu Offered in Both Vegetarian and Non-vegetarian Restaurant

Perceptions	Name of the Branded Restaurants				
	Rayappa's	Sampoorna	Haribhavanam	Anjappar	Anjali
Menu Theme					
Theme (Design)	4.23	4.12	4.02	4.07	4.28
Variety and Selection	4.09	4.01	3.98	3.99	3.95
Signature Item	3.84	3.85	4.02	3.81	3.55
Price Range and Value	3.86	3.84	3.59	3.74	3.50
Uniqueness	3.86	3.61	3.55	3.67	3.62
Food Quality					
Taste	4.61	4.49	4.40	4.36	4.56
Presentation	4.14	3.85	3.98	4.14	3.96
Portion Size	3.85	3.79	3.71	3.80	3.64
Maintaining Taste Consistency	3.89	3.61	3.66	3.61	3.57
Focus on Health Aspects	3.69	3.71	3.41	3.72	3.69
Price of Food					
Economically Priced	4.11	4.07	3.79	4.08	4.01
Customers' Paid More than Planned	3.83	3.96	3.76	3.78	3.63
Prices are Comparatively Competitive	3.91	3.73	3.55	3.73	3.66
Appearance / Comfort					
Exterior appearance and theme	4.07	4.12	4.12	3.99	4.16
Interior appearance and theme	3.93	3.80	3.62	3.85	3.74
Atmosphere	3.71	3.78	4.03	3.72	3.71
Cleanliness	3.94	3.77	3.62	3.96	3.53
Air condition quality	3.93	3.70	3.74	3.81	3.63
Physical Design					
Lighting in the restaurant	4.43	4.31	4.02	4.31	4.22
Adequate parking facilities	3.88	3.90	3.79	3.94	3.60
Restaurant cleanliness	3.92	3.93	3.84	3.99	3.74
Décor was visibility appealing (Ambiences)	3.87	3.67	3.78	3.82	3.50
Employee Responsiveness					
Employees attentiveness	4.27	4.30	4.03	4.13	4.46
Employees co-operatives	3.89	3.84	3.67	3.67	3.91
Promptness of service	3.82	3.80	3.59	3.73	3.81
Server's appearance (neat & presentable)	3.83	3.61	3.41	3.89	3.65
Employees understanding towards customers' needs	3.95	3.70	3.71	3.49	3.60
Courtesy of server	3.67	3.72	3.67	3.51	3.48
Server's knowledge about menu	3.97	3.83	3.48	3.91	3.61

Source: Developed from Primary Data

Table: 4.45 (B) Diners Level of Perception towards the Menu Offered in Both Vegetarian and Non-vegetarian Restaurant

Perceptions	Name of the Branded Restaurants				
	Rayappa's	Sampoorna	Haribhavanam	Anjappar	Anjali
Service Reliability					
Customers' receives exactly what they ordered the first time	4.36	4.19	4.09	4.11	4.30
Order served are error – free	3.81	3.90	3.72	3.75	3.90
The food was fresh	3.99	3.96	3.76	3.99	3.87
The temperature of the food was just right	3.72	3.71	3.33	3.86	3.58
Foods are Hygienically serviced	4.07	3.82	3.62	3.89	3.67
Service Time &Quality					
Days open (7 x 7 days)	4.35	4.25	3.86	4.26	4.34
Hours of Operation	4.03	3.86	3.67	3.91	3.75
Service style	4.08	3.95	3.79	3.89	3.72
Quality of Service	3.99	3.80	3.88	3.86	3.72
Speed of service	3.73	3.81	3.55	3.73	3.49
Extra services offered	3.91	3.77	3.53	3.71	3.43
Location					
Proximity to sources of demand	4.31	4.04	3.81	3.98	4.10
Accessibility	3.94	3.92	3.74	3.79	3.89
Visibility	3.85	3.78	3.88	3.85	3.61
Surrounding Neighbourhood	3.55	3.58	3.72	3.59	3.55
Parking Availability	3.62	3.66	3.62	3.76	3.66
Sign Visibility (location)	3.98	3.67	3.62	3.76	3.57

Source: Developed from Primary Data

The empirical data presented above clearly depicts individual non-vegetarian restaurant's strength and weakness. Among five restaurants compared it has been observed that diners have high perception for Rayappa's Chettinad restaurant in comparison to other non-vegetarian restaurants currently functioning in Coimbatore. This restaurant has long served Coimbatore and emerged in 90's as one of 'the place' to have a great evening dining. The food they offer is mostly of chettinad, Punjabi and Chinese which is their USP (Unique Selling Property).

Table 4.46 (A): Strength and Weakness of Non-Vegetarian Restaurant Services

Name of the Restaurant	Strength	Weakness
Rayappa's	Variety and Selection, Price Range and Value, Uniqueness, Taste, Presentation, Portion Size, Maintaining Taste Consistency, Economically Priced, Prices are Comparatively Competitive, Interior appearance and theme, Air condition quality, Lighting in the restaurant, Décor was visibility appealing (Ambiences), Promptness of service, Employees understanding towards customers' needs, Server's knowledge about menu, Customers' receives exactly what they ordered the first time, The food was fresh, Foods are Hygienically serviced, Days open (7 x 7 days), Hours of Operation, Service style, Quality of Service, Extra services offered, Proximity to sources of demand, Accessibility & Sign Visibility (location).	Theme (Design), Signature Item, Focus on Health Aspects, Customers' Paid More than Planned (High Price), Exterior appearance and theme, Atmosphere, Cleanliness, Adequate parking facilities, Restaurant cleanliness, Employees attentiveness, Employees co-operatives, Server's appearance (neat & presentable), Courtesy of server, Order served are error – free, The temperature of the food was just right, speed of service, Visibility, Surrounding Neighbourhood, Parking Availability.
Sampoorna	Signature Item, Customers' Paid More than Planned, Atmosphere, Courtesy of server, Order served are error – free, Speed of service.	Theme (Design), Variety and Selection, Price Range and Value, Uniqueness, Taste, Presentation, Portion Size, Maintaining Taste Consistency, Focus on Health Aspects, Economically Priced, Prices are Comparatively Competitive, Exterior appearance and theme, Interior appearance and theme, Cleanliness, Air condition quality, Lighting in the restaurant, Adequate parking facilities, Restaurant cleanliness, Décor was visibility appealing (Ambiences), Employees attentiveness, Employees co-operatives, Promptness of service, Server's appearance (neat & presentable), Employees understanding towards customers' needs, Server's knowledge about menu, Customers' receives exactly what they ordered the first time, The food was fresh, The temperature of the food was just right, Foods are Hygienically serviced, Days open (7 x 7 days), Hours of Operation, Service style, Quality of Service, Extra services offered, Proximity to sources of demand, Accessibility, Visibility, Surrounding Neighbourhood, Parking Availability, Sign Visibility (location).

Source: Developed from Descriptive Analysis

Table 4.46(B): Strength and Weakness of Non-vegetarian Restaurant Services

Name of the Restaurant	Strength	Weakness
Haribhavanam	Visibility, Surrounding Neighbourhood.	Theme (Design), Variety and Selection, Signature Item, Price Range and Value, Uniqueness, Taste, Presentation, Portion Size Maintaining Taste Consistency, Focus on Health Aspects, Economically Priced, Customers' Paid More than Planned, Prices are Comparatively Competitive, Exterior appearance and theme, Interior appearance and theme, Atmosphere, Cleanliness, Air condition quality, Lighting in the restaurant, Adequate parking facilities, Restaurant cleanliness, Décor was visibility appealing (Ambiences), Employees attentiveness, Employees co-operatives, Promptness of service, Server's appearance (neat& presentable), Employees understanding towards customers' needs, Courtesy of server, Server's knowledge about menu, Customers' receives exactly what they ordered the first time, Order served are error–free, The food was fresh, The temperature of the food was just right, Foods are Hygienically serviced, Days open (7x7 days), Hours of Operation, Service style, Quality of Service, Speed of service, Extra services offered, Proximity to sources of demand, Accessibility, Parking Availability, Sign Visibility (location).
Anjappar	Presentation, Focus on Health Aspects, Cleanliness, Adequate parking facilities, Restaurant cleanliness, Server's appearance (neat & presentable), The food was fresh, The temperature of the food was just right, Parking Availability.	Theme (Design),Variety and Selection, Signature Item, Price Range and Value, Uniqueness, Taste, Portion Size, Maintaining Taste Consistency, Economically Priced, Customers' Paid More than Planned, Prices are Comparatively Competitive, Exterior appearance and theme, Interior appearance and theme, Atmosphere, Air condition quality, Lighting in the restaurant, Décor was visibility appealing (Ambiences), Employees attentiveness, Employees co-operatives, Promptness of service, Employees understanding towards customers' needs, Courtesy of server, Server's knowledge about menu, Customers' receives exactly what they ordered the first time, Order served are error–free, Foods are Hygienically serviced, Days open (7x7 days), Hours of Operation, Service style, Quality of Service, Speed of service, Extra services offered, Proximity to sources of demand, Accessibility, Visibility, Surrounding Neighbourhood, Sign Visibility (location).

Source: Developed from Descriptive Analysis

Table 4.46 (C): Strength and Weakness of Non-vegetarian Restaurant Services

Name of the Restaurant	*Strength*	*Weakness*
Anjali	Theme (Design), Exterior appearance and theme, Employees attentiveness, Employees co-operatives, Order served are error – free, Customers' receives exactly what they ordered the first time, The food was fresh, The temperature of the food was just right, Foods are Hygienically serviced, Days open (7 x 7 days), Hours of Operation, Service style, Quality of Service, Speed of service, Extra services offered, Proximity to sources of demand, Accessibility, Visibility, Surrounding Neighbourhood, Parking Availability, Sign Visibility (location).	Variety and Selection, Signature Item, Price Range and Value, Uniqueness, Taste, Presentation, Portion Size, Maintaining Taste Consistency, Focus on Health Aspects, Economically Priced, Customers' Paid More than Planned, Prices are Comparatively Competitive, Interior appearance and theme, Atmosphere, Cleanliness, Air condition quality, Lighting in the restaurant, Adequate parking facilities, Restaurant cleanliness, Décor was visibility appealing (Ambiences), Promptness of service, Server's appearance (neat & presentable), Employees understanding towards customers' needs, Courtesy of server, Server's knowledge about menu

Source: Developed from Descriptive Analysis

The empirical data presented above clearly depicts individual restaurant's strength and weakness.

Consumers select their restaurants based on many factors. In the current study nine factors were considered an as important determinant that influences diners' choice for a restaurant and its services.

Based on the identified variables following hypothesis is framed that aims to measure whether there exists differences in the diners' preference towards foods and restaurant service features between vegetarian and non-vegetarian restaurants.

H4: There exists no differences in the diners' preference towards foods and restaurant service features between vegetarian and non-vegetarian restaurants.

Table 4.47(A): Independent Z-test Diners' Preference towards Vegetarian & Non Vegetarian Foods and their Perception on Restaurant Service

Particulars	Preference towards Vegetarian and Non-Vegetarian Foods						Z	Sig
	Veg		Non-veg		Both			
	Mean	SD	Mean	SD	Mean	SD		
Menu Offered								
Theme	1.70	0.92	1.76	1.03	1.90	0.94	.595	.441
Variety and selection	2.03	0.81	2.02	0.94	1.92	0.80	2.062	.152
Signature item	2.16	1.03	2.24	1.00	2.14	0.97	.141	.708
Price range and value	2.49	1.11	2.32	1.07	2.16	1.00	.636	.426
Uniqueness	2.35	1.28	2.41	1.23	2.31	1.13	.251	.617
Food Quality								
Taste	1.43	0.79	1.49	0.88	1.49	0.75	.693	.406
Presentation	1.98	0.89	2.08	0.85	1.94	0.74	.228	.633
Portion size	2.25	1.04	2.26	0.97	2.17	0.90	.694	.406
Consistency	2.38	1.12	2.38	1.04	2.24	0.99	.647	.422
Health aspects	2.38	1.27	2.45	1.27	2.21	1.24	.000	.983
Price								
Economically priced	1.67	0.85	1.88	1.07	2.11	1.01	4.918	.027
Customers' paid more than they had planned	2.15	0.96	2.11	0.90	2.27	0.93	2.474	.117
Prices are comparatively competitive	2.24	1.11	2.24	1.06	2.29	1.00	.095	.758
Appearance/Comfort								
Exterior appearance and theme	1.90	0.96	1.82	0.99	1.95	0.94	.263	.609
Interior appearance and theme	2.29	0.97	2.13	0.91	2.19	0.96	4.497	.035
Atmosphere	2.33	1.13	2.29	0.97	2.13	0.96	2.914	.089
Cleanliness	2.36	1.07	2.24	1.08	2.18	1.10	.037	.847
Air condition quality	2.15	1.23	2.42	1.10	2.20	1.17	.456	.500
Physical Design								
Lighting in the restaurant	1.73	0.90	1.72	0.98	1.70	0.83	.006	.939
Adequate parking facilities	2.15	0.82	2.14	0.96	2.20	0.89	3.131	.078
Restaurant cleanliness	2.11	1.05	2.22	1.00	2.05	0.98	1.383	.240
Décor was visibility appealing (Ambiences)	2.40	1.15	2.28	0.99	2.27	0.97	3.816	.052
Responsiveness								
Employees attentiveness	1.54	0.77	1.64	0.82	1.90	0.88	1.306	.254
Employees co-operatives	2.16	0.72	2.12	0.80	2.23	0.82	.367	.545
Promptness of service	2.15	0.91	2.15	0.93	2.30	0.96	.028	.867
Server's appearance (neat & presentable)	2.47	1.09	2.28	1.05	2.29	1.00	1.637	.202
Understanding towards customers' needs	2.27	1.08	2.36	1.08	2.33	1.09	.007	.932
Courtesy of server	2.55	1.00	2.29	1.01	2.38	0.95	.045	.833
Server's knowledge about menu	2.31	1.25	2.18	1.08	2.19	1.12	6.495	.011

Level of Significance: 5 per cent

Table 4.47(B): Independent Z-test Diners' Preference towards Vegetarian & Non Vegetarian Foods and their Perception on Restaurant Service

Particulars	Preference towards Vegetarian and Non-Vegetarian Foods							
	Veg		Non-veg		Both		Z	Sig
	Mean	SD	Mean	SD	Mean	SD		
Service Reliability								
Customers' receives exactly what they ordered the first time	1.71	0.86	1.71	0.97	1.83	0.87	1.828	.177
Order served are error – free	2.25	0.81	2.09	0.76	2.20	0.79	3.271	.072
The food was fresh	2.16	0.95	2.07	0.99	2.01	0.98	.080	.778
The temperature of the food was just right	2.45	1.11	2.32	1.07	2.31	1.01	.139	.709
Foods are Hygienically serviced	2.20	1.08	2.26	1.23	2.14	1.17	3.376	.067
Service Quality/ Service Timed Quality								
7x7 days	1.78	0.97	1.64	0.96	1.80	0.93	.001	.975
Hours of operation	2.09	0.85	2.11	0.88	2.14	0.76	.002	.968
Service style	2.08	1.00	2.10	0.95	2.08	0.96	.123	.726
Quality of service	2.31	1.08	2.20	1.03	2.06	0.97	.802	.371
Speed of service	2.46	1.23	2.36	1.17	2.25	1.09	.212	.646
Extra services offered	2.34	1.20	2.28	1.15	2.29	1.09	.541	.463
Location								
Proximity	1.83	0.91	1.93	1.04	1.96	0.91	.230	.632
Accessibility	2.23	0.91	2.05	0.87	2.12	0.90	3.754	.054
Visibility	2.22	0.98	2.26	0.94	2.19	0.92	.317	.574
Surrounding neighborhood	2.55	1.15	2.42	0.99	2.38	0.97	4.583	.033
Parking availability	2.40	1.16	2.41	1.12	2.35	1.12	.106	.744
Sign visibility	2.33	1.22	2.48	1.16	2.13	1.09	.338	.561

Level of Significance: 5 per cent

From the above empirical data analysis it has been clearly inferred that the vegetarian diners believe that the employees in the popular vegetarian restaurants are neat & presentable, courteous in nature and have proper knowledge about the menu. Followed by, the respondents' have opined that the popular restaurants provide error free services, fresh food and offers hot and delicious food to them. Similarly the respondents' have stated that the light settings and decorations of selected restaurants are delightful. Also, the sample populations' have opined that the selected vegetarian restaurants are located at accessible distance from their home. It has been found that the respondents' have said that the particular vegetarian restaurant provides pleasant interior appearance and theme, good atmosphere and ensure cleanliness. Subsequently it has been observed that the respondents' believe that the vegetarian restaurants offer wide variety and selection and also they also opined that the food is worth of the price. Further it has been observed that the sample populations' feel that the quality of food is consistent in the vegetarian restaurants. It has been clearly identified that the quality of service, speed of service and other extra services offered are good and satisfactory to its customers'.

From the above data discussion it has been observed that the non-veg diners have said that selected restaurants have proper understanding towards customers' needs, provide hygiene food and ensure cleanliness. Followed by, the sample populations' have said that particular restaurants are located at visible point and provide convenient parking services. Also, the respondents' have stated that the non-vegetarian restaurants offer ample air conditioning facility, signature items and provide unique customer service. Similarly the respondents' have opined that the selected non-vegetarian restaurants ensure promising food quality i.e., the taste, presentation, portion size, portion size and the health aspects are extremely good. Further it has been observed that the sample populations' have opened that the service style of selected non-vegetarian restaurants are reliable and enticing.

It is evident from the above data analysis that the diner who prefer to dine both vegetarian and non- vegetarian food have stated that the employees in selected restaurants are attentive, co-operative, prompt in their service and deliver exact order all the time. Subsequently it has been observed that the popular non-vegetarian restaurants provide adequate parking facilities and are located at reachable distance. Followed by the respondents' believe that the restaurants offer pleasant exterior appearance and theme, tasty food, 7x7 days service and extended working hours. However the vegetarian and non-vegetarian diners feel that price of the food in the selected restaurants are high in comparison to the other restaurants in Coimbatore.

From the above it has been inferred that the probability value of Z is not found to be significant at five per cent level. Therefore the hypothesis framed stands rejected and it is concluded that there exists differences in the diners' preference towards foods and restaurant service features between vegetarian and non-vegetarian restaurants. However it is exceptional in the case of interior appearance and theme, décor was visibility appealing (ambiences), server's knowledge about menu, accessibility and surrounding neighborhood.

Tucci and Talaga (1997)[1]conjoint analysis study aimed to determine the basic parameter on which a diner evaluates a service of restaurant. The study found that customer evaluates restaurant services based on different parameters like:price, speed of service, quality of food,

---

[1]Tucci, L.A. and Talaga J. (1997), *Service Guarantees and Consumers Evaluation of Services*, Journal of Services Marketing, Volume No.11, Issue No.1, PP. 10-18.

courtesy of server and service guarantee. The study also observed that customers evaluation norms varies from on category of restaurant to the other and it is not uniform in nature, it changes as per their desirability of the services. Drawing evidences from this study, following hypothesis is framed to measure there exist any differences in the diners' perception towards the service features of one restaurant in comparison to the other.

H5: There exist differences in the diners' perception towards the service features of one restaurant in comparison to the other.

Table 4.48: Measure of Dispersion Diners' Perception towards the Service Features of Annapoorna in Comparison to Other Vegetarian Restaurants

Perception	Mean(Annapoorna: 3.895)	SD(Annnapoorna: .201)	R	MD	SDD	Z	DF	Sig
Annapoorna Vs Anandha's	3.847	.231	.817	.048	.134	2.417	45	.020
Annapoorna Vs Aryaa's	3.826	.207	.819	.069	.123	3.808	45	.000
Annapoorna Vs Adyar Anandha Bhavan	3.842	.277	.807	.053	.165	2.175	45	.035
Annapoorna Vs RHR	3.606	.482	.565	.289	.404	4.848	45	.000

Level of significance: 5 per cent

(Note: MD-Mean Differences, SDD-Standard Deviation Differences)

From the above table it has inferred that probability values of z is found to be significant at 5 per cent level. Therefore the hypothesis framed stands accepted and it has been concluded that there exist differences in the diners' perception towards the service features of Annapoorna restaurant in comparison to the others.

Table 4.49: Measure of Dispersion Diners' Perception towards the Service Features of Anandha's in Comparison to Other Vegetarian Restaurants

Perception	Mean(Anandha's: 3.847)	SD(Anandha's: .231)	R	MD	SDD	Z	DF	Sig
Anandha's Vs annapoorna	3.895	.201	.817	.048	.134	2.417	45	**.020**
Anandha's Vs Aryaa's	3.826	.207	.772	.021	.149	.967	45	**.039**
Anandha's Vs Adyar Anandha Bhavan	3.842	.277	.834	.005	.153	.232	45	**.018**
Anandha's Vs RHR	3.606	.482	.519	.242	.413	3.968	45	**.000**

Level of significance: 5 per cent

(Note: MD-Mean Differences, SDD-Standard Deviation Differences)

From the above table it has inferred that probability values of z is found to be significant at 5 per cent level. Therefore the hypothesis framed stands rejected and it has been concluded that there exist differences in the diners' perception towards the service features of Anandha's restaurant in comparison to the others.

Table 4.50: Measure of Dispersion Diners' Perception towards the Service Features of Aryaa's in Comparison to other Vegetarian Restaurants

Perception	Mean(Aryaa's: 3.826)	SD(Aryaa's: .207)	R	MD	SDD	Z	DF	Sig
Aryaa's Vs Annapoorna	3.895	.201	.819	.069	.123	3.808	45	.000
Aryaa's Vs Anandha's	3.847	.231	.772	.021	.149	.967	45	.039
Aryaa's Vs Adyar Anandha Bhavan	3.842	.277	.649	.016	.212	.514	45	.010
Aryaa's Vs RHR	3.606	.482	.483	.220	.423	3.529	45	.001

Level of significance: 5 per cent

(Note: MD-Mean Differences, SDD-Standard Deviation Differences)

From the above table it has inferred that probability values of z is found to be significant at 5 per cent level. Therefore the hypothesis framed stands accepted and it has been concluded that there exist differences in the diners' perception towards the service features of Aryaa's restaurant in comparison to the others.

Table 4.51: Measure of Dispersion Diners' Perception towards The Service Features of Adyar Anandha Bhavan in Comparison to Other Vegetarian Restaurants

Perception	Mean(Adyar Anandha Bhyavan: 3.842)	SD(Adyar Anandha Bhyavan: .277)	R	MD	SDD	Z	DF	Sig
Adyar Anandha BhavanVs Annapoorna	3.895	.201	.807	.053	.165	2.175	45	.035
Adyar Anandha BhavanVs Anandha's	3.847	.231	.834	.005	.153	.232	45	.018
Adyar Anandha BhavanVs Aryaa's	3.826	.207	.649	.016	.212	.514	45	.010
Adyar Anandha BhavanVs RHR	3.606	.482	.480	.236	.426	3.766	45	.000

Level of significance: 5 per cent

(Note: MD-Mean Differences, SDD-Standard Deviation Differences)

From the above table it has inferred that probability values of z is found to be significant at 5 per cent level. Therefore the hypothesis framed stands rejected and it has been concluded that there exist differences in the diners' perception towards the service features of Adyar Anandha Bhavan restaurant in comparison to the others.

Table 4.52: Measure of Dispersion Diners' Perception towards the Service Features of RHR in Comparison to Other Vegetarian Restaurants

Perception	Mean(RHR:3.606)	SD(RHR:.482)	R	MD	SDD	Z	DF	Sig
RHRVs Annapoorna	3.895	.201	.754	.004	.181	.155	45	.047
RHRVs Anandha's	3.847	.231	.824	.043	.156	1.896	45	.054
RHRVs Aryaa's	3.826	.207	.714	.065	.192	2.284	45	.027
RHRVs Adyar Anandha Bhavan	3.842	.277	.456	.236	.205	4.467	45	.000

Level of significance: 5 per cent

(Note: MD-Mean Differences, SDD-Standard Deviation Differences)

From the above table it has inferred that probability values of z is found to be significant at 5 per cent level. Therefore the hypothesis framed stands rejected and it has been concluded that there exist differences in the diners' perception towards the service features of RHR restaurant in comparison to the others.

From the above Tables: 4.52- 4.56, it has been found that the hypothesis framed stands accepted and it has been concluded that there exists differences in the diners' perception towards the service features of one vegetarian restaurant in comparison to the other. The data analysis and summary presented in the Table: 4.43 (A) & (B) and 4.44 duly complement the conclusion drawn.

Table 4.53: Measure of Dispersion Diners' Perception towards the Service Features of Rayappa's in Comparison to other Non Vegetarian Restaurants

Perception	Mean(Rayappa's:3.963)	SD(Rayappa's:.218)	R	MD	SDD	Z	DF	Sig
Rayappa's Vs Sampoorna	3.872	.205	.847	0.091	0.118	5.244	45	.000
Rayappa's Vs Haribhavanam	3.755	.213	.647	0.208	0.181	7.774	45	.000
Rayappa's Vs Anjappar	3.868	.193	.834	0.095	0.121	5.320	45	.000
Rayappa's Vs Anjali	3.785	.281	.826	0.177	0.159	7.560	45	.000

Level of significance: 5 per cent

(Note: MD-Mean Differences, SDD-Standard Deviation Differences)

From the above table it has inferred that probability values of z is found to be significant at 5 per cent level. Therefore the hypothesis framed stands accepted and it has been concluded that there exist differences in the diners' perception towards the service features of Rayappa's restaurant in comparison to the others.

Table 4.54: Measure of Dispersion Diners' Perception towards the Service Features of Sampoorna in Comparison to Other Non Vegetarian Restaurants

Perception	Mean(Sampoorna:3.872)	SD(Sampoorna:.205)	R	MD	SDD	t	DF	Sig
Sampoorna Vs Rayappa's	3.963	.218	.847	.091	.118	5.244	45	.000
Sampoorna Vs Haribhavanam	3.755	.213	.737	.117	.152	5.214	45	.000
Sampoorna Vs Anjappar	3.868	.193	.831	.004	.116	.229	45	.820
Sampoorna Vs Anjali	3.785	.281	.889	.086	.136	4.293	45	.000

Level of significance: 5 per cent

(Note: MD-Mean Differences, SDD-Standard Deviation Differences)

From the above table it has inferred that probability values of z is found to be significant at 5 per cent level. Therefore the hypothesis framed stands accepted and it has been concluded that there exist differences in the diners' perception towards the service features of Sampoorna restaurant in comparison to the others. However it is exceptional in the case of Sampoorna Vs Others.

Table 4.55: Measure of Dispersion Diners' Perception towards the Service Features of Haribhavanam in Comparison to other Non Vegetarian Restaurants

Perception	Mean(Haribhavanam:3.755)	SD(Haribhavanam: .213)	R	MD	SDD	Z	DF	Sig
Haribhavanam Vs Rayappa's	3.963	.218	.647	.208	.181	7.774	45	.000
Haribhavanam Vs Sampoorna	3.872	.205	.737	.117	.152	5.214	45	.000
Haribhavanam Vs Anjappar	3.868	.193	.605	.113	.181	4.217	45	.000
Haribhavanam Vs Anjali	3.785	.281	.758	.003	.068	3.425	45	.001

Level of significance: 5 per cent

(Note: MD-Mean Differences, SDD-Standard Deviation Differences)

From the above table it has inferred that probability values of z is found to be significant at 5 per cent level. Therefore the hypothesis framed stands accepted and it has been concluded that there exist differences in the diners' perception towards the service features of Haribhavanam restaurant in comparison to the others. However it is exceptional in the case of Haribhavanam Vs Anjali.

Table 4.56: Measure of Dispersion Diners' Perception towards the Service Features of Anjappar in Comparison to other Non Vegetarian Restaurants

Perception	Mean(Anjappar:3.868)	SD(Anjappar: .193)	R	MD	SDD	Z	DF	Sig
Anjappar Vs Rayappa's	3.963	.218	.834	.095	.121	5.320	45	.000
Anjappar Vs Sampoorna	3.872	.205	.831	.004	.116	.229	45	.020
Anjappar Vs Haribhavanam	3.755	.213	.605	.113	.020	4.217	45	.000
Anjappar Vs Anjali	3.785	.281	.781	.082	.178	3.145	45	.003

Level of significance: 5 per cent

(Note: MD-Mean Differences, SDD-Standard Deviation Differences)

From the above table it has inferred that probability values of z is found to be significant at 5 per cent level. Therefore the hypothesis framed stands accepted and it has been concluded that there exist differences in the diners' perception towards the service features of Anjappar restaurant in comparison to the others.

Table 4.57: Measure of Dispersion Diners' Perception towards the Service Features of Anjali in Comparison to Other Non Vegetarian Restaurants

Perception	Mean(Anjali:3.785)	SD(Anjali: .281)	R	MD	SDD	Z	DF	Sig
Anjali Vs Rayappa's	3.963	.218	.826	.177	.159	7.560	45	**.000**
Anjali Vs Sampoorna	3.872	.205	.889	.086	.136	4.293	45	**.000**
Anjali Vs Haribhavanam	3.755	.281	.826	.062	.166	2.551	45	**.014**
Anjali Vs Anjappar	3.868	.193	.781	-082	.178	3.145	45	**.003**

Level of significance: 5 per cent

(Note: MD-Mean Differences, SDD-Standard Deviation Differences)

From the above table it has inferred that probability values of z is found to be significant at 5 per cent level. Therefore the hypothesis framed stands accepted and it has been concluded that there exist differences in the diners' perception towards the service features of Anjali restaurant in comparison to the others. From the above Tables: 4.57-4.61, it has been found that the hypothesis framed stands accepted and it has been concluded that, there exist differences in the diners' perception towards the service features of one non-vegetarian restaurant in comparison to the other. Thus from the above table Tables: 4.52-4.61 it has been concluded that there exist differences in the diners' perception towards the service features of one restaurant in comparison to the other. The data analysis and summary presented in the Table: 4.45 (A) & (B) and 4.46(A)-(C) duly complement the conclusion drawn. Factor analysis technique has been applied to find the underlying dimension (factors) that exists among 46 variables relating to identify the diners' perception towards the service features of vegetarian restaurants and their preferences towards particular restaurant.

Table 4.58: KMO and Bartlett's Test Diners' Perception towards the Service Features of Vegetarian Restaurants

Kaiser-Meyer-Olkin Measure of Sampling Adequacy	.781
Bartlett's Test of Sphericity Approx. Chi-Square	18653.495
DF	351
Sig	.000

Level of Significance: 5 per cent

In the present study, Kaiser-Meyer-Oklin (KMO) Measure of Sampling Adequacy (MSA) and Bartlett's test of Sphericity were applied to verify the adequacy or appropriateness of data for factor analysis. In this study, the value of KMO for overall matrix was found to be excellent (0.781) and Bartlett's test of Sphericity was highly significant (p<0.05). Bartlett's Sphericity test was effective, as the chi-square value draws significance at five per cent level. The results thus indicated that the sample taken was appropriate to proceed with a factor analysis procedure. Besides the Bartlett's Test of Sphericity and the KMO Measure of sampling Adequacy, Communality values of all variables were also observed.

Table 4.59(A): Cumulative Diners' Perception towards the Service Features of Vegetarian Restaurants

Variables	Initial	Extraction
Menu Offered		
Theme	1.000	.822
Variety and selection	1.000	.866
Signature item	1.000	.839
Price range and value	1.000	.865
Uniqueness	1.000	.905
Food Quality		
Taste	1.000	.944
Presentation	1.000	.554
Portion size	1.000	.807
Consistency	1.000	.924
Health aspects	1.000	.948
Price		
Economically priced	1.000	.925
Customers' paid more than they had planned	1.000	.965
Prices are comparatively competitive	1.000	.659
Appearance/Comfort		
Exterior appearance and theme	1.000	.882
Interior appearance and theme	1.000	.564
Atmosphere	1.000	.845
Cleanliness	1.000	.877
Air condition quality	1.000	.904
Physical Design		
Lighting in the restaurant	1.000	.952
Adequate parking facilities	1.000	.517
Restaurant cleanliness	1.000	.651
Décor was visibility appealing (Ambiences)	1.000	.938
Responsiveness		
Employees attentiveness	1.000	.551
Employees co-operatives	1.000	.753
Promptness of service	1.000	.730
Server's appearance (neat & presentable)	1.000	.584
Understanding towards customers' needs	1.000	.684
Courtesy of server	1.000	.851
Server's knowledge about menu	1.000	.935

Table 4.59(B): Cumulative Diners' Perception towards the Service Features of Vegetarian Restaurants

Variables	Initial	Extraction
Service Reliability		
Customers' receives exactly what they ordered the first time	1.000	.585
Order served are error – free	1.000	.857
The food was fresh	1.000	.911
The temperature of the food was just right	1.000	.986
Foods are Hygienically serviced	1.000	.969
Service Quality/ Service Timed Quality		
7x7 days	1.000	.933
Hours of operation	1.000	.926
Service style	1.000	.612
Quality of service	1.000	.886
Speed of service	1.000	.952
Extra services offered	1.000	.722
Location		
Proximity	1.000	.969
Accessibility	1.000	.737
Visibility	1.000	.792
Surrounding neighborhood	1.000	.778
Parking availability	1.000	.971
Sign visibility	1.000	.888

In order to provide a more parsimonious interpretation of the results, 46-item scale was then Factor analyzed using the Principal Component method with Equamax rotation.

Factor analysis attempts to identify underlying variables, or factors, that explain the pattern of correlations within a set of observed variables. Factor analysis is often used in data reduction to identify a small number of factors that explain most of the variance observed in a much larger number of manifest variables. In the current study rotation factor analysis is performed to measure the diners' perception towards the service features of vegetarian restaurants and their preferences towards particular restaurant. The significance of relationship between the variables is depicted in the following table

Table 4.60(A): Rotated Component Matrix Diners' Perception towards the Service Features of Vegetarian Restaurants

Factors	Vegetarian Restaurants				
	Annapoorna	Anandha's	Aryaa's	Adyar Anandha Bhavan	RHR
Menu Offered					
X_1-Theme	-	-	.722	-	-
X_2-Variety and selection	-	-	-	.817	-
X_3-Signature item	-	-	.691	-	-
X_4-Price range and value	.563	.685	-	-	-
X_5-Uniqueness	-	.761	-	-	-
Food Quality					
X_6-Taste	.560	-	-	-	.708
X_7-Presentation	-	-	-	-	.545
X_8-Portion size	.545	-	-	-	-
X_9-Consistency	.579	-	.543	-	-
X_{10}-Health aspects	.789	-	-	-	-
Price					
X_{11}-Economically priced	-	-	.897	-	-
X_{12}-Customers' paid more than they had planned	-	-	.711	-	-
X_{13}-Prices are comparatively competitive	.764	-	-	-	-
Appearance/Comfort					
X_{14}-Exterior appearance and theme	-	-	-	-	.855
X_{15}-Interior appearance and theme	-	-	-	-	.626
X_{16}-Atmosphere	-	-	-	.856	-
X_{17}-Cleanliness	.617	-	-	-	-
X_{18}-Air condition quality	.709	-	-	-	-
Physical Design					
X_{19}-Lighting in the restaurant	.587	-	-	-	-
X_{20}-Adequate parking facilities	-	-	-	-	-
X_{21}-Restaurant cleanliness	-	-	-	.666	-
X_{22}-Décor was visibility appealing (Ambiences)	.921	-	-	-	-
Responsiveness					
X_{23}-Employees attentiveness	-	-	-	-	-
X_{24}-Employees co-operatives	-	-	-	-	.808
X_{25}-Promptness of service	-	-	-	-	.500
X_{26}-Server's appearance (neat & presentable)	-	-	.726	-	-
X_{27}-Understanding towards customers' needs	-	-	.596	-	-
X_{28}-Courtesy of server	.530	.601	-	-	-
X_{29}-Server's knowledge about menu	-	-	.538	.713	-

Level of Significance: 5 per cent

Table 4.60(B): Rotated Component Matrix Diners' Perception towards the Service Features of Vegetarian Restaurants

Factors	Vegetarian Restaurants				
	Annapoorna	Anandha's	Aryaa's	Adyar Anandha Bhavan	RHR
Service Reliability					
X_{30}-Customers' receives exactly what they ordered the first time	-	.719	-	-	-
X_{31}-Order served are error – free	-	-	-	.715	-
X_{32}-The food was fresh	-	-	.556	-	.757
X_{33}-The temperature of the food was just right	-	.782	-	-	-
X_{34}-Foods are Hygienically serviced	-	.792	-	-	-
Service Quality/ Service Timed Quality					
X_{35}-7x7 days	-	-	.616	-	-
X_{36}-Hours of operation	-	-	.620	.657	-
X_{37}-Service style	.588	-	-	-	-
X_{38}-Quality of service	-	.717	-	-	-
X_{39}-Speed of service	-	.922	-	-	-
X_{40}-Extra services offered	-	.577	-	-	-
Location					
X_{41}-Proximity	,840	-	-	-	-
X_{42}-Accessibility	-	-	-	-	.832
X_{43}-Visibility	-	-	-	.815	-
X_{44}-Surrounding neighborhood	.590	-	-		-
X_{45}-Parking availability	.507	-	-	.638	-
X_{46}-Sign visibility	-	-	-	-	.761
Eigen value	*8.598*	*7.575*	*7.495*	*6.997*	*6.95*
% of Variance	*18.691*	*16.467*	*16.293*	*15.211*	*15.109*
Cumulative%	*18.691*	*35.159*	*51.452*	*66.663*	*81.772*

Level of Significance: 5 per cent

Five factors extracted together account for 81.772 percent of the total variance (information contained in the original 46 variables). This is pretty good, because the researcher are able to economize on the number of variables (from 46 researcher have reduced them to five underlying factors), while the data lost only about 18.228 percent of the information content (81.772 percent is retained by the five factors extracted out of the 46 original variables). Since the idea of factor analysis is to identify the factors that meaningfully summarize the sets of closely related variables, the rotation phase of the factor analysis attempts to transfer initial matrix into one that is easier to interpret. Equamax rotation method is used to extract meaningful factors.

Five factors were identified as being maximum percentage variance accounted. The variables X_4, X_6, X_8, X_9, X_{10}, X_{13}, X_{17}, X_{18}, X_{19}, X_{22}, X_{28}, X_{37}, X_{41}, X_{44} and X_{45} are grouped as factor I and it accounts for 18.691 per cent of the total variance. The variables X_4, X_5, X_{28}, X_{30}, X_{33}, X_{34}, X_{38}, X_{39} and X_{40} constitute the factor II and it accounts for 16.467 per cent of the total variance. The variables X_1, X_3, X_9, X_{11}, X_{12}, X_{26}, X_{27}, X_{29}, X_{32}, X_{35} and X_{36} are grouped as factor III and it accounts for 16.293 per cent of the total variance. The variables X_2, X_{16}, X_{21}, X_{29}, X_{31}, X_{36}, X_{43} and X_{45} are grouped as factor IV and it accounts for 15.211 per cent of the total variance. The variables X_6, X_7, X_{14}, X_{15}, X_{24}, X_{25}, X_{32}, X_{42} and X_{46} constitute the factor V and it accounts for 15.109 per cent of the total variance.

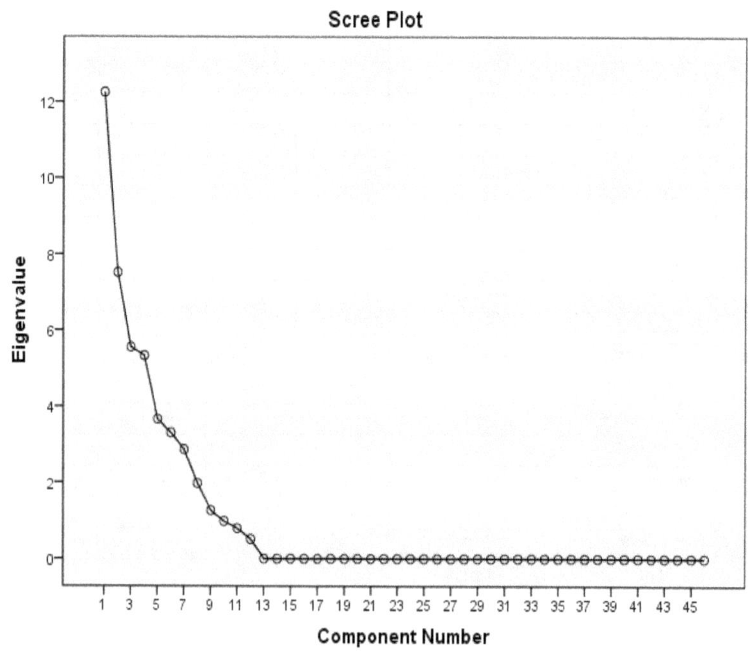

Exhibit 4.11: Screen Plot Diners' Perception towards the Service Features of Vegetarian Restaurants

Table 4.61: Summary of Rotation Factor Analysis & Cronbach's Alpha Diners' Perception towards the Service Features of Vegetarian Restaurants

Factors	Factor Interpretation	Variables included in the factors	Cronbach's Alpha
F_1	Annapoorna	Price range and value, taste, portion size, consistency, health aspects, prices are comparatively competitive, cleanliness, air condition quality, lighting in the restaurant, décor was visibility appealing (ambiences), Courtesy of server, service style, proximity, surrounding neighborhood and parking availability.	.932
F_2	Anandha's	Price range and value, uniqueness, Courtesy of server, customers' receives exactly what they ordered the first time, the temperature of the food was just right, foods are hygienically serviced, quality of service, speed of service and extra services offered.	.904
F_3	Aryaa's	Theme, signature item, consistency, economically priced, customers' paid more than they had planned, server's appearance (neat & presentable), understanding towards customers' needs, server's knowledge about menu, the food was fresh, 7*7 days and hours of operation.	.798
F_4	Adyar Anandha Bhavan	Variety & selection, atmosphere, Restaurant cleanliness, server's knowledge about menu, order served is error–free, hours of operation, visibility and parking availability.	.738
F_5	RHR	Taste, presentation, exterior appearance and theme, interior appearance and theme, employee's co-operatives, promptness of service, the food was fresh, accessibility and sign visibility.	.718

Source: Computed From Primary Data

Factor analysis was used to find out the diners level of perception towards the service features of vegetarian restaurants and their preferences towards particular restaurant. The Cronbach's reliability values (.932, .904, .798, .738 and.718) indicate significant correlation between the variables tested.

Factor analysis technique has been applied to find the underlying dimension (factors) that exists among 46 variables relating to identify the diners' perception towards the service features of non-vegetarian restaurants and their preferences towards particular restaurant.

Table 4.62: KMO and Bartlett's Test Diners' Perception towards the Service Features of Non-Vegetarian Restaurants

Kaiser-Meyer-Olkin Measure of Sampling Adequacy	.723
Bartlett's Test of Sphericity Approx. Chi-Square	2083.028
DF	1035
Sig	.000

Level of Significance: 5 per cent

In the present study, Kaiser-Meyer-Oklin (KMO) Measure of Sampling Adequacy (MSA) and Bartlett's test of Sphericity were applied to verify the adequacy or appropriateness of data for factor analysis. In this study, the value of KMO for overall matrix was found to be excellent (0.723) and Bartlett's test of Sphericity was highly significant (p<0.05). Bartlett's Sphericity test was effective, as the chi-square value draws significance at five per cent level. The results thus indicated that the sample taken was appropriate to proceed with a factor analysis procedure. Besides the Bartlett's Test of Sphericity and the KMO Measure of sampling Adequacy, Communality values of all variables were also observed.

Table 4.63(A): Cumulative Diners' Perception towards the Service Features of Non-vegetarian Restaurants

Variables	Initial	Extraction
Menu Offered		
Theme	1.000	.614
Variety and selection	1.000	.546
Signature item	1.000	.674
Price range and value	1.000	.724
Uniqueness	1.000	.586
Food Quality		
Taste	1.000	.600
Presentation	1.000	.642
Portion size	1.000	.638
Consistency	1.000	.686
Health aspects	1.000	.687
Price		
Economically priced	1.000	.614
Customers' paid more than they had planned	1.000	.549
Prices are comparatively competitive	1.000	.541
Appearance/Comfort		
Exterior appearance and theme	1.000	.713
Interior appearance and theme	1.000	.653
Atmosphere	1.000	.640
Cleanliness	1.000	.549
Air condition quality	1.000	.643
Physical Design		
Lighting in the restaurant	1.000	.531
Adequate parking facilities	1.000	.568
Restaurant cleanliness	1.000	.535
Décor was visibility appealing (Ambiences)	1.000	.650
Responsiveness		
Employees attentiveness	1.000	.675
Employees co-operatives	1.000	.667
Promptness of service	1.000	.545
Server's appearance (neat & presentable)	1.000	.504
Understanding towards customers' needs	1.000	.603
Courtesy of server	1.000	.798
Server's knowledge about menu	1.000	.556

Table 4.63(B): Cumulative Diners' Perception towards the Service Features of
Non-vegetarian Restaurants

Variables	Initial	Extraction
Service Reliability		
Customers' receives exactly what they ordered the first time	1.000	.637
Order served are error – free	1.000	.564
The food was fresh	1.000	.504
The temperature of the food was just right	1.000	.668
Foods are Hygienically serviced	1.000	.506
Service Quality/ Service Timed Quality		
7*7 days	1.000	.590
Hours of operation	1.000	.557
Service style	1.000	.632
Quality of service	1.000	.585
Speed of service	1.000	.694
Extra services offered	1.000	.613
Location		
Proximity	1.000	.539
Accessibility	1.000	.681
Visibility	1.000	.586
Surrounding neighborhood	1.000	.785
Parking availability	1.000	.554
Sign visibility	1.000	.541

In order to provide a more parsimonious interpretation of the results, 46-item scale was then Factor analyzed using the Principal Component method with Equamax rotation.

Factor analysis attempts to identify underlying variables, or factors, that explain the pattern of correlations within a set of observed variables. Factor analysis is often used in data reduction to identify a small number of factors that explain most of the variance observed in a much larger number of manifest variables. In the current study rotation factor analysis is performed to measure the diners' perception towards the service features of non-vegetarian restaurants and their preferences towards particular restaurant. The significance of relationship between the variables is depicted in the following table

Table 4.64(A): Rotated Component Matrix Diners' Perception towards the Service Features of Non-vegetarian Restaurants

Factors	Non-vegetarian Restaurants				
	Rayappa's	Sampoorna	Haribhavanam	Anjappar	Anjali
Menu Offered					
X_1-Theme	.654	-	-	-	-
X_2-Variety and selection	-	-	-	-	-
X_3-Signature item	-	-	.637	-	-
X_4-Price range and value	-	-	-	-	-
X_5-Uniqueness	-	-	.567	-	-
Food Quality					
X_6-Taste	.587	-	-	-	-
X_7-Presentation	-	.558	-	-	-
X_8-Portion size	-	-	-	-	-
X_9-Consistency	-	-	-	-	.554
X_{10}-Health aspects	-	-	.518	-	-
Price					
X_{11}-Economically priced	.761	-	-	-	-
X_{12}-Customers' paid more than they had planned	-	.687	-	-	-
X_{13}-Prices are comparatively competitive	-	-	.502	-	-
Appearance/Comfort					
X_{14}-Exterior appearance and theme	.820	-	-	-	-
X_{15}-Interior appearance and theme	-	.678	-	-	-
X_{16}-Atmosphere	-		-	-	.504
X_{17}-Cleanliness	-	.529	-	-	-
X_{18}-Air condition quality	-	-	.633	-	-
Physical Design					
X_{19}-Lighting in the restaurant	.699	-	-	-	-
X_{20}-Adequate parking facilities	-	-	-	-	-
X_{21}-Restaurant cleanliness	-	-	-	-	.551
X_{22}-Décor was visibility appealing (Ambiences)	-	-	.615	-	-
Responsiveness					
X_{23}-Employees attentiveness	-	-	-	.600	-
X_{24}-Employees co-operatives	-	-	-	.648	-
X_{25}-Promptness of service	-	-	-	.547	-
X_{26}-Server's appearance (neat & presentable)	-	-	-	-	-
X_{27}-Understanding towards customers' needs	-	-	-	-	-
X_{28}-Courtesy of server	-	-	-	.539	-
X_{29}-Server's knowledge about menu	-	-	-	.595	-

Level of Significance: 5 per cent

Table 4.64(B): Rotated Component Matrix Diners' Perception towards the Service Features of Non-Vegetarian Restaurants

Factors	Non-vegetarian Restaurants				
	Rayappa's	Sampoorna	Haribhavanam	Anjappar	Anjali
Service Reliability					
X_{30}-Customers' receives exactly what they ordered the first time	-	-	-	.575	-
X_{31}-Order served are error – free	-	-	-	-	-
X_{32}-The food was fresh	-	-	-	-	-
X_{33}-The temperature of the food was just right	-	-	-	-	.565
X_{34}-Foods are Hygienically serviced	-	-	-	-	-
Service Quality/ Service Timed Quality					
X_{35}-7*7 days	.611	-	-	-	-
X_{36}-Hours of operation	-	-	-	-	-
X_{37}-Service style	-	-	-	-	-
X_{38}-Quality of service	-	-	-	-	-
X_{39}-Speed of service	-	-	-	-	-
X_{40}-Extra services offered	-	-	-	-	-
Location					
X_{41}-Proximity	.657	-	-	-	-
X_{42}-Accessibility	-	.588	-	-	-
X_{43}-Visibility	-	-	-	-	-
X_{44}-Surrounding neighborhood	-	-	-	-	-
X_{45}-Parking availability	-	-	-	-	-
X_{46}-Sign visibility	-	.500	-	-	.517
Eigen value	*6.987*	*6.903*	*6.780*	*6.585*	*6.510*
% of Variance	*15.189*	*15.006*	*14.740*	*14.314*	*14.152*
Cumulative%	*15.189*	*30.196*	*44.935*	*59.250*	*73.402*

Level of Significance: 5 per cent

Five factors extracted together account for 73.402 percent of the total variance (information contained in the original 46 variables). This is good, because the researcher are able to economize on the number of variables (from 46 researcher have reduced them to five underlying factors), while the data lost only about 26.598 percent of the information content (73.402 percent is retained by the five factors extracted out of the 46 original variables). Since the idea of factor analysis is to identify the factors that meaningfully summarize the sets of closely related variables, the rotation phase of the factor analysis attempts to transfer initial matrix into one that is easier to interpret. Equamax rotation method is used to extract meaningful factors. Five factors were identified as being maximum percentage variance accounted. The variables X_1, X_6, X_{11}, X_{14}, X_{19}, X_{35} and X_{41} are grouped as factor I and it accounts for 15.189 per cent of the total variance. The variables X_7, X_{12}, X_{15}, X_{17}, X_{42} and X_{46} constitute the factor II and it accounts for 15.006 per cent of the total variance. The variables X_3, X_5, X_{10}, X_{13}, X_{18} and X_{22} are grouped as factor III and it accounts for 14.740 per cent of the total variance.

The variables X_{23}, X_{24}, X_{25}, X_{28}, $X_{29}$and X_{30} are grouped as factor IV and it accounts for 14.314 per cent of the total variance. The variables X_9, X_{16}, X_{21},X_{33} and X_{46} constitute the factor V and it accounts for 14.152 per cent of the total variance.

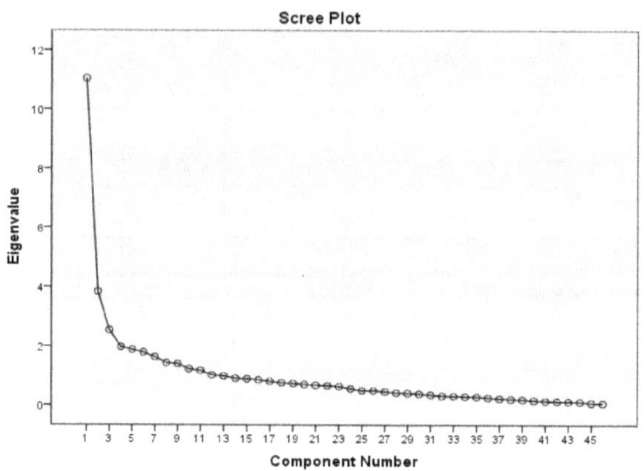

Exhibit 4.12: Scree Plot Diners' Perception towards the Service Features of Non-vegetarian Restaurants

Table 4.65: Summary of Rotation Factor Analysis & Cronbach's Alpha Diners' perception towards the Service Features of Non-vegetarian Restaurants

Factors	Factor Interpretation	Variables included in the factors	Cronbach's Alpha
F_1	Rayappa's	Theme, taste, economically priced, exterior appearance and theme, lighting in the restaurant, 7*7 days and proximity.	.932
F_2	Sampoorna	Presentation, customers' paid more than they had planned, interior appearance and theme, cleanliness, accessibility and sign visibility.	.904
F_3	Haribhavanam	Signature item, uniqueness, health aspects, prices are comparatively competitive, air condition quality and décor was visibility appealing (ambiences).	.798
F_4	Anjappar	Employees attentiveness, employees co-operatives, promptness of service, courtesy of server, server's knowledge about menu and customers' receives exactly what they ordered the first time.	.738
F_5	Anjali	Consistency, atmosphere, restaurant cleanliness, the temperature of the food was just right and sign visibility.	.718

Source: Computed from Primary Data

Factor analysis was used to find out the diners' level of perception towards the service features of non-vegetarian restaurants and their preferences towards particular restaurant. The Cronbach's reliability values (.932, .904, .798, .738 and .718) indicate significant correlation between the variables tested.

Customers' satisfaction is measured often by determining the experiences and expectations of customers. However, it is very difficult to measure customer satisfaction in restaurant services, because the products, customers' feelings as well as perceptions of equity have effects on satisfaction. Products and services include some intangible features such as ambience of a store. In addition, peoples' moods and their feelings play a big role on how satisfied they are: when an individual is very happy, he or she reacts positively to a product or service. Based on this conceptual understanding following table discussion and hypothesis testing were performed.

Table 4.66: Diners Level of Satisfaction towards the Service Features of Vegetarian and Non-Vegetarian Restaurant

Factors	Very High	High	Moderately	Low	Very Low	Sum	Mean	Rank
Menu offered	176 (29.33)	211 (35.17)	149 (24.83)	42 (7.00)	22 (3.67)	2277	3.80	8
Food quality	223 (37.17)	184 (30.67)	123 (20.50)	50 (8.33)	20 (3.33)	2340	3.90	3
Price of food items	172 (28.67)	200 (33.33)	162 (27.00)	47 (7.83)	19 (3.17)	2259	3.77	9
Appearance / comfort	179 (29.83)	216 (36.00)	156 (26.00)	38 (6.33)	11 (1.83)	2314	3.86	5
Ambience (Physical design)	182 (30.33)	198 (33.00)	184 (30.67)	29 (4.83)	7 (1.17)	2319	3.87	4
Responsiveness of employee	299 (49.83)	185 (30.83)	100 (16.67)	7 (1.17)	9 (1.50)	2558	4.26	1
Service reliability	170 (28.33)	260 (43.33)	147 (24.50)	11 (1.83)	12 (2.00)	2365	3.94	2
Service quality	200 (33.33)	201 (33.50)	119 (19.83)	43 (7.17)	37 (6.17)	2284	3.81	6
Location of restaurants	184 (30.67)	191 (31.83)	171 (28.50)	36 (6.00)	18 (3.00)	2287	3.81	6

Source: Primary Data

Values in parenthesis are in per cent

From the above table that it has been found that, majority of the sample subjects' exhibit high degree of satisfaction towards the responsiveness of employees in particular hotel, it is ranked in first place with the mean score of 4.26.Similarly the respondents' are pleased with the service reliability, food quality and ambience of particular restaurant. These variables are ranked in second, third and fourth position with the mean score of 3.94, 3.90 and 3.87, respectively. It has been found that the sample populations' exhibit moderate satisfaction levels on the appearance/comfort, service quality and location of specific restaurant. These factors are ranked in fifth and sixth place with the mean score of 3.86 and 3.81, respectively. Whereas the diners have stated that the menu and price of food items offered in particular restaurant is not convincing to them. These variables are ranked in eighth and ninth place with an average score of 3.80 and 3.77.

Hence it has been concluded that majority of the sample subjects' exhibit high degree of satisfaction towards the responsiveness of employees i.e., employees react fast to customers' wishes and helping them willingly, their service reliability (Keeping a promise which means that the service is accurate and provided at correct time without making any mistakes. Billing and records are recorded accurate and kept correct) and food quality.

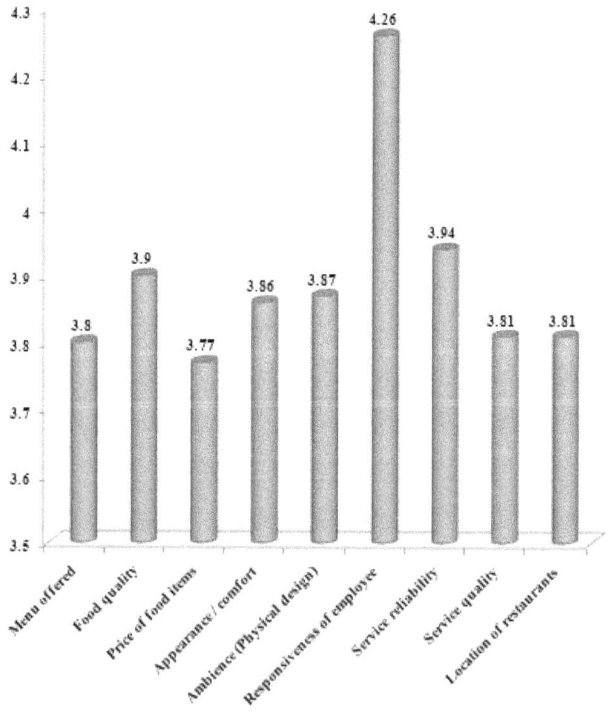

Exhibit 4.13: Diners Level of Satisfaction towards the Service Features of Vegetarian and Non-Vegetarian Restaurant

Table 4.67: Diners Level of Satisfaction towards the Service Features of Vegetarian and Non-vegetarian Restaurant

Variables	Vegetarian														
	Annapoorna			Anandha's			Arya's			Adyar Anandha Bhavan			RHR		
	Sum	Mean	Rank	Sum	Mean	Rank	Sum	Mean	Rank	Sum	Mean	Rank	Sum	Mean	Rank
Menu offered	790	3.80	4	615	3.82	3	313	3.68	5	243	3.86	2	270	3.91	1
Food quality	828	3.98	1	634	3.94	2	333	3.92	3	236	3.75	5	261	3.78	4
Price of food items	807	3.88	1	597	3.71	4	323	3.80	3	223	3.54	5	263	3.81	2
Appearance / comfort	815	3.92	2	623	3.87	3	319	3.75	4	225	3.57	6	281	4.07	1
Ambience (Physical Design)	808	3.88	3	631	3.92	2	341	4.01	1	231	3.67	5	265	3.84	4
Responsiveness of employee	879	4.23	3	707	4.39	2	347	4.08	5	277	4.40	1	291	4.22	4
Service reliability	830	3.99	2	628	3.90	4	320	3.76	5	250	3.97	3	289	4.19	1
Service quality	796	3.83	3	599	3.72	5	332	3.91	2	237	3.76	4	272	3.94	1
Location of restaurants	798	3.84	2	611	3.80	4	316	3.72	5	241	3.83	3	274	3.97	1

Non-Vegetarian															
Variables	Rayappa's			Sampoorna			Haribhavanam			Anjappar			Anjali		
	Sum	Mean	Rank	Sum	Mean	Rank	Sum	Mean	Rank	Sum	Mean	Rank	Sum	Mean	Rank
Menu offered	457	3.81	3	624	3.76	5	225	3.88	2	321	3.78	4	392	3.73	6
Food quality	475	3.96	2	659	3.97	1	218	3.76	6	328	3.86	4	402	3.83	5
Price of food items	469	3.91	1	626	3.77	2	214	3.69	6	316	3.72	4	388	3.70	5
Appearance / comfort	471	3.93	1	649	3.91	2	215	3.71	6	325	3.82	4	399	3.80	5
Ambience (Physical Design)	479	3.99	1	647	3.90	3	227	3.91	2	329	3.87	4	388	3.70	6
Responsiveness of employee	530	4.42	1	716	4.31	2	229	3.95	6	356	4.19	5	449	4.28	3
Service reliability	496	4.13	1	648	3.90	4	220	3.79	6	335	3.94	2	406	3.87	5
Service quality	480	4.00	1	625	3.77	3	212	3.66	6	328	3.86	2	391	3.72	5
Location of restaurants	459	3.83	4	641	3.86	3	206	3.55	6	329	3.87	2	408	3.89	1

Source: Computed from Primary Data

The above table discusses about the diners level of satisfaction towards the service features of particular restaurant in Coimbatore city.

Vegetarian Restaurants

Majority of the respondents' exhibit high degree of satisfaction towards the service features such as service reliability, location, appearance/comfort, menu offered and service quality of RHR hotel. Similarly the Annapoorna customers' have stated that they are satisfied with the price and quality of food items offered in the hotel. Followed by, the diners are found to be satisfied with the ambience and decoration of Arya's hotel and Adyar Anandha

Bhavan customers' have stated that they are pleased with the responsiveness of employees in the hotel.

Non Vegetarian Restaurants

It is evident from the above table that, most of the sample populations' express high degree of satisfaction towards the services like responsiveness of employee, service reliability, ambience, price range, appearance/comfort and service quality of Rayappas's restaurant. Similarly the respondents' are found to be satisfied with the food quality of Sampoorna restaurant. Followed by, the sample populations' have said that they prefer Anjali for its location.

According to Steadman (1991) customers at dining restaurants want to be made to feel special. Service quality is a critical component of customers' value perceptions that, in turn, become a determinant of customer satisfaction. Drawing both theoretical and empirical evidences from the above statement, following hypothesis is framed to measure whether there exists any differences in the diners' satisfaction towards foods and restaurant service features between vegetarian and non-vegetarian restaurants.

H6: There exists differences in the diners' satisfaction towards foods and restaurant service features between vegetarian and non-vegetarian restaurants.

Table 4.68: Independent Z-test Diners' Satisfaction towards Foods and Restaurant Service Features between Vegetarian and Non-vegetarian Restaurants

Particulars	Preference towards Vegetarian and Non-Vegetarian Foods							
	Veg		Non-veg		Both		Z	Sig
	Mean	SD	Mean	SD	Mean	SD		
Menu offered	2.30	1.11	2.27	1.01	2.13	1.06	.439	.008
Food quality	2.22	1.18	2.16	1.11	2.02	1.05	1.072	.001
Price of food items	2.27	1.04	2.23	1.10	2.22	1.03	.347	.056
Appearance / comfort	2.21	.86	2.13	1.05	2.13	.98	5.414	.021
Ambience (Physical design)	2.20	1.03	2.17	.90	2.09	.94	3.814	.052
Responsiveness of employee	1.68	.85	1.54	.82	1.87	.91	.368	.045
Service reliability	2.06	.93	2.03	.93	2.08	.84	.039	.043
Service quality/ Service Timed Quality	2.31	1.17	2.34	1.22	2.06	1.10	.212	.046
Location of restaurants	2.12	1.03	2.37	1.07	2.11	1.00	1.503	.021

Level of Significance: 5 per cent

From the above cross-sectional data analysis it has been clearly identified that the Vegans' exhibit high degree of satisfaction towards the service features of selected restaurants in Coimbatore. It has been observed that vegetarians' are found to be satisfied with the ambience (physical design and appearance), price range, appearance / comfort, menu and quality of food offered in the popular restaurants. On the other hand, the non-vegans' are found to be satisfied with the location and service quality of the restaurants. Further it has been observed that the veg and non-veg diners express high satisfaction levels on the responsiveness and service reliability of the selected restaurants in Coimbatore.

From the above it has been inferred that the probability value of Z is found to be significant at five per cent level. Therefore the hypothesis framed stands accepted and it has been concluded that there exists differences in the diners' satisfaction towards foods and restaurant service features between vegetarian and non-vegetarian restaurants. However there exist differences in diners' satisfaction towards ambience, appearance and comfort between vegetarian and non-vegetarian restaurants.

Johns and Pine (2002) comment that the fundamental factors that contribute to customer satisfaction in restaurants include the food (hygiene, balance, and healthiness), physical provision (layout, furnishing, and cleanliness), the atmosphere (feeling and comfort), and the service received (speed, friendliness, and care) during the meal experience and this experiences may differ from one restaurant to other in same category or may differ from one category to other. To draw empirical justification to this earlier study in relevance to current situation prevailing in India, following hypothesis is framed and tested.

H7: There exist differences in the diners' satisfaction towards the service features of one restaurant in comparison to the other.

Table 4.69: Measure of Dispersion Diners' Satisfaction towards the Service Features of Annapoorna in Comparison to Other Vegetarian Restaurants

Satisfaction	Mean(Annapoorna: 3.928)	SD(Annnapoorna: .130)	R	MD	SDD	t	DF	Sig
Annapoorna Vs Anandha's	3.897	.202	.924	.031	.096	.972	8	.049
Annapoorna Vs Aryaa's	3.848	.138	.625	.080	.117	2.058	8	.034
Annapoorna Vs Adyar Anandha Bhavan	3.817	.258	.755	.111	.181	1.842	8	.003
Annapoorna Vs RHR	3.970	.160	.618	-.042	.129	-.978	8	.047

Level of significance: 5 per cent

(Note: MD-Mean Differences, SDD-Standard Deviation Differences)

From the above table it has inferred that probability values of t is found to be significant at 5 per cent level. Therefore the hypothesis framed stands accepted and it has been concluded that there exist differences in the diners' satisfaction towards the service features of Annapoorna restaurant in comparison to the others.

Table 4.70: Measure of Dispersion Diners' Satisfaction towards the Service Features of Anandha's in Comparison to Other Vegetarian Restaurants

Satisfaction	Mean(Anandha's: 3.897)	SD(Anandha's: .202)	R	MD	SDD	t	DF	Sig
Anandha's Vs Annapoorna	3.928	.130	.924	.031	.096	.972	8	.049
Anandha's Vs Aryaa's	3.848	.138	.655	.049	.153	.959	8	.046
Anandha's Vs Adyar Anandha Bhavan	3.817	.258	.827	.080	.145	1.651	8	.037
Anandha's Vs RHR	3.970	.160	.580	.073	.170	1.292	8	.032

Level of significance: 5 per cent

(Note: MD-Mean Differences, SDD-Standard Deviation Differences)

From the above table it has inferred that probability values of t is found to be significant at 5 per cent level. Therefore the hypothesis framed stands accepted and it has been concluded that there exist differences in the diners' satisfaction towards the service features of Anandha's restaurant in comparison to the others.

Table 4.71: Measure of Dispersion Diners' Satisfaction towards the Service Features of Aryaa's in Comparison to Other Vegetarian Restaurants

Satisfaction	Mean(Aryaa's: .848)	SD(Aryaa's: .138)	R	MD	SDD	t	DF	Sig
Aryaa's Vs Annapoorna	3.928	.130	.625	.080	.117	2.058	8	.034
Aryaa's Vs Anandha's	3.897	.202	.655	.049	.153	.959	8	.046
Aryaa's Vs Adyar Anandha Bhavan	3.817	.258	.414	.031	.237	.394	8	.004
Aryaa's Vs RHR	3.970	.160	.057	.122	.205	1.786	8	.012

Level of significance: 5 per cent

(Note: MD-Mean Differences, SDD-Standard Deviation Differences)

From the above table it has inferred that probability values of t is found to be significant at 5 per cent level. Therefore the hypothesis framed stands accepted and it has been concluded that there exist differences in the diners' satisfaction towards the service features of Aryaa's restaurant in comparison to the others.

Table 4.72: Measure of Dispersion Diners' Satisfaction towards the Service Features of Adyar Anandha Bhavan in Comparison to other Vegetarian Restaurants

Satisfaction	Mean(Adyar Anandha Bhavan:3.817)	SD(Adyar Anandha Bhavan: .258)	R	MD	SDD	t	DF	Sig
Adyar Anandha BhavanVs Annapoorna	3.928	.130	.755	.111	.181	1.842	8	.003
Adyar Anandha BhavanVs Anandha's	3.897	.202	.827	.080	.145	1.651	8	.037
Adyar Anandha BhavanVs Aryaa's	3.848	.138	.414	.031	.237	.394	8	.004
Adyar Anandha BhavanVs RHR	3.970	.160	.698	.153	.186	2.475	8	.008

Level of significance: 5 per cent

(Note: MD-Mean Differences, SDD-Standard Deviation Differences)

From the above table it has inferred that probability values of t is found to be significant at 5 per cent level. Therefore the hypothesis framed stands accepted and it has been concluded that there exist differences in the diners' satisfaction towards the service features of Adyar Anandha Bhavan restaurant in comparison to the others.

Table 4.73: Measure of Dispersion Diners' Satisfaction towards the Service Features of RHR in Comparison to other Vegetarian Restaurants

Satisfaction	Mean(RHR: 3.970)	SD(RHR: .160)	R	MD	SDD	t	DF	Sig
RHRVs Annapoorna	3.928	.130	.618	.042	.129	.978	8	.047
RHRVs Anandha's	3.897	.202	.580	.073	.170	1.292	8	.032
RHRVs Aryaa's	3.848	.138	.057	.122	.205	1.786	8	.012
RHRVs Adyar Anandha Bhavan	3.817	.258	.698	.153	.186	2.475	8	.008

Level of significance: 5 per cent

(Note: MD-Mean Differences, SDD-Standard Deviation Differences)

From the above table it has inferred that probability values of t is found to be significant at 5 per cent level. Therefore the hypothesis framed stands rejected and it has been concluded that there exist differences in the diners' satisfaction towards the service features of RHR restaurant in comparison to the others.

From the above Tables: 4.73-4.77, it has been found that the hypothesis framed stands accepted and it has been concluded that there exists differences in the diners' satisfaction towards the service features of one vegetarian restaurant in comparison to the other. The list of strength and weakness of five sample restaurants listed in the Table: 4.67 duly complement this statistical conclusion.

Table 4.74: Measure of Dispersion Diners' Satisfaction towards the Service Features of Rayappa's in Comparison to Other Non vegetarian Restaurants

Satisfaction	Mean(Rayappa's: 3.998)	SD(Rayappa's: .185)	R	MD	SDD	t	DF	Sig
Rayappa's Vs Sampoorna	3.906	.169	.858	.092	.095	2.897	8	.020
Rayappa's Vs Haribhavanam	3.767	.130	.547	.231	.157	4.408	8	.002
Rayappa's Vs Anjappar	3.879	.132	.912	.119	.084	4.244	8	.003
Rayappa's Vs Anjali	3.836	.182	.813	.162	.112	4.337	8	.002

Level of significance: 5 per cent

(Note: MD-Mean Differences, SDD-Standard Deviation Differences)

From the above table it has inferred that probability values of t is found to be significant at 5 per cent level. Therefore the hypothesis framed stands accepted and it has been concluded that there exist differences in the diners' satisfaction towards the service features of Rayappa's restaurant in comparison to the others.

Table 4.75: Measure of Dispersion Diners' Satisfaction towards the Service Features of Sampoorna in Comparison to Other Non Vegetarian Restaurants

Satisfaction	Mean(Sampoorna: 3.906)	SD(Sampoorna: .169)	R	MD	SDD	t	DF	Sig
Sampoorna Vs Rayappa's	3.998	.185	.858	.092	.095	2.897	8	.020
Sampoorna Vs Haribhavanam	3.767	.130	.518	.139	.151	2.768	8	.024
Sampoorna Vs Anjappar	3.879	.132	.913	.027	.072	1.107	8	.001
Sampoorna Vs Anjali	3.836	.182	.924	.070	.069	3.023	8	.016

Level of significance: 5 per cent

(Note: MD-Mean Differences, SDD-Standard Deviation Differences)

From the above table it has inferred that probability values of t is found to be significant at 5 per cent level. Therefore the hypothesis framed stands accepted and it has been concluded that there exist differences in the diners' satisfaction towards the service features of Sampoorna restaurant in comparison to the others.

Table 4.76: Measure of Dispersion Diners' Satisfaction towards the Service Features of Haribhavanam in Comparison to Other Non Vegetarian Restaurants

Satisfaction	Mean(Haribhavanam: 3.767)	SD(Haribhavanam: .130)	R	MD	SDD	t	DF	Sig
Haribhavanam Vs Rayappa's	3.998	.185	.547	.231	.157	4.408	8	.002
Haribhavanam Vs Sampoorna	3.906	.169	.518	.139	.151	2.768	8	.024
Haribhavanam Vs Anjappar	3.879	.132	.477	.112	.134	2.511	8	.036
Haribhavanam Vs Anjali	3.836	.182	.338	.069	.184	1.122	8	.004
Haribhavanam Vs Others	3.866	.156	.703	.099	.113	2.631	8	.030

Level of significance: 5 per cent

(Note: MD-Mean Differences, SDD-Standard Deviation Differences)

From the above table it has inferred that probability values of t is found to be significant at 5 per cent level. Therefore the hypothesis framed stands accepted and it has been concluded that there exist differences in the diners' satisfaction towards the service features of Haribhavanam restaurant in comparison to the others.

Table 4.77: Measure of Dispersion Diners' Satisfaction towards the Service Features of Anjappar in Comparison to Other Non Vegetarian Restaurants

Satisfaction	Mean(Anjappar: 3.879)	SD(Anjappar: .132)	R	MD	SDD	t	DF	Sig
Anjappar Vs Rayappa's	3.998	.185	.912	.119	.084	4.244	8	.003
Anjappar Vs Sampoorna	3.906	.169	.913	.027	.072	1.107	8	.001
Anjappar Vs Haribhavanam	3.767	.130	.477	.112	.134	2.511	8	.036
Anjappar Vs Anjali	3.836	.182	.923	.043	.078	1.658	8	.036

Level of significance: 5 per cent

(Note: MD-Mean Differences, SDD-Standard Deviation Differences)

From the above table it has inferred that probability values of t is not found to be significant at 5 per cent level. Therefore the hypothesis framed stands rejected and it has been concluded that there exist no differences in the diners' satisfaction towards the service features of Anjappar restaurant in comparison to the others.

Table 4.78: Measure of Dispersion Diners' Satisfaction towards the Service Features of Anjali in Comparison to other Non Vegetarian Restaurants

Satisfaction	Mean(Anjali: .836)	SD(Anjali: .182)	R	MD	SDD	t	DF	Sig
Anjali Vs Rayappa's	3.998	.185	.813	.162	.112	4.337	8	.002
Anjali Vs Sampoorna	3.906	.169	.924	.070	.069	3.023	8	.016
Anjali Vs Haribhavanam	3.767	.130	.338	.069	.184	1.122	8	.004
Anjali Vs Anjappar	3.879	.132	.923	.043	.078	1.658	8	.036

Level of significance: 5 per cent

(Note: MD-Mean Differences, SDD-Standard Deviation Differences)

From the above table it has inferred that probability values of t is not found to be significant at 5 per cent level. Therefore the hypothesis framed stands rejected and it has been concluded that there exist no differences in the diners' satisfaction towards the service features of Anjali restaurant in comparison to the others. From the above Tables: 4.78 To 4.82, it has been found that the hypothesis framed stands accepted and it has been concluded that, there exist differences in the diners' satisfaction towards the service features of one non-vegetarian restaurant in comparison to the other.

Thus from the above table Tables: 4.73 to 4.82 it has been concluded that there exist differences in the diners' satisfaction towards the service features of one restaurant in comparison to the other. The list of strength and weakness of five sample restaurants listed in the Table: 4.67 duly complement this statistical conclusion.

The restaurant industry is one of the most competitive industries in the world. As the restaurant industry continues to expand, the issue of service quality has received increasingly more attention. Providing and maintaining customer satisfaction is one of the biggest challenges of management in restaurant industries. In order to provide a constructive suggestion in this regards to the various casual dine restaurants operating in the Coimbatore city, following hypothetical test is performed to assess whether there exist any differences in diners perception and satisfaction towards restaurant services.

H8: There exist no differences in diners perception and satisfaction towards restaurant services.

Table 4.79: Measures of Dispersion Diners Perception and Satisfaction towards Vegetarian Restaurant Services

Variables	Perception		Satisfaction		Correlation
	Mean	SD	Mean	SD	
Menu Offered	3.877	.055	3.814	.086	.172
Food Quality	3.941	.051	3.874	.102	.162
Price of Food Items	3.861	.054	3.748	.131	.210
Appearance / Comfort	3.842	.043	3.836	.188	.384
Ambience (Physical Design)	3.935	.067	3.864	.125	-.543
Responsiveness of Employee	3.809	.082	4.264	.134	-.107
Service Reliability	3.899	.079	3.962	.156	.918
Service Quality	3.861	.046	3.832	.094	-.422
Location of Restaurants	3.771	.060	3.832	.090	-.388

Level of significance: 5 per cent

From the above table it has been observed that the diners had high expectations towards the services of selected vegetarian restaurants. However, the vegetarian restaurants failed to satisfy the diners' needs which are reflected on the above results. The results of correlation co-efficient reveal that there exists negative association between the diners' perception and satisfaction towards the vegetarian restaurant services.

Table 4.80: Result of Paired T Test Diners Perception and Satisfaction towards Vegetarian Restaurant Services

Perception Vs Satisfaction	Mean	SD	t	DF	Sig
Menu offered	.063	.093	1.502	4	.208
Food quality	.067	.107	1.409	4	.232
Price of food items	.113	.131	1.925	4	.127
Appearance / comfort	.006	.176	.071	4	.947
Ambience (Physical Design)	.071	.171	.922	4	.409
Responsiveness of employee	-.455	.164	-6.192	4	.003
Service reliability	-.063	.089	-1.586	4	.188
Service quality	.029	.121	.542	4	.617
Location of restaurants	-.061	.126	-1.075	4	.343

Level of significance: 5 per cent

From the above table it has inferred that probability value of 't' is not found to be significant at 5 per cent level of significance. Therefore the hypothesis framed stands rejected and it has been concluded that there exist differences in diners perception and satisfaction towards vegetarian restaurant services. However it is exceptional in the case of responsiveness of employee in the vegetarian restaurants.

Table 4.81: Measures of Dispersion Diners Perception and Satisfaction towards

Non-Vegetarian Restaurant Services

Variables	Perception		Satisfaction		Correlation
	Mean	SD	Mean	SD	
Menu offered	3.866	.073	3.792	.057	-.228
Food quality	3.914	.079	3.876	.089	-.689
Price of food items	3.840	.105	3.758	.090	-.806
Appearance / comfort	3.839	.059	3.834	.089	-.527
Ambience (Physical Design)	3.923	.111	3.874	.107	-.789
Responsiveness of employee	3.789	.096	4.230	.177	-.980
Service reliability	3.879	.107	3.926	.127	-.861
Service quality	3.854	.125	3.802	.133	-.928
Location of restaurants	3.780	.059	3.800	.141	-.321

Level of significance: 5 per cent

The data presented in the above table indicates that the diners express low satisfaction levels on the services offered by the selected non-vegetarian. The results of correlation co-efficient reveal that there exists negative association between the diners' perception and satisfaction towards the non-vegetarian restaurant services.

Table 4.82: Result of Paired T Test Diners Perception and Satisfaction towards

Non-vegetarian Restaurant Services

Perception Vs Satisfaction	Mean	SD	t	DF	Sig
Menu offered	.074	.082	2.028	4	.112
Food quality	.038	.067	1.271	4	.273
Price of food items	.082	.062	2.939	4	.042
Appearance / comfort	.005	.077	.152	4	.887
Ambience (Physical Design)	.049	.071	1.550	4	.196
Responsiveness of employee	-.441	.085	-11.624	4	.000
Service reliability	-.047	.064	-1.641	4	.176
Service quality	.052	.050	2.348	4	.079
Location of restaurants	-.020	.135	-.332	4	.756

Level of significance: 5 per cent

From the above table it has inferred that probability value of 't' is not found to be significant at 5 per cent level of significance. Therefore the hypothesis framed stands rejected and it has been concluded that there exist differences in diners' perception and satisfaction towards non-vegetarian restaurant services. However it is exceptional in the case of price of food items and responsiveness of employee in the non-vegetarian restaurants.

From the above Tables: 4.1-4.4 it has been concluded that there exist differences in diners perception and satisfaction towards restaurant services. The study has observed that diners expectation towards food menu offered, food quality, price of food items, appearance/

comfort level inside the restaurants and restaurant ambience (physical design) has not meet efficiently by the restaurant managers and operators in Coimbatore city. Factor analysis technique has been applied to find the underlying dimension (factors) that exists among 9 variables relating to identify the diners' satisfaction towards the service features of vegetarian restaurants and their preferences towards particular restaurant.

Table 4.83: KMO and Bartlett's Test Diners' Satisfaction towards the Service Features of Vegetarian Restaurants

Kaiser-Meyer-Olkin Measure of Sampling Adequacy	.794
Bartlett's Test of Sphericity Approx. Chi-Square	142.524
DF	36
Sig	.000

Level of Significance: 5 per cent

In the present study, Kaiser-Meyer-Oklin (KMO) Measure of Sampling Adequacy (MSA) and Bartlett's test of Sphericity were applied to verify the adequacy or appropriateness of data for factor analysis. In this study, the value of KMO for overall matrix was found to be excellent (0.794) and Bartlett's test of Sphericity was highly significant ($p<0.05$). Bartlett's Sphericity test was effective, as the chi-square value draws significance at five per cent level. The results thus indicated that the sample taken was appropriate to proceed with a factor analysis procedure. Besides the Bartlett's Test of Sphericity and the KMO Measure of sampling Adequacy, Communality values of all variables were also observed.

Table 4.84: Cumulative Diners' Satisfaction towards the Service Features of Vegetarian Restaurants

Variables	Initial	Extraction
Menu offered	1.000	.630
Food quality	1.000	.723
Price of food items	1.000	.875
Appearance / comfort	1.000	.764
Ambience	1.000	.700
Responsiveness of employee	1.000	.957
Service reliability	1.000	.895
Service Quality/ Service Timed Quality	1.000	.709
Location of restaurants	1.000	.780

In order to provide a more parsimonious interpretation of the results, 9-item scale was then Factor analyzed using the Principal Component method with Equamax rotation.

Factor analysis attempts to identify underlying variables, or factors, that explain the pattern of correlations within a set of observed variables. Factor analysis is often used in data reduction to identify a small number of factors that explain most of the variance observed in a much larger number of manifest variables. In the current study rotation factor analysis is performed to measure the diners' satisfaction towards the service features of vegetarian restaurants and their preferences towards particular restaurant. The significance of relationship between the variables is depicted in the following table

Table 4.85: Rotated Component Matrix Diners' Satisfaction towards the Service Features of Vegetarian Restaurants

Factors	Vegetarian Restaurants				
	Annapoorna	Anandha's	Aryaa's	Adyar Anandha Bhavan	RHR
X_1-Menu offered	-	.541	-	-	-
X_2-Food quality	-	.745	-	-	-
X_3-Price of food items	-	-	-	-	.913
X_4-Appearance / comfort	-	.778	-	-	-
X_5-Ambience	.722	-	-	-	-
X_6- Responsiveness of employee	-	-	-	.965	-
X_7-Service reliability	-	-	.896	-	-
X_8-Service Quality/ Service Timed Quality	.666	-	-	-	-
X_9-Location of restaurants	.580	-	.582	-	-
Eigen value	1.640	1.535	1.507	1.182	1.169
% of Variance	18.227	17.060	16.743	13.132	12.994
Cumulative%	18.227	35.286	52.029	65.161	78.155

Level of Significance: 5 per cent

Five factors extracted together account for 78.155 percent of the total variance (information contained in the original 9 variables). This is good, because the researcher are able to economize on the number of variables (from 9 researcher have reduced them to five underlying factors), while the data lost only about 21.845 percent of the information content (78.155 percent is retained by the five factors extracted out of the 9 original variables). Since the idea of factor analysis is to identify the factors that meaningfully summarize the sets of closely related variables, the rotation phase of the factor analysis attempts to transfer initial matrix into one that is easier to interpret. Equamax rotation method is used to extract meaningful factors.

Five factors were identified as being maximum percentage variance accounted. The variables X_5, X_8 and X_9 are grouped as factor I and it accounts for 18.227 per cent of the total variance. The variables X_1, X_2 and X_4 constitute the factor II and it accounts for 17.060 per cent of the total variance. The variable X_7 and X_9 is grouped as factor III and it accounts for 16.743 per cent of the total variance. The variable X_6 is grouped as factor IV and it accounts for 13.132 per cent of the total variance. The variables X_3 constitute the factor V and it accounts for 12.994 per cent of the total variance.

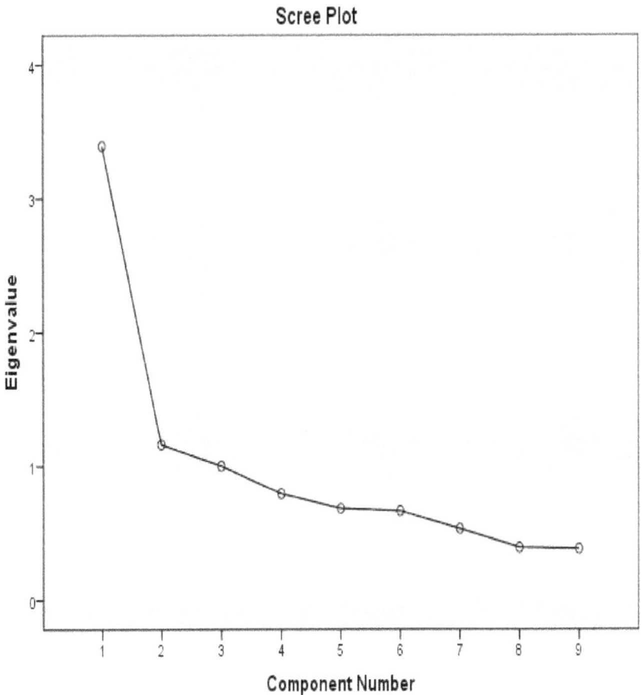

Exhibit 4.14: Scree Plot Diners' Satisfaction towards the Service Features of Vegetarian Restaurants

Table 4.86: Summary of Rotation Factor Analysis & Cronbach's Alpha Diners' Satisfaction towards the Service Features of Vegetarian Restaurants

Factors	Factor Interpretation	Variables included in the factors	Cronbach's Alpha
F_1	Annapoorna	Ambience, service quality/ service timed quality and location of restaurants.	.793
F_2	Anandha's	Menu offered, food quality and appearance / comfort.	.787
F_3	Aryaa's	Service reliability and location of restaurants	.618
F_4	Adyar Anandha Bhavan	Responsiveness of employee	.595
F_5	RHR	Price of food items	.520

Source: Computed From Primary Data

Factor analysis was used to find out the diners' level of satisfaction towards the service features of vegetarian restaurants and their preferences towards particular restaurant. The Cronbach's reliability values (.793, .787, .618, .595 and .520) indicate significant correlation between the variables tested.

Factor analysis technique has been applied to find the underlying dimension (factors) that exists among9 variables relating to identify the diners' satisfaction towards the service features of non-vegetarian restaurants and their preferences towards particular restaurant.

Table 4.87: KMO and Bartlett's Test Diners' Satisfaction towards the Service Features of Non-vegetarian Restaurants

Kaiser-Meyer-Olkin Measure of Sampling Adequacy	.761
Bartlett's Test of Sphericity Approx. Chi-Square	203.149
DF	36
Sig	.000

Level of Significance: 5 per cent

In the present study, Kaiser-Meyer-Oklin (KMO) Measure of Sampling Adequacy (MSA) and Bartlett's test of Sphericity were applied to verify the adequacy or appropriateness of data for factor analysis. In this study, the value of KMO for overall matrix was found to be excellent (0.761) and Bartlett's test of Sphericity was highly significant (p<0.05). Bartlett's Sphericity test was effective, as the chi-square value draws significance at five per cent level. The results thus indicated that the sample taken was appropriate to proceed with a factor analysis procedure. Besides the Bartlett's Test of Sphericity and the KMO Measure of sampling Adequacy, Communality values of all variables were also observed.

Table 4.88: Cumulative Diners' Satisfaction towards the Service Features of Non-vegetarian Restaurants

Variables	Initial	Extraction
Menu offered	1.000	.594
Food quality	1.000	.731
Price of food items	1.000	.755
Appearance/comfort	1.000	.829
Ambience	1.000	.732
Responsiveness of employee	1.000	.751
Service reliability	1.000	.806
Service Quality/Service Timed Quality	1.000	.765
Location of restaurants	1.000	.889

In order to provide a more parsimonious interpretation of the results, 9-item scale was then Factor analyzed using the Principal Component method with Equamax rotation.

Factor analysis attempts to identify underlying variables, or factors, that explain the pattern of correlations within a set of observed variables. Factor analysis is often used in data reduction to identify a small number of factors that explain most of the variance observed in a much larger number of manifest variables. In the current study rotation factor analysis is performed to measure the diners' satisfaction towards the service features of non-vegetarian restaurants and their preferences towards particular restaurant. The significance of relationship between the variables is depicted in the following table

Table 4.89: Rotated Component Matrix Diners' Satisfaction towards the Service Features of Non-vegetarian Restaurants

Factors	Non-vegetarian Restaurants				
	Rayappa's	Sampoorna	Haribhavanam	Anjappar	Anjali
X_1-Menu offered	-	.606	-	-	-
X_2-Food quality	.755	-	-	-	-
X_3-Price of food items	.818	-	-	-	-
X_4-Appearance/ comfort	-	-	-	-	.891
X_5-Ambience	-	.599	.533	-	-
X_6-Responsiveness of employee	-	.747	-	-	-
X_7-Service reliability	-	-	-	.863	-
X_8-Service Quality/ Service Timed Quality	-	-	-	.556	-
X_9-Location of restaurants	-	-	.926	-	-
Eigen value	1.464	1.408	1.365	1.319	1.297
% of Variance	16.272	15.641	15.164	14.652	14.412
Cumulative%	16.272	31.913	47.077	61.728	76.140

Level of Significance: 5 per cent

Five factors extracted together account for 76.140 percent of the total variance (information contained in the original 9 variables). This is good, because the researcher are able to economize on the number of variables (from 46 researcher have reduced them to five underlying factors), while the data lost only about 23.860 percent of the information content (76.140 percent is retained by the five factors extracted out of the 9 original variables). Since the idea of factor analysis is to identify the factors that meaningfully summarize the sets of closely related variables, the rotation phase of the factor analysis attempts to transfer initial matrix into one that is easier to interpret. Equamax rotation method is used to extract meaningful factors.

Five factors were identified as being maximum percentage variance accounted. The variables X_2 and X_3 are grouped as factor I and it accounts for 16.272 per cent of the total variance. The variables X_1, X_5 and X_6 constitute the factor II and it accounts for 15.641 per cent of the total variance. The variables X_5 and X_9 are grouped as factor III and it accounts for 15.164 per cent of the total variance. The variables X_7 and X_8 are grouped as factor IV and it accounts for 14.652 per cent of the total variance. The variable X_4 constitute the factor V and it accounts for 14.412 per cent of the total variance.

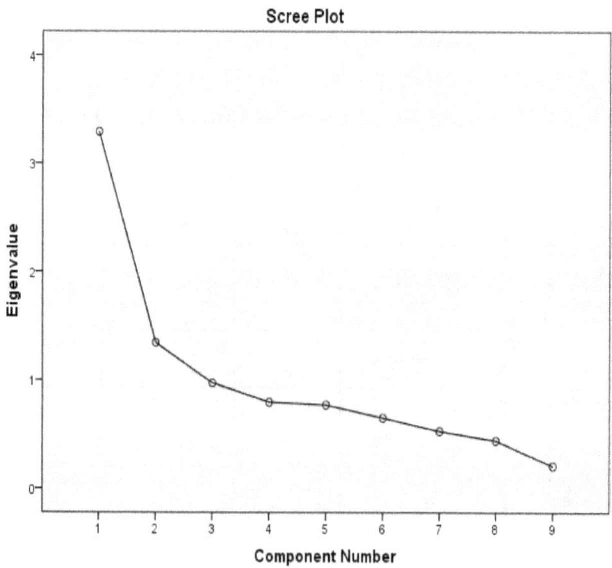

Exhibit 4.15: Scree Plot Diners' Satisfaction towards the Service Features of Non-vegetarian Restaurants

Table 4.90: Summary of Rotation Factor Analysis & Cronbach's Alpha Diners' Satisfaction towards the Service Features of Non-vegetarian Restaurants

Factors	Factor Interpretation	Variables included in the factors	Cronbach's Alpha
F_1	Rayappa's	Food quality and price of food items.	.793
F_2	Sampoorna	Menu offered, ambience and responsiveness of employee.	.787
F_3	Haribhavanam	Ambience and location of restaurants	.618
F_4	Anjappar	Service reliability and service quality/ service timed quality.	.595
F_5	Anjali	Appearance / comfort	.520

Source: Computed From Primary Data

Factor analysis was used to find out the diners' level of satisfaction towards the service features of non-vegetarian restaurants and their preferences towards particular restaurant. The Cronbach's reliability values (.793, .787, .618, .595 and .520) indicate significant correlation between the variables tested.

4.2. Conclusion

From the empirical data analysis it has been observed that, 58 per cent of diners are employees working in various public and private organizations and most of the respondents' earn between `.10001 to `.20000 per month. It has been observed that majority of the diners' prefer to eat both vegetarian and non-vegetarian food items at the time visiting popular restaurants. It has been found that the respondents' prefer to visit restaurants mostly on special occasions and like to visit with their family members & friends to have a pleasant dining experience. When coming to the restaurant selection, majority of the diners' in Coimbatore city prefer to visit Annapoorna and Sampoorna restaurant for its delicious taste. It has been inferred that most of the sample populations' do not fix budgets before visiting restaurants.

From the detailed data discussion it has been found that 79.09 per cent of the respondents' believe that popular restaurant ensure enable that they offer good food, innovative dishes, delicious& taste food with reasonable price, pleasant ambience, lighting decorations, attentiveness of servers, 7x7 days working and promptness in delivery, so they like to visit restaurants rather than ordinary hotels. Further it has been observed that most of the sample subjects' exhibit high degree of satisfaction towards the responsiveness of employees in popular vegetarian and non-vegetarian restaurants.

However the diners' perceptions and satisfaction levels differ after visiting those vegetarian and non-vegetarian restaurants. Thus it has been clearly understood that the service quality of popular restaurants are not up to the standards and they deceive their customers' by giving fake promotions.

CHAPTER V

SUMMARY, FINDINGS, SUGGESTION AND CONCLUSION

The final and fifth chapter of this elaborate empirical study aims to present a brief summary of the statement of the problem, the purpose of the study and methodology used in the investigation, the findings, suggestion proposed by the researcher and conclusion are presented.

5.1. Summary of the Study

Restaurants play a significant role in modern lifestyle, and dining out is a favourite social activity. Everyone like to eat, so, to enjoy good food and perhaps unique taste in the company of friends and in pleasant surroundings is one of life's buyout pleasures. Eating out has become a way of life for families these days. Today, more meals potential than ever are being eaten away from home.India is in the midst of the restaurant revolution. Individual dine in restaurants for different reasons and the casual dining customer has many choices when diningout in restaurants i.e., in selection of restaurants for dining. Thus, it can be rightly claimed that restaurateurs are increasingly concerned with satisfying customers. To draw empirical confirmation to the above discussions this study aims to analyse diners' preference towards restaurant services in Coimbatore City.

The study has addressed the issues of analysing diners' preference towards restaurant services with a well-defined five objectives. They are: to study the demographic and socio-economic habits of restaurant diners in Coimbatore city, to analyse the food consumption habits of Coimbatorians and the factors that determine the restaurant selection by the diners, to measure diners' level of perception towards prominent restaurants located at Coimbatore city, to measure level of satisfaction experienced by the diners' in the prominent restaurants and to evaluate the prevailing gap between diners' level of perception and satisfaction derived by them.

The current study is both explorative and descriptive in nature. Explorative research form part of desk work carried for collection of review of literature. Through detailed secondary data search on: food consumption, influences of demographic variables on restaurant service selections, consumers' perceptions and satisfaction towards restaurant service were collected and summarised. The collected review of literature forms the basis for preparing the structured questionnaire to the next stage of the research. The second stage of the research was descriptive in nature, conducted by applying a survey method i.e., fact finding investigation with adequate interpretations. Structured questionnaire was framed consisting of five segments comprising, complete details about the socio-economic profile of the restaurant diners, their dining preference, motivating factors for dining practices, their level of perception and satisfaction towards restaurant service of restaurants located at Coimbatore city.

The current study is mainly concentrated on the leading restaurants located at Coimbatore city. It is the third largest city of Tamil Nadu. There are 214 restaurants (bakery, café and desserts, casual dining, desserts parlour, quick eat, fast food, fine dine and others) currently operating in Coimbatore city. Current study is purely focused on the 158 casual dine restaurants currently functioning in the city. At the beginning of data collection a pilot survey was conducted among the sample population with two objectives. One to identify the most popular and frequently visited casual dine restaurants by the households in Coimbatore city and second, purpose was to test the feasibility and adoptability of the questionnaire framed. Based the pilot survey results five vegetarian and non-vegetarian restaurants were identified, that where more preferred by the Coimbatorians. An option of "others" was provided to gather information about other most preferred and visited casual dine restaurants. Samples of five vegetarian and non-vegetarian hotels were selected for the effective conduct of the study. The most popular and prominent vegetarian restaurants were chosen for study: Annapoorna's, Anandha's, Aryaa's, Adyar Anandha Bhavan, RHR and others. Five most popular and prominent non-vegetarian restaurants were chosen for study: Rayappa's, Sampoorna, Haribhavanam, Anjappar, Anjaliand others. A sample of sixty (60) diners where chose in each category of hotels, since researcher found it very difficult in identification of restaurant diners and collection of data were restricted on 60 diners from each sample restaurants was summed to 600 samples subjects. Both primary and secondary data were used for the effective conduct of this study. According to Orme. B (2010) [1]sample size for conjoint studies generally can ranges from about 150 to 1,200 respondents and it largely depends on the purpose of research. The author also claims that for investigational work and developing hypotheses about a market, between thirty and sixty respondents may be sufficient. Based on this concept, the sampling framework of the study is constructed.

---

[1]Orme, B. (2010) Getting Started with Conjoint Analysis: Strategies for Product Design and Pricing Research. Second Edition, Madison, Wis.: Research Publishers LLC

5.2. Major Findings of the Study

Major findings of the study are summarized below.

Life Style Profile of Customers

- Majority i.e., 51.40 per cent of dinners' in Coimbatore city are female and the study findings indicates that majority of diners surveyed are young fall within the age grouping of 20 years or less than that to 30-40 years of age i.e., 70.16 per cent. Further, it has been observed that35.33 per cent of respondents' have gained either Degree or Diploma degrees as their highest level of educational qualification.

- It has been inferred that 58 per cent of respondents' live in nuclear families consisting of a pair of adults with their children and 29per cent of the respondents' surveyed are employees working in various public and private organizations.

- From the elaborate data discussion it has been found that 33.17 per cent of sample subjects' monthly income ranges between `.10001 to `.20000.

- The study observed that majority of the respondents surveyed are married i.e., 63.33 per cent and only 36.67 per cent were found to either bachelors or spinsters or singles. Further, it was observed that 43.83 per cent of respondents' family size constitutes of four members and 37.50 per cent of respondents' have said that both husband and wife are earning for the family.

- From the results of ANOVA test it has been concluded that the diners' choice of the vegetarian restaurant is purely influenced by their demographic and socio-economic status.

- With the conduct of ANOVA test it has been revealed that the diners' choice of the non-vegetarian restaurant is purely influenced by their demographic and socio-economic status.

Dinners' Opinion on Food Consumption Habits (Eating at Outlets)

- From the elaborate data discussion it has been observed that majority i.e., 50.67 per cent of dinners' prefers to eat both vegetarian and non-vegetarian food items while visiting popular restaurants.

- Similarly 41.33 per cent of respondents' prefer to visit restaurants during special occasions and 41 per cent of sample populations' like to visit restaurants with both family members & friends to have a pleasant dinning.

- It has been inferred that 35 per cent of dinners' in Coimbatore city often visit Annapoorna hotel for its delicious taste and29.83 per cent of respondents' prefer to visit Sampoorna hotel for having non-vegetarian dishes.

- From the elaborate data discussion it has been found that 36 per cent of respondents' have said that they visit restaurants at any time as per their wish and 35.67 per cent of sample subjects' like to dine in restaurants at late evenings to have a pleasant dinner.

- It is evident from the empirical data analysis that majority i.e., 51.70 per cent of sample populations' does not fix budgets before visiting restaurants.

- The study has observed that diners were influences by restaurant features like: the food quality, menu varieties, price and value for money, least waiting time and prompt services.

- The results of ANOVA test reveal that there exists close association between food consumption habits of the diners' and factors that motivated them to visit restaurants.

Dinners Level of Perception and Satisfaction towards Restaurant Service

- The study has concluded that the diners give more preferences and have high perception towards food themes presented in the menu, the type of food varieties listed in the menu and major signature dishes offered by the restaurants.

- It has been clearly identified that most of the sample populations' have said that they are influenced by the delicious taste of dishes served in the restaurant, its food presentation manner and portion of food served.

- The study identified that identified that most of the respondents' prefer those restaurants that offer economic priced food services, suit to their budget and priced competitively.

- The study claim that majority of the diners in Coimbatore are attracted by the both exterior and interior appearance and theme of specific restaurant. Moreover, the study it has been concluded that most of the diners are attracted by the lightings and cleanliness of particular restaurant.

- It has been found that majority of the diners are inspired by the attentiveness of servers, their co-operation with the diners and servers knowledge about the menu.

- The dinners' in Coimbatore city have said that specific restaurant delivers exactly what they ordered the first time and they are impressed by ordered the first time and food are served fresh.

- The study observed that majority respondents have agreed that they prefer to dine in those restaurants that are opened for all 7x7 days, it has unique service style and long hour of operations i.e., opening.

- The study observed that majority of the diners prefer to visit those restaurant (s) that has proximity in its location i.e., nearby their residence or work place and it is convenient for them to access easily to those restaurant(s) as it is very much visible to traveller and paddlers.

- From the empirical results of Independent 'Z' test it has been it is concluded that there exists differences in the diners' preference towards foods and restaurant service features between vegetarian and non-vegetarian restaurants.

- The results of Paired 'Z' test indicates that there exist differences in the diners' perception towards the service features of one restaurant in comparison to the other.

- The study declared that majority of the sample subjects' exhibit high degree of satisfaction towards the responsiveness of employees i.e., employees react fast to customers' wishes and helping them willingly, their service reliability (Keeping a promise which means that the service is accurate and provided at correct time without making any mistakes. Billing and records are recorded accurate and kept correct) and food quality.

- With the conduct of Independent 'Z' test it has been concluded that there exists differences in the diners' satisfaction towards foods and restaurant service features between vegetarian and non-vegetarian restaurants.

- From the empirical results of Paired 't' test it has been found that there exist differences in the diners' satisfaction towards the service features of one restaurant in comparison to the other.

- From the empirical results of Paired 't' test it has been concluded that there exist differences in diners perception and satisfaction towards restaurant services. The study has observed that diners expectation towards food menu offered, food quality, price of food items, appearance/comfort level inside the restaurants and restaurant ambience (physical design) has not meet efficiently by the restaurant managers and operators in Coimbatore city.

5.3.   Suggestion

The study has observed that diners expectation towards food menu offered, food quality, price of food items, appearance/comfort level inside the restaurants and restaurant ambience (physical design) has not meet efficiently by the restaurant managers and operators in Coimbatore city. Based on this findings following suggestions are proposed.

Focus on Food Menu, Design and Inclusion of Signature Dishes etc.

- Food menu is the index and face identity of a restaurant services. The study has identified that many popular restaurants in Coimbatore like: Annapoorna, Shree Anandha's, A2B, Arya's, Rayappa's, Sampoorna, Haribhavanam and Anjappar does not draft any strategies for defining their menu theme. Thus, it is suggested to these restaurant owners to focus on menu design. For, example the Annapoorna though functioning in Coimbatore since 1968, it do not have a well-designed menu or in fact menu card is not offered to its customers.

- Moreover, in today's competitive business environments, well design of menu card are very important to communicate to the customers about various cuisines and food of various culture serviced in a restaurant.

- Highlighting the signature dishes in menu and those food items referred by Chief or celebrities can offer competitive advantage in attracting the customers.

- The restaurant managers and owners should realise the fact that when most people choose to eat in their restaurant (or order takeout), they are looking for new and unique culinary experiences. With that in mind, they are suggested to refresh their menu at least seasonally to give their guests a flavour that may be a bit different than what they are already accustomed to ordering in a particular restaurant.

- Restaurant managers are suggested for new menu introductions as it supports in restaurant's marketing and promotions.

Focus on Food Quality

- Food quality is one of the major factors in determining a restaurant's success. This study has focused on the five elements of food quality i.e., taste, presentation, food portion served, consistency in food taste and focus on health aspects. It is suggested to the various vegetarian and non-vegetarian restaurateurs, manager and others to focus on food quality.

  - In modern day life-style many people (both male and females) do not have time to cook at home or taste/make variety of dishes at home due to want of time. Restaurants are the last resort for these potential foodies and diner. Thus, it is the duty at time opportunities for restaurateurs to service taste and variety of food to attract more customers.

- It is the more responsibility of the restaurateurs to ensure that the foods served by them are healthy to the consumers who dine in their restaurants. As it supports in retaining the customers and also expecting them to frequency visit the restaurants either for dining or order take-away home foods.

- The restaurateurs are also suggested to offer variety and taste differences in food items served by them, but by maintaining the consistency of food taste. As many diners claim that they do not find any differences in food taste of North Indian food served at many non-vegetarian restaurants like: Rayappa's, Sampoorna, Haribhavanam, Anjappar or Anjali though it is served in different names.

Focus on Redesigning Appearance/ Comfort Level inside the Restaurants and Restaurant Ambience (Physical Design)

A successful restaurant has an environment that matches the food it is serving and the customers it attracts. Based on study findings it is suggested:

- To Annapoorna and Haribhavanam have to focus on redesigning its building structure, restaurant layout both inside and outside according to modern tend to ensure that their restaurant ambience feature offers a cozy and comfortable feel to its diners. The exterior appearance and theme, interior appearance and theme, atmosphere, cleanliness, air condition quality, lighting quality in the restaurant have to be enhanced.

- The study has also observed that Haribhavanam, Anjappar and Sampoorna lack skills in maintaining their restaurant clean and Hygiene. Thus, they are suggested to ensure utmost cleanliness, hygiene and oudur free environment to their regular and future diners.

Ensure value for Money (Price of Food Items)

The study has observed that majority of the sample respondents surveyed are very price conscious and their always seek value for every rupee spend by them. It is reality that due to outbreak of global economic crisis and mounting of inflation common have started cutting down all his/her unwanted expenses including dining at restaurants, this in situation it is suggested to the casual dine restaurant owners and managers to focus on:

- Pricing their menu card according to the pocket size of the consumers, i.e., the restauranteur have to reduce the price s of various food they offer, this in turn can support in more walk-in diners and results in maximisation of revenues for the restaurants.

- To overcome the prevailing issues of customer dissatisfaction with high price menus, the restauranteur are suggested to introduce innovative foods, where fewer Ingredients can be used so the price hike can be control at the same time customers can be treated to their utmost satisfactions.

v. Innovative Marketing Practices to Experience the feel of Casual Dining

While, it is true that with more Middle class Indian consumers are patronising causal dine restaurants; it is the true to claim that restaurant sector is experiencing a high evolution in the country, But still the casual dine restaurant practices are still in nascent stage as far as India is considered. The study has found that41.33 per cent of respondents' prefer to visit restaurants during special occasions. Thus it is suggested to the restaurant manager and entrepreneurs to offer an innovative service, but at the same time very much a casual dining feel to the customers i.e., the diners that support in frequent visit to the restaurant.

- By way of implementation of new technologies: like offering a wi-fi zones, where a diner can dine at the same time can manage his/her personal or official works.
- Changing the menu very frequency and spreading its information through newspaper, hoardings and food blogs on net.
- Price moderation with the small quantity of food services. This will help in attracting youth and young population who have limited spending capacities.

5.4.   Conclusion

In India casual dining establishments provides full table service that is more upscale than fast-casual restaurants, but also more affordable than fine dining restaurants. They appeal to a wide customer base and are usually family-friendly. Industrial experts predict that his casual dining restaurants, which are worth $430 million will continue to grow even in 2016. This empirical study finding reveals that It has been observed that majority of the diners' prefer to eat both vegetarian and non-vegetarian food items at the time visiting popular restaurants. It has been found that the respondents' prefer to visit restaurants mostly on special occasions and like to visit with their family members & friends to have a pleasant dining experience. When coming to the restaurant selection, majority of the diners' in Coimbatore city prefer to visit Annapoorna and Sampoorna restaurant for its delicious taste. It has been inferred that most of the sample populations' do not fix budgets before visiting restaurants.

From the detailed data discussion it has been found that 79.09 per cent of the respondents' believe that popular restaurant ensure enable that they offer good food, innovative dishes, delicious& taste food with reasonable price, pleasant ambience, lighting decorations, attentiveness of servers, 7x7 days working and promptness in delivery, so they like to visit restaurants rather than ordinary hotels. Further it has been observed that most of the sample subjects' exhibit high degree of satisfaction towards the responsiveness of employees in popular vegetarian and non-vegetarian restaurants. However the diners' perceptions and satisfaction levels differ after visiting those vegetarian and non-vegetarian restaurants. Thus it has been clearly understood that the service quality of popular restaurants are not up to the standards and they deceive their customers' by giving fake promotions.

The study concludes by stating that restaurant customers today seek the thrill of deriving maximum pleasure for their taste-buds. Restaurants the market size of fine dine and casual dine model of Food and Beverages sector entirely depends upon the location. Fine dine is only phenomenal in metros while the culture of casual and fast, casual mid-segment format are very popular in tier II and tier III cities across India. The future looks bright for this sector. As cconsumers' are more interested in tasting innovative dishes than yester year diners and they like to taste both modern, authentic cuisine that is affordable for the family. Local and sustainable concepts are also in high demand as citizens become more socially and environmentally responsible.

5.5.   Future Scope for the Study

The geographical limitations and simple size limitation of this study offer feasible scope effective conduct future researchers in this area, i.e., diners' preference towards restaurant services. The future researchers can focus their study on:

- Diners' preference towards restaurant services in various cities in Tamil Nadu.
- Diners' preference towards restaurant services in Metropolitan city (Chennai) and Industrial City (Coimbatore).
- A Comparative Study on Fine and Casual diners' preference and satisfaction towards restaurant services in Coimbatore city.
- A Comparative Study on Fine, Casual and Quick diner's preference and satisfaction towards restaurant services in Coimbatore city.
- Diners' preference towards restaurant services offered across India.

ANNEXURE–I

CLASSIFICATION OF LIST OF RESTAURANT

Table 1: List of Restaurants in Coimbatore City (Bakery)

Sl.No.	Name	Location	Cuisines
1	Ranis	Town Hall	Pure Veg, Bakery, South Indian, Fast Food

Table 2: List of Restaurants in Coimbatore City (Cafe)

Sl.No.	Name	Location	Cuisines
1.	Café Totaram	Race Course	Cafe, Fast Food
2.	Cocoabay	Saibaba Colony	Cafe, Bakery
3.	V's Café	Saibaba Colony	Café
4.	Hot Chocolate	Race Course	Cafe, Italian, French, Continental, America
5.	Kites Café	Peelamedu	Café
6.	ChockoChoza	Peelamedu	Café
7.	Buddies Café	Peelamedu	Café
8.	Pavilion	Race Course	Chinese, Continental, South Indian, North Indian, Mexica
9.	Hot Chocolate	RS Puram	Café
10.	Hot Chocolate	Saibaba Colony	Cafe, Italian, French, Continental, America
11.	Seasons	RS Puram	Pure Veg, Cafe, Continental
12.	Chai n Gupshup	RS Puram	Pure Veg, Cafe
13.	Bazaar	Lakshmi Mills	South Indian, North Indian, Chinese, Italian, Continental, American, Thai

Table 3: Category of Casual Dining (Vegetarian & Non-vegetarian)

Sl.No	Name	Location	Cuisines	Category
1	On the Go	Race Course	Italian, North Indian, Desserts	Non-Vegetarian
2	Kovai Biryani	RS Puram	Biryani, South Indian	Non-Vegetarian
3	Tangerine	Race Course	Steakhouse, Continental, Italian	Non-Vegetarian
4	Barneque Nation	Town Hall	North Indian, European, Mediterranean	Non-Vegetarian
5	The Cascade	Peelamedu	Chinese	Non-Vegetarian
6	SreeGowrishankar	Peelamedu	Pure Veg, South Indian, Chinese, North India	Vegetarian
7	Little Italy	Ramanathapuram	Pure Veg, Italian	Vegetarian
8	Wok This Way	Peelamedu	Chinese	Non-Vegetarian
9	That's Y Food	RS Puram	North Indian, Biryani	Non-Vegetarian
10	SMS Hotel	Peelamedu	North Indian, South Indian, Chinese, Seafood	Non-Vegetarian

Sl.No	Name	Location	Cuisines	Category
1	Yari	Saibaba Colony	Pure Veg, North Indian, Chinese, Street Food	Vegetarian
2	MotiMahal	Race Course	North Indian	Non-Vegetarian
3	ValarmathiKongunaatu Samayal	Race Course	South Indian, Biryani	Non-Vegetarian
4	ShahiGril	Peelamedu	Chettinad, North Indian, Chinese	Non-Vegetarian
5	Yolo Food	Peelamedu	Continental, South Indian, Chinese	Non-Vegetarian
6	Cream Centre	Race Course	Pure Veg, North Indian, Chinese, Italian, Mexican	Vegetarian
7	Mexitoes	Peelamedu	Mexican, Chinese, Continental, Italian	Non-Vegetarian
8	Greens and Grains	RS Puram	Pure Veg, North Indian, Chinese	Vegetarian
9	Atom	Saibaba Colony	South Indian, North Indian, Chinese	Non-Vegetarian
10	Haribhavanam	Peelemedu, Gandhipuram	South Indian, Chettinad, North Indian, Chinese, Sea food	Non-Vegetarian
11	Hotel Junior Kuppanna	Gandhipuram	Chettinad, South India	Non-Vegetarian
12	Bird on Tree	Race Course	North Indian, South Indian, Chinese, Continental	Non-Vegetarian
13	My Place	Ramanathapuram	North Indian, South Indian, Chines	Non-Vegetarian
14	Tiffinys	Nehru Stadium	North Indian, Chinese, Cafe	Non-Vegetarian
15	RHR	Ramanathapuram, Race Course	Pure Veg, South Indian, North India	Vegetarian
16	The Cascade	RS Puram	Chines	Non-Vegetarian
17	SreeAnnapoorna	Peelamedu, Gandhipuram	Pure Veg, South Indian, Chinese, North India	Vegetarian
18	Dr.Grill	Lakshmi Mills	Mughlai	Non-Vegetarian
19	AnjapparChettinad	Saibaba Colony	Chettinad, South India	Non-Vegetarian
20	Peking	RS Puram, Nehru Stadium	Chines	Non-Vegetarian
21	10 BiriyaniMandi	Gandhipuram	South American, Biryani	Non-Vegetarian
22	Hotel Arrunnachala	Peelamedu	North Indian, Chinese	Non-Vegetarian
23	The Afghan Grill	Race Course	North Indian	Non-Vegetarian
24	SrinidhiAmmayiVeedu Pot Cook	Siddhapudur	Chettinad	Non-Vegetarian
25	Hotel Sri Surya	Ramanathapuram	Chinese, South Indian, North India	Non-Vegetarian
26	The Parries Hotel	Nehru Stadium	North Indian, Chinese, Fast Foo	Non-Vegetarian
27	SitaPaani	Avinashi Road	Arabian, North Indian, Chinese, Biryan	Non-Vegetarian
28	Tangy Cuisines	Peelamedu	North Indian, Chinese, Chettina	Non-Vegetarian
29	Aryaas	PeelameduRamanathapuram,Vadavalli,Saibaba Colony	Pure Veg, North Indian, South India	Vegetarian
30	SreeAnandhaas	Gandhipuram	Pure Veg, Chinese, South Indian, Chettinad	Vegetarian

Sl.No	Name	Location	Cuisines	Category
1	Malabar	Gandhipuram	Kerala, South India	Non-Vegetarian
2	Ayyappa's Peal Veg	Kavundampalayam	Pure Veg, South Indian, North Indian, Chines	Vegetarian
3	Hotel Anghappas	Gandhipuram	Chinese, South Indian, North Indian, Biryan	Non-Vegetarian
4	Sri Rayappas	Gandhipuram	Chettinad, South Indian, North Indian, Chines	Non-Vegetarian
5	Zafran Hotel Aloft	Singanallur	North Indian, Mughlai, South India	Non-Vegetarian
6	Swadh	Avinashi Rd, Sitra	South Indian, Chettinad, Kerala, Chines	Non-Vegetarian
7	Denmark Drive INN	Nehru Stadium	North Indian, Chines	Non-Vegetarian
8	Hotel Nalan	Ramanathapuram	Pure Veg, South India	Vegetarian
9	Apex Garden	Nehru Stadium	North Indian, South Indian, Chinese, Continental	Non-Vegetarian
10	Lakshmi Shankar	Peelamedu	South Indian	Vegetarian
11	Nila	Gandhipuram	North Indian, Chinese, South India	Non-Vegetarian
12	AdyarAnandaBhavan	Gandhipuram	Pure Veg, Street Food, Dessert	Vegetarian
13	Symphony	Race Course	Chinese, Continental, South India	Non-Vegetarian
14	24x7 Bytes – Clarion	ChinniayamPalayam	Indian, Continental, South Indian, North Indian, Chinese, Cafe	Non-Vegetarian
15	Nallas	Kavundampalayam	North Indian, Biryani, South India	Non-Vegetarian
16	Jagan'sBiriyani	Gandhipuram	Biryani, North India	Non-Vegetarian
17	Sampoorna	Race Course	Biryani, North Indian, Seafood	Non-Vegetarian
18	MuthuRowther	Ukkadam, Nehru Stadium	Biryani, South India	Non-Vegetarian
19	Akshya Park	Thudiyallur	North Indian, Arabian, Chines	Non-Vegetarian
20	Rathina	Race Course	Pure Veg, Continental, South Indian, Chinese, North India	Vegetarian
21	Lalkudi	Gandhipuram	Fast Food, North Indian, Seafood	Non-Vegetarian
22	Comfort's Relish	Saibaba Colony	Pure Veg, North Indian, South India	Vegetarian
23	Yummy	Thudiyalur	North Indian, Chinese	Non-Vegetarian
24	Saffron	Podanur	North Indian, South Indian, Chines	Non-Vegetarian
25	Sri Amuthaas	Thudiyalur	Pure Veg, North Indian, South Indian, Chines	Vegetarian
26	Sri Lalitha's	Kavundampalayam	Pure Veg, South Indian, North India	Vegetarian
27	Eton	Thudiyalur	Indian, Continental, Italian, Chines	Non-Vegetarian
28	Kavitha	Vadavalli	South Indian, Fast Foo	Non-Vegetarian
29	Spice	Ramanathapuram,	North Indian, Chines	Non-Vegetarian
30	Bells	Kalapatti	South Indian, North Indian, Chines	Non-Vegetarian
31	MarwadiBhojanalay	Town Hall	Rajasthani	Vegetarian
32	Parambriym	Peelamedu	South Indian, North Indian, Chines	Non-Vegetarian
33	Seven Elevel	Ramanathapuram	South Indian, North Indian, Chines	Non-Vegetarian

Sl.No	Name	Location	Cuisines	Category
1	SreeVeluBiriyani	Gandhipuram	Biryani, North Indian, Chinese, Seafood	Non-Vegetarian
2	Velu Grand	Race Course	North Indian, Chinese, Seafood, Biryani	Non-Vegetarian
3	Nivin	Kalapatti	North Indian, Chinese, South India	Non-Vegetarian
4	Donne Biryani	RS Puram	Chinese, North India	Non-Vegetarian
5	SavariBhavan	Kavundampalayam	Chettinad, Chinese, South India	Non-Vegetarian
6	Spice9	Kavundampalayam	Chinese, North India	Non-Vegetarian
7	Fusion	Town Hall	North Indian, Chinese, South Indian, Continental	Non-Vegetarian
8	Anghappas	Ganapathy	Biryani, Chinese, South Indian, North India	Non-Vegetarian
9	Denmark Drive INN	Ganapathy	North Indian, Chines	Non-Vegetarian
10	Ramanaas	Maruthamalai	Pure Veg, Fast Food	Vegetarian
11	City	Avinashi Road, Sitra	South Indian, North Indian, Fast Food	Non-Vegetarian
12	Murali	Town Hall	North India	Non-Vegetarian
13	Rooftop	Nehru Stadium	North Indian, Chinese, South India	Non-Vegetarian
14	Shower & Showers Lounge	Saibaba Colony	North Indian, Chinese, South India	Non-Vegetarian
15	ParuvaaMulticuisine	Nehru Stadium	North Indian, South Indian, Chinese, Continental	Non-Vegetarian
16	Super Needs	Town Hall	Chettinad, Chinese, North India	Non-Vegetarian
17	Jaisalmer	RS Puram	Pure Veg, North Indian, Chinese, South Indian, Street Food	Vegetarian
18	Palms	Town Hall	North Indian, South Indian, Chines	Non-Vegetarian
19	Spice Tree	Nehru Stadium	North Indian, South Indian, Chines	Non-Vegetarian
20	Sri Krishna	Thudiyalur	Pure Veg, South Indian, North India	Vegetarian
21	Akshayaas	Peelamedu	Pure Veg, North Indian, Chinese, South India	Vegetarian
22	Abbirami	Gandhipuram	Pure Veg, South India	Vegetarian
23	MayuraBiriyani	Gandhipuram	Fast Food, South Indian, Desserts, Chinese, North India	Non-Vegetarian
24	Annavaasal	Ondipudur	South Indian, North India	Non-Vegetarian
25	Grill & Chill	Town Hall	North Indian, Chinese, Fast Foo	Non-Vegetarian
26	Dewz	Peelamedu	South Indian, Chinese, North Indian, Continental	Non-Vegetarian
27	Vinod Chicken Spot	Kavundampalayam	North Indian, Chinese, Fast Food, Seafood	Non-Vegetarian
28	Manasu	Nehru Stadium	Kerala, North Indian, South India	Non-Vegetarian
29	SreeAnnalakshmi	Thudiyalur	Pure Veg, South Indian	Vegetarian
30	Comfort	RS Puram	Pure Veg, North Indian, South Indian	Vegetarian
31	New SitaPaani	Peelamedu	Arabian, North Indian, Chinese, Biryani	Vegetarian
32	Orchard	Gandhipuram	Pure Veg, North Indian, Chinese, South Indian	Vegetarian

Sl.No	Name	Location	Cuisines	Category
1	City Heights – Rooftop	Peelamedu	South Indian, Chinese, North Indian	Non-Vegetarian
2	Silver Spoon	Gandhipuram	North Indian, South Indian, Chinese, Continental	Non-Vegetarian
3	Sri Pondia Mess	Podanur,	South Indian	Vegetarian
4	Hotel Chola	Town Hall, Singanallur	North Indian, Chinese	Non-Vegetarian
5	Covai Grand	RS Puram	North Indian, South Indian, Mughlai, Chinese	Non-Vegetarian
6	City Pride	Gandhipuram	North Indian, Mughlai, South Indian, Chinese	Non-Vegetarian
7	A-1 KonguChettinad	Thudiyalur	South Indian, North Indian	Non-Vegetarian
8	Mubarak Biryani	Podanur	North Indian, Chinese	Non-Vegetarian
9	Nanjai	Ramanathapuram	South Indian, North Indian	Non-Vegetarian
10	Pink Pepper	Peelamedu	Continental, Italian, South Indian, Chinese	Non-Vegetarian
11	Sri Raja Biriyani	Gandhipura	South India	Non-Vegetarian
12	Irani	Town Hall, RS Puram, Ukkadam	North Indian, Mughlai, South India	Non-Vegetarian
13	Cloud 9	Gandhipura	North Indian, Mughlai, Chinese, South India	Non-Vegetarian
14	Kannapar	Gandhipuram	South Indian, North India	Non-Vegetarian
15	Anjali Chettinad Mess	Kavundampalayam	South Indian, Fast Food	Non-Vegetarian
16	Bay Leaf	Peelamedu	South Indian, North Indian, Chinese	Non-Vegetarian
17	Ayyappa's Peal	Kavundampalayam	Pure Veg, South Indian	Vegetarian
18	Kasturi	Podanur	South Indian	Vegetarian
19	Valayapatti	Town Hall	Chettinadu	Non-Vegetarian
20	Rice n Spice	Gandhipuram	North Indian, South Indian, Chines	Non-Vegetarian
21	ShaliniChettinadu	Gandhipura	Chettinad, South India	Non-Vegetarian
22	Jenny's Dunasty	Peelamed	South Indian, Chinese, North India	Non-Vegetarian
23	Tiffanys	Nehru Stadiu	South Indian, North Indian, Chinese, Continental, Chettina	Vegetarian
24	Karuppanna	RS Puram	North Indian, South Indian, Chines	Non-Vegetarian
25	Aahaaram	Chinniayampalaya	South India	Vegetarian
26	Vasantham	Kavundampalaya	South Indian, North India	Vegetarian
27	Amrutha	Peelamedu	South Indian, North Indian, Chines	Vegetarian
28	Aishwarya Hyderabad	Avinashi Road, Sitr, Thudiyalur	Biryani, North Indian, Fast Food	Non-Vegetarian
29	Mahalakshmi	Vadavalli	Pure Veg, South India	Non-Vegetarian
30	ShriAbhinaya	Saibaba Colony	South Indian, Chettinadu	Vegetarian
31	Madurai Amma mess	Gandhipuram	South India	Vegetarian
32	Grand Gunas	RS Puram	North Indian, South Indian, Chinese, Continental	Non-Vegetarian

Sl. No.	Name	Location	Cuisines	Category
1	Roja Mess	Peelamedu	South Indian, Chines	Non-Vegetarian
2	Denmarrk Drive – Inn	Nehru Stadiu	South India	Vegetarian
3	Madurai Aby's	Thudiyalu	South Indian, Seafood	Non-Vegetarian
4	Suvaigam	Sitra	South India	Vegetarian
5	KaraikudiChettinadu Unavagam	Kavundampalayam	North Indian, South Indian	Non-Vegetarian
6	New MadhumithaChettinadu	Gandhipuram	Chettinad, South Indian	Non-Vegetarian
7	KasthuriBhavan	Gandhipuram,	Pure Veg, South Indian	Vegetarian
8	Annalakshmi Foods	Thudiyalur, Ramanathapuram	Pure Veg, South Indian, North Indian	Vegetarian
9	Tiffen House	Kavundampalayam	Pure Veg, South Indian	Vegetarian
10	DMF	Singanallur	South Indian, North Indian	Vegetarian
11	SAM Nalaas	Gandhipuram	Pure Veg, Chinese	Non-Vegetarian
12	SreeSelvamani Canteen	Town Hall	South Indian	Vegetarian
13	Park Inn Multi – Cuisine	Town Hall	South Indian, North Indian, Chinese	Non-Vegetarian
14	Food Park	Ramanathapuram,	South Indian, North Indian	Non-Vegetarian
15	Best Biriyani Corner	Saibaba Colon	Biryani	Non-Vegetarian
16	AkshayaaDharshini	Thudiyalu	South Indian, Fast Foo	Non-Vegetarian
17	Anandha	Singanallu	Pure Veg, South Indian, North India	Vegetarian
18	Bells Drive Inn	Nehru Stadiuam	Fast Food, South India	Non-Vegetarian
19	Nest Cafe	Race Course	Asian, Continental, North Indian, Thx	Non-Vegetarian
20	Rollacosta	RS Puram	Lebanese, Italian	Vegetarian
21	Kannappa	Chinniayampalayam	Chettinad	Non-Vegetarian

Table 4: List of Restaurants in Coimbatore City (Dessert Parlor)

Sl.No.	Name	Location	Cuisines
1	Bakeroe	Race Course	Desserts, Baker
2	Boomerang	Peelamedu	Pure Veg, Desserts, Ice Cream
3	Ajay's Delhi Wala Sweet Home	Gandhipuram	Pure Veg, North Indian, Desserts, Street Foo
4	Ibaco	Peelamedu	Pure Veg, Ice Cream, Dessert

Table 5: List of Restaurants in Coimbatore City (Quick Bites)

Sl.No.	Name	Location	Cuisines
1.	Kovai Biryani	Saibaba Colony	Biryani, South Indian
2.	Let's Eat Meat	Saibaba Colony	Biryani, North Indian, Afghani
3.	Leiden	Peelamedu	Fast Food
4.	Burger KaBaap	Peelamedu	Fast Food
5.	SreeAnnapoorna	RS Puram	Pure Veg, South Indian, North Indian, Chines
6.	Snack Street	RS Puram	Pure Veg, South Indian, Chinese, Street Food, North India
7.	Subway	Race Course	Fast Food, America
8.	The Village	RS Puram	Pure Veg, South India
9.	Kowloon	Saibaba Colony	Chinese
10.	Cock Ra Co	RS Puram	North Indian, Chinese, South India
11.	DindigulVenu Biryani	Gandhipuram	Biryani
12.	SreeAnnapoorna	Saibaba Colony	Pure Veg, South Indian, North Indian, Chines
13.	Early	RS Puram	Pure Veg, South India
14.	Shree Anandhaas	Vadavalli	Pure Veg, South Indian, North India (7 location)
15.	Alam Grilled Wraps	Ganapathy	Fast Food
16.	KFC	Peelamedu	Fast Food
17.	Burger Hub	Peelamedu	Fast Food
18.	Priya Juice & Cakes	Town Hall	Fast Food, Baker
19.	TN38	Saibaba Colony	South Indian
20.	Subway	RS Puram	Fast Food, America
21.	Calcutta Chats	RS Puram	Pure Veg, Street Foo
22.	Sri MaduralMeemakshi	Singanallur	South Indian

Table 6: List of Restaurants in Coimbatore City (Food Court)

Sl.No.	Name	Location	Cuisines
1	ID	RS Puram	Pure Veg, South Indian
2	Shree Anandhaas	RS Puram	Pure Veg, South India
3	Zucca Pizzeria	Peelamedu	Pizza
4	Pizza Hut	RS Puram	Pizza
5	Domino's Pizza	Peelamedu	Pizza (6 location)
6	Pizza Hut	Peelamedu	Pizza
7	Tuscany Pizza	Peelamedu	Pizza

Table 7: List of Restaurants in Coimbatore City (Fine Dining)

Sl.No.	Name	Location	Cuisines
1.	Grain of Salt	Peelamedu	North Indian, Chinese, Italian, Continental
2.	Bombay Brasserie	Race Course	North Indian
3.	Latest Recipe - Le Meridien	Neelambur	North Indian, Continental, South Indian, Chinese
4.	Latitude – Vivanta By Taj	Race Course	North Indian, South Indian, Continental

Table 8: List of Restaurants in Coimbatore City (Others)

Sl.No.	Name	Location	Cuisines
1.	Bawarchi	RS Puram	North Indian, South Indian, Chines
2.	Indulge Cupcakes	Ganapathy	Bakery
3.	Annalakshmi	Race Course	Pure Veg, South India
4.	Sri Sarvanabava	Peelamedu	Pure Veg, South Indian, Chines
5.	Sri Raja Chettinadu Mess	-	-

Table 9: Category of Dining Centers Functioning in India

Sl.No	Category of Dining Center	Numbers	Percentage
1.	Bakery	1	0.47
2.	Café Desserts	13	6.07
3.	Causal Dinning	158	73.83
4.	Dessert Parlor	4	1.87
5.	Quick Eat	22	10.28
6.	Fast Foods	7	3.27
7.	Fine Dine	4	1.87
8.	Others	5	2.34
	Total	214	100

PROFILE OF THE SELECTED VEGETARIAN AND NON-VEGETARIAN RESTAURANTS OPERATING IN COIMBATORE

Sree Annapoorna

For many years Sree Annapoorna has been Coimbatore's most favorite restaurant. Sree Annapoorna Sree Gowrishankar chain of restaurants that is located at various hearts of Coimbatore city serving traditional South Indian vegetarian cuisine since the 1960s. A family run business, we believe in delivering food with absolutely no compromise on quality and standards. Currently, more than 16 restaurants are operating in Coimbatore and other important cities of Tamil Nadu.

Shree Anandhaas

Shree Anandhaas Restaurants have taken shape from diner's family legacy in the restaurant business which started half a century ago. Initially based in Tirunelveli, the group's first restaurant in Coimbatore was set up in 1998. Anandhaas is run by a team of five young professionals. A unique blend of traditional hospitality and modern professionalism sets diners restaurants apart. Shree Anandhaas now have branches at seven prestigious locations spread over

the city. The continued support of diner patrons speaks volumes for diners commitment to provide the best food and the best service at all times. At all Shree Anandhaas restaurants, they focus on taste, service, ambience and cleanliness to give diners patrons an enjoyable dining experience. Restaurant at Puliakulam offers ample parking space. With gracious interiors and personalised service, this restaurant has a seating capacity of 250 and gives its diners a wide choice of dining options.

Shree Anandhaas bring to its customers a wide variety of tasty vegetarian food. Shree Anandhaas constant commitment to quality has brought us to the forefront in diners field and made us a respected brand in the city. Shree Anandhaas ensure that the food that reaches diners table at diners' restaurants is prepared under stringent controls for quality and hygiene. The restaurant have a dedicated eco-friendly central kitchen spread over 12000 sq.ft, where the restaurant have upgraded to imported machines to ensure quality and hygiene during the production process. From kitchen to table, the food is handled with the greatest care to ensure the best levels of cleanliness. Shree Anandhaas spare no effort to give you a dining experience diner will want to savdiners again and again.

PROFILE OF THE SELECTED VEGETARIAN AND NON-VEGETARIAN RESTAURANTS OPERATING IN COIMBATORE

Hotel Aryaas

Hotel Aryaas, one of the best hangout places in Coimbatore and Kerala. Hotel Aryaas offers mouthwatering and healthy recipes for diners customers on valuable prices. Hotel Aryaas takes pride to introduce itself as one of the leading Authentic High Class A/C Vegetarian Restaurant in Coimbatore. Hotel Aryaaas was established during late 1990's and on existence for several years. Hotel Aryaas have two branches in Coimbatore and extend diners service in Alappuzha, Ernakulam, Trichur and Tiruvalla. Hotel Aryaas have attracted thousands of customers by providing them healthy and tasty foods. Hotel Aryaas have more than 50 employees ready to serve diners needs at the most.

Hotel Aryaas have talented chefs to provide healthy foods which you have ever tasted in and around the city. Hotel Aryaas have specialized in Millet Foods. Hotel Aryaas ensure diners customers are diners' strength and make them feel at home when they are with us. An outlet to be great with friends or all by diners self. Diner can eat in, take it to go, or have it catered right to you. The feeling is friendly and the food is fabulous. Hotel Aryaas offer Party Hall for free on diners special occasions such as Birthday parties, Reception, family-friend's get-together, Official-Business meeting, etc. Diners Party Hall is spacious to more than 200 accommodate with fulfilling all diners needs.

Hotel Aryaas do offer food packages on dining occasions to make it more special. Hotel Aryaas have packages for Breakfast, Lunch and Dinner on affordable prices. Hotel Aryaas ensure diners food satisfy not only diners budget also diners taste buds.

AdyarAnandaBhavan

A2B was founded by late Thiru.K.S. Thirupathi Raja founder of Guru Sweets in Rajapalayam, Srinivasa sweets in Bangalore and Sri AnandaBhavan in Vannarapettai, Chennai. This was followed by the opening of a branch in Adyar which prompted the company to add Adyar to the name AnandaBhavan which is now called Adyar Ananda Bhavan. Adyar Ananda Bhavan, now operates with 93 branches spread all over India, majorly in South India. Adyar Ananda Bhavan is now managed & run by Thiru. K.T.Venkatesan & Thiru.K.T.Srinivasa raja, sons of Founder Late Thiru.K.S.Thirupathi Raja.

PROFILE OF THE SELECTED VEGETARIAN AND NON-VEGETARIAN RESTAURANTS OPERATING IN COIMBATORE

RHR

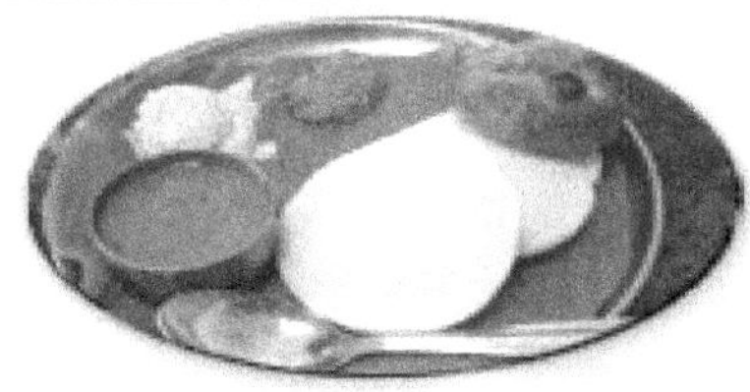

RHR Hotels Pvt.Ltd Restaurant is the best place for Vegetarian food Service in Coimbatore. RHR stands for Royal Hindu Restaurant started by Royal Group of Concerns. R.H.R was started in the year 1931 and is one of the noted old and traditional Vegetarian restaurants in Coimbatore. There were items like Idly, Vada, Pongal, Kichadi, Roast, Poori Masala, Variety Rice, Chapatti, Parota, Chilly Idly, Aappam, Family Roast, Coffee, Tea, Veg Cutlet, Samosa and more under the breakfast menu. Fresh Juices made of fruits like Mango, Musambi, Orange, Grape, Dates, Pineapple, Apple, Water Melon, Pomegranate, MulamPazham, Carrot and Tomato were also there in the menu. Diners can enjoy a tasty Breakfast, Lunch & Dinner. There is this RHR Sweet shop adjacent to the hotel where Hot JILAEBI is very famous. There is a bakery nearby too. Aappam and Paniyaram is the center of attraction. There is a live Aappam section and you can see the chef/staff demonstrating the live preparation in Aappamkadai. The staffs are friendly and hospitable. The place is clean and the food served is yummy. The best thing about RHR is that it is affordable, hygienic and offers quality food in a big hall. The items up on the menu are good. Food quality and taste is worth mentioning too. Cost wise, it's moderate. Delicious food, Tidiness of the place and their super-fast service is an added advantage. Even their parcel services are very quick with great packaging. Overall, RHR is a Reliable Restaurant for South Indian food.

PROFILE OF THE SELECTED VEGETARIAN AND NON-VEGETARIAN RESTAURANTS OPERATING IN COIMBATORE

Sree Anjali Restaurant	
	The Anjali is the best place to have a lunch and dinner in Coimbatore. It provides the cheapest food services in this area. It offers dishes like Chinese and Non-Veg and some others mouth-watering dishes that make diner lights and impressive dining table.
Anjappar	
	Established in Chennai in the year 1964, Anjappar is the pioneer in bringing the food of the famed Chettiars to the people world around. Over the years they mastered the art of using spice to give one's taste buds the best food experience. With more than 45 years of experience and 25 outlets to date, Anjappar is spreading its wings to give customers a homely dining experience. The freshness of its products and the use of secret home ground recipes bring the food lovers in search of those unique dishes that can be found only at Anjappar. Anjappar's humble beginnings started in Chennai more than 45 years back offering the Chennaites some typical Chettinad food. As time passed Anjappar became synonym for Chettinad cuisine. The people's demand has led us to take this experience overseas. Anjappar has been accommodating the changes of time by increasing their standards to cater the ever-growing necessities of today's taste hunters. And now Anjappar Restaurants have preserved the culinary traditions and served as one of the most outstanding Ambassadors of Chettinad Cuisine. Anjappar's humble beginnings started in Chennai more than 45 years back offering the Chennaites some typical Chettinad food. Now Anjappar keep diners foot prints in Coimbatore. Anjappar also proud on announcing that they are one of the Multi Cuisine Chettinadu Restaurant. Anjappar placed diners' restaurant in Bharathiar Road, Gandhipuram.

PROFILE OF THE SELECTED VEGETARIAN AND NON-VEGETARIAN RESTAURANTS OPERATING IN COIMBATORE

Sri RayappasChettinad Restaurant

 	Rayappas Restaurant Established in 14th march 1996 & Rayappas Chittinad Restaurant in 14th December 1997, Rayappas Restaurant is situated at the prominent place of Coimbatore. Rayappas Restaurant is located in crosscut road Gandhipuram, the commercial hub of Coimbatore. This restaurant listen to diners guests to refine food offerings and menus constantly. Born from and firmly rooted in the local culture and customs, At Rayappas diners will find these values in menus, service, and total presentation. Rayappas level of service and quality of food will keep diner satisfied. A real treat for diners taste buds with all Indian and international cuisine in one roof. In Rayappas can customize food to diners taste with diners interactive team of chef every day.
Chicken Sampoorna	
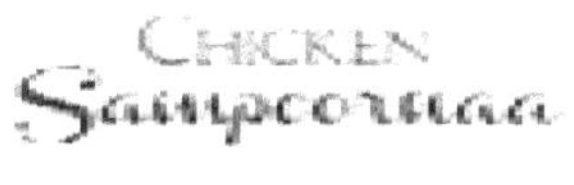	The Chicken Sampoorna is also the best place to have a lunch and dinner in Coimbatore. It provides the cheapest food services in this area. The Chicken Sampoorna is located in Near Women Polytecnique College, Coimbatore, Tamil Nadu that provides customers the best quality food services. It offers dishes like Chinese and Non-vegetarian watering dishes that make diners feel delighted. Besides, it has great interior that is well furnished and equipped with amazing lights and impressive dining table. With its proper location and address details provided in net diners in the city post their review and rating to Chicken Sampoorna Coimbatore and make us serve the better.

Haribhavanam	
	Haribhavanam–Trusted Taste since 1971: Specialist in Indian and Chinese cuisine, diners wide variety of menu and trusted taste caters diners taste buds at all occasions. Every day is special so as customers, check diners Today's special to have a healthy and tasty food. Haribhavanam Hotels started in 1971 was founded and managed by Mr. S. Raju who rewritten the service industry with homely care and rich heritage in the city of Coimbatore. Commitment to quality and transparency to the customers by providing homely food is the core values you can feel in diners' restaurants. These values continue to drive the inspiration at hotel. This restaurant listen to diners quests closely and constantly and are always upgrading diners services, facilities and infrastructure to keep pace with their changing needs.

I. Life style Profile of Customers'

1. Gender:
   - Male
   - Female

2. Age:
   - Below 20 years
   - 21-25 years
   - 26-30 years
   - 30-40 years
   - 40-50 years
   - Above 50 years

3. Educational Qualification :
   - School Level
   - Higher Secondary Level
   - Degree/Diploma
   - Professionals

4. Life style:
   - Nuclear Family
   - Joint Family

5. Occupation:
   - Business
   - Employees
   - Professional
   - Home Maker
   - Student

6. Income (Monthly):
   - Less than Rs.10000
   - Rs.10001- Rs.20000
   - Rs.20001- Rs.30000
   - Above Rs.30000

7. Family size
   - 2 member's
   - 3 member's
   - 4 member's
   - Above 4 member's
8. Earning Members
   - Husband only
   - Both Husband and Wife

II. Food Consumption Habits (Eating at Outlets)

9. State your Preferences for foods
   - Pure Vegetarian
   - Non-Vegetarian
   - Both
10. How often you prefer to dine in restaurant
    - Once in a week.
    - Once in a month
    - Occasionally
11. With whom do you prefer to dine?
    - Alone
    - With Friends
    - With Family Members
    - Both Family Members &Friends
12. Which these restaurant do you visit frequently
    - Pure Vegetarian Hotels /Restaurants
      - Annapoorna
      - Anandha's
      - Arya's
      - AdyarAnandhaBhavan
      - RHR
      - Otherspl. specify _______________
    - Both Vegetarian - Non-Vegetarian Hotels /Restaurants
      - Rayappa's
      - Sampoorna

- Haribhavanam
- Anjappar
- Anjali
- Otherspl.specify _______________

13. State when do you prefer to visit the restaurant

- Saturday Evenings
- Sundays' (Lunch/Dinner)
- Special Occasions
- Festive Seasons
- Any time

14. State your preferred time of visit to the restaurant

- Early Morning
- Morning Break-Fast
- After-noon Lunch
- Early Evening
- Late Evening

15. Do you fix budget for dinning per visit?

- Yes
- No

16. State the factors that motivated for visiting the particular restaurant

Sl.No	Service Features	Rank
1.	Food quality	
2.	Menu selection (Variety)	
3.	Menu pricing and value	
4.	Waiting times	
5.	Promptness of service	
6.	Professionalism and friendliness of server(s)	
7.	Server's knowledge of menu	
8.	Décor (Ambience)	
9.	Restaurant location	
10.	Special places for kids to play	
11.	Overall restaurant experience	

III. Dinners' Level of Perception and Satisfaction towards Restaurant Service

17. State your level of perception towards the responsiveness of employee restaurant employees

Sl.No	Factors	Very High	High	Moderate	Low	Very Low
1.	Employees attentiveness					
2.	Employees co-operatives					
3.	Promptness of service					
4.	Server's appearance (neat & presentable)					
5.	Employees understanding towards customers' needs					
6.	Courtesy of server					
7.	Server's knowledge about menu					

18. State your level of perception towards the service reliability at the restaurant

Sl.No	Factors	Very High	High	Moderate	Low	Very Low
1.	Customers' receives exactly what they ordered the first time					
2.	Order served are error-free					
3.	The food was fresh					
4.	The temperature of the food was just right					
5.	Foods are Hygienically Serviced					

19. State your level of perception towards the physical design and appearance of the restaurant

Sl. No	Particulars	Very High	High	Moderate	Low	Very Low
1.	Lighting in the restaurant					
2.	Adequate parking facilities					
3.	Restaurant cleanliness					
4.	Decor was visibility appealing(Ambiences)					

20. State your level of perception towards the price of food items offered at the (preferred) restaurant

Sl.No	Factors	Very High	High	Moderate	Low	Very Low
1.	Economically Priced					
2.	Customers' paid more than they had planned					
3.	Prices are comparatively competitive					

21. State your level of perception towards the location of the (preferred)restaurants

Sl. No	Factors	Very High	High	Moderate	Low	Very Low
1.	Proximity to sources of demand					
2.	Accessibility					
3.	Visibility					
4.	Surrounding neighborhood					
5.	Parking availability					
6.	Sign visibility (location)					

22. State your level of perception towards the appearance/comfort in the restaurant.

Sl. No	Factors	Very High	High	Moderate	Low	Very Low
1.	Exterior appearance and theme					
2.	Interior appearance and theme					
3.	Atmosphere					
4.	Cleanliness					
5.	Air condition quality					

23. State your level of perception towards the menu offered in the restaurant.

Sl. No	Factors	Very High	High	Moderate	Low	Very Low
1.	Theme					
2.	Variety and selection					
3.	Signature item					
4.	Price range and value					
5.	Uniqueness					

24. State your level of perception towards the food quality in the restaurant.

Sl. No	Factors	Very High	High	Moderate	Low	Very Low
1.	Taste					
2.	Presentation					
3.	Potion size					
4.	Consistency					
5.	Health aspects					

25. State your level of perception towards the service quality of their preferred restaurants.

Sl. No	Factors	Very High	High	Moderate	Low	Very Low
1.	Days open (7x7 days)					
2.	Hours of operation					
3.	Service style					
4.	Quality of service					
5.	Speed of service					
6.	Extra services offered					

26. State your overall satisfaction towards the restaurant features

Sl. No	Factors	Very High	High	Moderate	Low	Very Low
1.	Responsiveness of employee					
2.	Service reliability					
3.	Ambience (Physical design and appearance)					
4.	Price of food items					
5.	Location of restaurants					
6.	Appearance/comfort					
7.	Menu offered					
8.	Food quality					
9.	Service quality					

Thank U

ANNEXURE-IV

STATISTICAL TOOLS APPLIED

Statistics is the science of collecting, analyzing and making inference from data. Statistics is a particularly useful branch of mathematics that is not only studied theoretically by advanced mathematicians but one that is used by researchers in many fields to organize, analyze, and summarize data. Statistical methods and analyses are often used to communicate research findings and to support hypotheses and give credibility to research methodology and conclusions. It is important for researchers and also consumers of research to understand statistics so that they can be informed, evaluate the credibility and usefulness of information, and make appropriate decisions.

The data collected through the questioner were classified and tabulated for analysis in accordance with the outline laid down for the purpose of justifying the objective and the hypotheses framed at the time of developing research design. According to the nature of data and interpretations required, appropriate statistical tools have been applied. The following tools have been applied in the study: Frequency distribution, Weighted Average, One-way ANOVA, Independent' 'Z' test, Chi-Square, Paired 'Z' Test, Rotation Factor Analysis and Reliability test.

a. Frequency Distribution

The frequency distribution of the variables were calculated with help of simple percentage, by writing the formula *FD = F/N x 100*. Where f1 denotes the number of respondents, and n denotes the total number of sample population.

b. Weighted Arithmetic Mean

One of the most important objectives of statistical analysis is to get one single value that describes the characteristic of the entire mass of entire data. Such a value is called the central value or an "average" means or the expected value of the variable, what the statisticians call the arithmetic mean. The process of computing mean in case of individual observation (i.e), where frequencies are not given is very simple. Add together the various values of the variable and divide the total by the number of items. The researcher has applied weighted mean, instead of calculating the simple mean to obtain a realistic average.

$$\bar{x} = \frac{\sum W i X j}{\sum W i}$$

Where $\bar{X}$ = Weighted mean

Wi = Weight of i th item X

Xj= value of the jth item of X

c. Summated Scales (Likert's-scales)

Summated scales (or Likert-type scales) are developed by utilizing the item analysis approach where in a particular item is evaluated on the basis of how well it discriminates between those persons whose total score is high and those whose score is low. Those items or statements that best meet this sort of discrimination test are included in the final instrument. In a Likert Scale, the respondent is asked to respond to each statement in terms of several degrees, usually five degree of agreement (or) disagreement. Each point on the scale carries a score of 5, 4, 3, 2, and 1. Scaling describes the procedure of assigning numbers to various degrees of opinion, attitude and other concepts.

d. ANOVA (F-Test)

Two way ANOVA techniques are used when the data are classified on the basis of two factorsANOVA. The F-test is named in honour of the great statistician R.A. Fisher. The objective of the F-test is to find out whether the two independent estimates of population variance differ significantly, or whether the two samples may be regarded as drawn from the normal populations having the same variance. The formula used in the analysis of variance (ANOVA table) classification model is:

$$\text{The ratio of F} = \frac{Between - column\ variance}{Within - column\ variance}$$

$$\text{i.e., F} = \frac{V_1^2}{V_2^2}$$

e. Chi-square Test

The chi-square test is an important test amongst the several tests of significance developed by statisticians. Chi-square, symbolically written as $\chi 2$ (pronounced as ki-square). As a non-parametric test, it can be used to determine if categorical data shows dependency or the two classifications are independent.

Chi-square as a test of independence enables a researcher to explain whether or not two attributes are associated.

$\chi 2$ are calculated as follows:

$$\chi 2 = \frac{\Sigma (Oij - Eij)2}{Eij}$$

Where o_{ij} =observed frequency of the cell in ith row and jth column

e_{ij}=expected frequency of the cell in ith row and jth column

The $\chi 2$ values obtained as such should be compared with relevant table value of $\chi 2$ and the inference can be drawn. If the calculated value is greater than the table value the hypothesis framed will be rejected, otherwise accepted.

The entire hypothesis test in this study was carried out at 5 percent level of significance. In research we quit often face measurement problem (since we want a valid measurement but may not obtain it), especially when the concepts to be measured are complex and abstract and we do not possess the standardized measurement tools.

f. Paired Z-Test

Paired Z-test is a way to test for comparing two related samples, involving small values of n that does not require the variances of the two populations to be equal, but the assumption that the two populations are normal and must continue to apply. For a paired t-test, it is necessary that the observations in the two samples be collected in the form of what is called matched pairs i.e. "each observation in the one sample must be paired with an observation in the other sample in such a manner that these observations are somehow "matched" or related, in an attempt to eliminate extraneous factors which are not of interest in test",

$$Z = \frac{\bar{D} - 0}{\sigma\, diff\, / \sqrt{n}} \text{ with (n-1) degrees of freedom}$$

Where,

$\bar{D}$= Mean of differences

$\sigma\, diff$=Standard deviation of differences

g. Independent 'Z' test

The independent Z-test, also called the two sample Z-test or student's Z-test, is an inferential statistical test that determines whether there is a statistically significant difference between the means in two unrelated groups. In this study year of exports and value of cotton yarn exports are considered as two variables.

$$Z = \frac{\bar{x}1 - \bar{x}2}{\sqrt{\frac{s1^2 + s2^2}{n}}}$$

h. Reliability Analysis

Reliability analysis may be used to construct reliable measurement scales, to improve existing scales, and to evaluate the reliability of scales already in use. Specifically, Reliability & Item Analysis will aid in the design and evaluation of sum scales, that is, scales that are made up of multiple individual measurements (e.g., different items, repeated measurements, different measurement devices, etc.). It can be compute numerous statistics that allows researcher to build and evaluate scales following the so-called classical testing theory model.

From the above discussion, one can easily infer a measure or statistic to describe the reliability of an item or scale. Specifically, we may define an *index of reliability* in terms of the proportion of true score variability that is captured across subjects or respondents, relative to the total observed variability. In equation form, we can say:

$$\text{Reliability} = \sigma^2_{(\text{true score})} / \sigma^2_{(\text{total observed})}$$

Cronbach's Alpha: The proportion of true score variance that is captured by the items by comparing the sum of item variances with the variance of the sum scale. Specifically, can be

$$\text{Computed: } \alpha = (k/(k-1)) * [1 - \Sigma\ (s^2_i)/s^2_{\text{sum}}]$$

If the sum scale is perfectly reliable, it would expect that the two halves are perfectly correlated (i.e., $r = 1.0$). Less than perfect reliability will lead to less than perfect correlations.

i. Rotation Factor Analysis

The factor analysis is another multivariate technique. It is an extremely powerful and useful analytic approach to psychological, behavioral, financial and other types of data. It is a statistical technique for determining the underlying factors or forces among a large number of interdependent variables of measures. It is a method for extracting common factor variances from a set of observations. It groups the number of variables of smaller set of uncorrelated factors potentially conveying a great deal of information.

- Factor: A factor is an underlying dimension that accounts for several observed variables. There can be one or more factors, depending upon the nature of the study and the number of variables involved in it.
- Factor –loading: Factor-loading is those values which explain how closely the variables are related to each one of the factors discovered. They are also known as factors-

variable correlations. In fact, factor-loadings work as a key to the understanding what the factors mean. It is the absolute size (rather than the signs, plus or minus) of the loading that is important in the interpretation of a factor.

- Communality (h^2): Communality, symbolized as h^2, shows how much of each variable is accounted for by the underlying factors taken together. A high value of communality means that not much of the variable is left over after whatever the factors represent is taken into consideration. It is worked out in respect of each variable as under:

  H^2 of the ith variable= (ith factor loading of factor A)^2= (ith factor loading of factor B)^2

- Eigen Value: Eigen value (or Latent Root) is the sum of squared values of factor loadings relating to a factor. It indicates the relative importance of each in accounting for the particular set of variables under study.

- Total sum of squares: When Eigen values of all factors are totaled, the resulting value is called the total of squares. Rotations reveal different structures in the data. If the factors are independent, orthogonal rotation is done, and if they are corrected, an oblique rotation is made. Factor score represents the degree to which each respondent gets high scores on the group of item that load high on each factor. Factor scores are used in several other multivariate analyses.